The Flavor of Wood

The Flavor of Wood

IN SEARCH OF THE WILD TASTE OF TREES
FROM SMOKE AND SAP TO ROOT AND BARK

Artur Cisar-Erlach

Abrams Press, New York

Cataloging-in-Public ation Data is available from the Library of Congress
Book design and typeformatting by Bernard Schleifer
Manufactured in the United States of America
ISBN 978-1-4683-1672-8
eISBN 978-1-4683-1673-5

10 9 8 7 6 5 4 3 2 1

Abrams books are available at special discounts when purchased in quantity for premiums and promotions as well as fundraising or educational use. Special editions can also be created to specification. For details, contact specialsales@abramsbooks.com or the address below.

Abrams Press® is a registered trademark of Harry N. Abrams, Inc.

ABRAMS The Art of Books
195 Broadway, New York, NY 10007
abramsbooks.com

This book couldn't have been completed without the incredible support of my girlfriend, Carmen; it wouldn't have been started without the wonderful encouragement by my parents; and it couldn't have been filled page to page without the help of the greatest friends imaginable.

Thank you, Kira!

CONTENTS

INTRODUCTION
What Is Wood?

What is wood?

The answer to this question very much depends on who you ask.

Foresters, cabinetmakers, and the broader public alike generally use the technical definition of wood that classifies it as a raw material[1] and as an energetic resource with many technical and artisanal applications.[2] It is used to construct everything from bridges to the frameworks of houses, intricate pieces of furniture, musical instruments, and sculptures. When burned, its energy is used to heat our homes, or even melt iron or glass.

Biologists on the other hand see wood as a key player in the world of plants. Defined as "the principal strengthening and nutrient-conducting tissue of trees and other plants and one of the most abundant and versatile natural materials,"[3] wood gives plants stability and strength, provides the transport infrastructure for nutrient-rich fluids, and offers protection. If compared to the human body, wood would have the combined functions of our bones, flesh, blood vessels, and skin.

Being a cabinetmaker as well as a biologist I would like to use a combination of both definitions.

In my opinion, wood is the tree as a whole, which includes roots, trunk, branches, leaves, the environment it grows in, the ecosystem it sustains, and its relation to the people working and living with it. I propose to understand the word "wood" in a much broader sense, which includes its technical meaning, its integral role in the plant world, its importance to the environment, and its huge socioeconomic significance.

Trees have always had a profound influence on humans. We started off as small, tree-dwelling insect eaters living in the great tropical forests of what is today known as North America, Africa, Asia, and Europe. Only later, when a cooling world climate turned the forests of Africa into savannas and open woodlands, did we come down from the trees and start to evolve into the bipedal, agrarian and urban beings we are now.[4] Nevertheless, those open woodlands and savannas must have left a lasting impression on us. We try to recreate them in our parks and gardens, wide-open green spaces with carefully selected and positioned trees and shrubs.

The close relationship between trees and humans is also evident in religious contexts. In shamanic religions the tree is regularly regarded as the symbol of life itself. In the Bible as well as the Torah, a symbolic tree is placed in the center of the Garden of Eden. The Quran has the same narrative; there it is called the tree of eternity. Interestingly, the word "Eden" stems from the ancient Sumerian word *edin-na,* which means plain or steppe.[5] A steppe, by definition, is a wide-open grassland with only a few trees surrounding a source of water. So what religious writings describe as the Garden of Eden, remarkably, is the very landscape we humans evolved in.

Similarly, Hinduism and Buddhism worship a large and impressive species of the fig tree with the fitting scientific name *Ficus religiosa.* In Hinduism, the tree is a trinity; the roots are Brahma (the Creator), the trunk is Vishnu (the preserver), and the leaves are Shiva (the destroyer or transformer). In Buddhism the fig tree is called "Bodhi," or "tree of enlightenment," as Buddha was sitting beneath one when he reached enlightenment. It is for this reason that there are fig trees in almost every Buddhist monastery.[6]

In addition to the stately tree symbolizing life in many religions, parts of trees, like twigs, leaves, flowers, and fruits, are also frequently used as metaphors by those very same religions. The Christian motifs of the olive branch (a peace symbol) or the forbidden fruit (symbolizing temptation), as well as cherry blossoms in Shintoism (a symbol of delicate earthly life[7]), are just a few examples. Furthermore, in Norse mythology the tree "Yggdrasil" embodies nothing less than the whole cosmos. Its worldly influence is still visible on many farms in the Scandinavian countries, where a big tree is planted right in the center of the yard. Caring for it symbolizes respect for one's ancestors and is a moral reminder to tend to the farm and land.[8]

On a related note, the family tree is used to visualize one's ancestry. Visual and organizational representations of trees are also used to schematize the increasingly complex structures of corporations, organizations, and governments.

Famed Swiss psychiatrist and psychotherapist Carl Jung spent many years exploring symbols in the unconscious mind stemming from different cultures. A frequent image in dreams was a tree. Jung discovered that the meaning of trees in dreams corresponded to the use of trees in ancient scriptures, myth, and poetry of which the dreamers had no previous knowledge. Therefore he concluded that the tree is a human archetype, a symbol hardwired into the brains of people of every culture.[9] Several studies even suggest that by simply looking at pictures of forests and verdant landscapes we become relaxed, and our mood improves.[10] Even the use of wood as a decorative finish for houses, interiors, and furnishings seems to have a positive impact on people.[11] Experiments with students, patients, and office workers showed their stress levels were reduced and their general senses of well-being increased in rooms containing wood.[12] Japanese scientists researching the impact of taking a walk in the forest, called "Shinrin-yoku," or forest bathing, found that it gave an actual and measurable boost to the immune system through exposure to chemical compounds naturally released by trees.[13]

The pressing issue of climate change is unquestionably related to the global decline of major wooded areas, including the Amazon rainforest and the Russian boreal forests. Environmental organizations like the World Wide Fund for Nature (WWF) and Greenpeace regularly use the imagery of deforested areas in their campaigns, stressing the importance of trees and forests for the reduction of atmospheric CO_2 concentrations as well as for the world's biodiversity and water availability. Trees are also crucial for overall socioeconomic development. The Food and Agricultural Organization of the United Nations goes so far as to estimate that the annual value of fuelwood and wood-based forest products represent about 2 percent of the gross domestic product of the planet, with a growth rate of 2.5 percent per year.[14] Furthermore, estimated numbers of people who derive direct and indirect benefits from forests—through employment, forest products, and direct or indirect contributions to livelihoods and income—range between 1 and 1.5 billion, which is roughly one-seventh of the world population. So unlike almost all other economic sectors, forests and sustainable forestry not only provide jobs, resources, and products but also benefit the ecosystem in ways that are crucial, if difficult to quantify in economic terms, by creating clean water, fresh air, and healthy soils, all of which are indispensable for humans.[15]

To put it simply, trees and wood are everywhere. They are a constant human companion, be it as a symbol in religion, construction material, fuel source, mood booster, or as an immensely important factor for our economy. They are even in our dreams.

But are they in our food?

And if so, what is the flavor of wood? Can it be described? Is it a stand-alone, simple flavor, like sweet or sour? Or is it a complex, exotic one consisting of many different components? Which food products out there are influenced by wood? Who are the people producing them? How would you go about finding the answers to those questions?

It was during my graduate studies in gastronomy, while working on a creative writing assignment on whisky and wine, that I suddenly began to wonder about the wooden barrel.

Why is it that discussions of wine and whisky focus on the quality of ingredients, the producer's knowledge, and the importance of aging, but rarely analyze the vessel in which these components combine: the wooden barrel? After all, a lot of knowledge and craftsmanship goes into making one. As wood is a living material, the barrel surely must add flavor to the liquids it holds. In addition to the familiar flavor of vanilla, a flavor produced as a byproduct of the chemical transformations of wood components when exposed to alcohol[16] do wooden barrels produce other flavors? Do they share a common flavor profile? And why is everyone only using barrels made from oak when there are so many other tree species out there?

The more I thought about it, the more I realized that it was not only wine and whisky that come into contact with wood or parts of the tree. Some foods, like maple syrup or tea, are actually made from trees. Others, including meat, fish, and even chocolate or pasta, are both preserved and flavored by wood smoke. Also, if I thought about the flavor of wood, I subsequently had to think about the smell of wood, as scent and flavor are interconnected. Are there any perfumes derived from trees?

My thoughts were on fire, and I instantly knew that I would blow past the maximum word limit of my assignment.

Looking back, my sudden flaring interest for the flavor of wood was only the natural course of events having had an almost lifelong exposure to wood and forests. Growing up in the most northern part of Austria, an area called *Waldviertel*, or "wooded district," and spending all my summers in Nova Scotia, the woodland-rich Canadian east coast province, many of my favorite childhood moments took place in forests of all shapes and sizes. When I enrolled in high school, a fantastic boarding school in the Austrian province of Salzburg, I did so because it gave me the rare possibility to additionally train as a cabinetmaker.

Later, at the University of Vienna, I majored in biology, specializing in woodland ecology. So it almost came naturally that, during my studies in the graduate program of Food Culture and Communication at the University of Gastronomic Sciences in Pollenzo, I found a way to connect my two passions: wood and food.

For my aforementioned writing assignment I would not only need way more than a thousand words to write about my hunt for the elusive flavor of wood, but I would also have to figure out where to start. Little did I know that those questions spurred by a creative writing prompt would lead me on a mental and physical journey around the world starting in Italy and Austria where I lived at the time of writing.

Over the next three years, I met with lively Neapolitan pizza makers, balsamic vinegar producers in Modena, Piemontese truffle hunters, south Tyrolean winemakers, and mountain pine chefs, Austrian whisky distillers, Bavarian brewers, German pickle producers, and central London tea merchants. Beyond Europe, I visited Indian tea farmers, Kenyan yoghurt producers, Canadian maple syrup producers, Argentinian engineers, and rebellious Vietnamese scent hunters. Mine was a journey brimming with fascinating encounters, unexpected turns, beautiful landscapes, scientific discoveries, and historic connections, all in the quest for the elusive flavor of wood. Would I find it?

PART I

Wood,
Passion,
Flavor

CHAPTER 1

Inspired by Beavers

After my oak barrel epiphany, I started to become slightly obsessed with discovering the flavor of wood. For weeks I researched every source I could think of, searching the web and talking with friends and colleagues, as well as many food producers and scientists. Each conversation contributed another idea, insight, or clue. Soon, it became increasingly apparent that there was no single answer. Some sources strongly supported the thesis that wood affects the food products it comes in contact with; others categorically disagreed. To complicate things further, those that did note the influence (and these affirmers only existed in the realms of wine and spirits) were split into two camps: One deemed the influence of wood to be very positive, and the other thought it was altogether a negative thing, ruining the flavor of a given food item. After a while it also became clear that most took "wood" to mean "oak"; no other species of tree was discussed, particularly when it came to storage barrels.

Determined to find conclusive evidence of the flavor of wood, I continued with my research, always hoping to find the one lead that would definitively confirm—or deny—my hypothesis that wood did indeed flavor our foods. Quite to the contrary, though, every source I consulted just led in another possible direction.

Frustrated with my lack of progress, I decided to visit my parents in Nova Scotia, Canada, where I had spent most of my childhood summers hiking and canoeing. With its vast forests and seemingly endless waterways and lakes, it was the perfect place to clear my head: There is nothing more beautiful and relaxing than wandering through the aromatic, evergreen canopy of towering white pine, hemlock, and maple trees alongside lively streams and glassy lakes, particularly during a crisp autumn morning, when you get out on the lake before sunrise in your canoe, gliding silently through the landscape. Surrounded by mist rising from the water, you can watch as nature slowly wakes up around you. Birds make their first short morning flights from tree to tree. Deer stand close to the water's edge for a drink. A family of river otters, returning from a night of hunting, noisily splashes into the lake.

On one especially picturesque, early-morning canoe trip during my visit, I met a family of four beavers munching away on the shoreline vegetation. I was delighted to see them, but the feeling wasn't mutual, as they stated loud and clear by forcefully splashing their tails on the water's surface before making a dive for it. On my treks I'd regularly come across their dams, which were masterfully crafted to keep all entrances to their burrow underwater, thereby making it very hard for any enemies, as well as the cold air, to enter. Constructed from nearby tree limbs, sticks, mud, stones, and other vegetation, these dams can last for centuries and change landscapes profoundly. The architectural capability of a beaver, I reflected, was probably unmatched by any other single animal on this planet, humans of course—and unfortunately—excluded. And they do all this hard work in cold water, on a diet consisting mostly of trees.

Then it hit me—this could be the one lead I had been looking for! Who better than beavers to address questions regarding food and trees? They basically chew trees for a living—and, judging from some pictures, can even get quite fat off them.

As perfect as this source might seem, there was one fatal flaw. How would I communicate with an animal that likes to swim extensively in cold water, preferably during nighttime, chews trees with iron-colored and reinforced teeth, reingests its feces for optimal nutrient extraction,[17] and purposefully floods its home? There is literally no common ground between the behavior of beavers and humans.

After a bit of thinking I came to the conclusion that I had to resort to studying their behavior to make assumptions about their likes and dislikes in trees. At first sight, judging from the small trees and bushes cut down around their dams, they were not very discriminating. Vicinity rather than taste preference seemed to have been the main deciding factor in their choice of wood. Yet when I took a closer look at what tree species were actually used in the building of the dams and compared them to the ones missing from the banks, there were a few noticeably absent. (I would later read that this had to do with the beavers' so-called "central-place foraging behavior," where they would not eat small trees, branches, and bushes at the place of growth but would rather bring them back to a specific central place—their burrows—for consumption.[18] This meant that they had brought the trees of their liking back to their burrow while they used the ones they didn't like to eat for the construction of their dam.)

Some large, heavy trees that were impossible to move back to their burrow had all their bark chewed off, while some (probably the unappetizing ones) still had all their bark. Following one particular construction project—a dam that suffered some damage after strong rainfalls and had to be partly rebuilt—I could narrow down which trees were missing and which were debarked. Wild raisin and dogwood seemed to be only used as building materials, while evergreen trees like larch, spruce, and balsam fir were understandably shunned completely. Why? Imagine you had only your teeth to cut down a tree. Which one would you prefer: the sticky one that freshens your breath, yet won't allow you to open your mouth for days, or the one that doesn't glue your teeth together? As it turned out, my not-very-scientific observations about a single dam were confirmed by scientific literature and internet sources alike. I had found the beavers' preferred trees: willow, poplar, maple, and birch.

Now to the question of taste. How do you taste a tree? Here, the beaver inspired me again. He only eats the bark and the nutrient-conducting underlying cambium, the layer sandwiched between the outer bark and the inner hardwood. Furthermore, he is known for being a bit of a tree connoisseur; he actually tastes the bark of a tree before deciding to use it.[19] This casual tree-tasting approach of the beaver became my shared plan of attack. Knowing that the bark from mature trees would be very tough, and also to avoid damaging them, I opted to taste samples from young trees growing in ditches that were regularly cleared. Thanks to a knife (my replacement for the beaver's iron-reinforced teeth), I obtained a small piece of bark, cambium included, from each of the four trees and simply tried them.

I expected it to be a rather unpleasant experiment, but most surprisingly, it wasn't. The poplar bark initially tasted faintly like rhubarb and then grew more bitter, but still with a hint of sweetness that strongly reminded me of Manuka honey (honey made from the flowers of the Manuka tree, native to New Zealand and with antibacterial and antioxidant properties).[20] The birch bark had a very crunchy texture and tasted surprisingly like salad greens, while the maple bark had, unexpectedly, no taste whatsoever. The most unpleasant one was the willow bark, which tasted like green potatoes still covered in some soil. Altogether, it was fascinating to discover how very different tree barks taste and how varied the beavers' taste landscape actually is.

But I suspect I was not the first person to observe animals eating bark and decide to sample it as well. Tree bark in general has had a hugely important role in human history. Most aboriginal people from Africa, Asia, Australia, Europe, and the Americas have used it for a myriad of purposes, including for making clothing, pots, paper, medicine, fibers for fishing lines and nets, and wrappers for cooking. The Native Americans' use of birch bark for the outer skin of canoes and their tipis is probably best known, but the Aboriginal Australians also used eucalyptus bark for making canoes and shelters.[21] Native Americans made their own tobacco from willow bark (simultaneously taking advantage of its analgesic effects thanks to the presence of *acetylsalicylic acid*, more commonly known as aspirin)[22] and dyed their cloth a brownish red with alder bark.[23]

More importantly and interestingly for this book, in addition to their many uses of tree products, several North American tribes were actually eating trees or parts thereof. This tradition, which was first described in 1792 by the trader and explorer Alexander MacKenzie and a little later by members of the famous Lewis and Clark expedition, has even found its way into modern vocabulary[24]: The word "Adirondack" stems from the old Mohawk Indian word *atirú:taks,* meaning "tree eaters."[25] The Mohawks used this word to speak in a rather derogatory fashion about some Algonquin tribes who were known to eat tree bark. More specifically, they were not eating the bark itself but rather the soft cambium underneath, which was rich in carbohydrates, vitamins, fiber, and minerals. Harvesting of the bark happened only in springtime (the Coeur d'Alene people called May the "bark loose on tree month") and mostly focused on trees from the pine genus.[26] Other tribes were also known to dry the cambium of hemlock and spruce trees and then grind it into a kind of flour used in the making of a specific cake.[27]

Using pine cambium for food was also a tradition practiced by the indigenous Sami people of Scandinavia. Considered quite a delicacy and brought as a special gift when visiting relatives living in pine-free areas, it was the perfect complement to their protein-rich diet. Also, due to its high vitamin C content, it kept them from getting scurvy.[28] By today's definition, pine cambium would have definitely been branded a "superfood."

I am almost certain that the first Native Americans and their Scandinavian counterparts who thought of bark as food had previously observed the natural behavior of beavers. They basically had started from the same point as I had, yet they had obviously spent much more time finding the best method for eating trees. Namely, they did not eat the bark as a whole but only the soft cambium that lies beneath, and even that only in springtime, when it's most tender.

Of course, I wanted to sample cambium immediately. However, it didn't feel right to partly or fully cut a pine tree just for tasting purposes. Also, it wasn't spring. And as the edibility of pine cambium had already been proven by a wealth of sources, I wanted to try something new anyway. So I returned to the four saplings I had already cut and carefully separated some soft cambium from the tough outer bark. Disappointingly, it didn't taste very different from the whole bark. The flavor was slightly milder and the cambium was softer and easier to chew, which reminded me of a survival technique I'd heard of many years before: If you were to find yourself stranded in a remote woodland without any food, it is supposedly possible to make a kind of spaghetti from birch cambium strips cooked in boiling water. Would this transform the raw taste of the bark or cambium?

Conveniently, I had already cut the cambium into narrow strips, and a pot with boiling water was quite easily procured. I threw the birch cambium into the boiling water and tried it at regular intervals to see if it had become softer. After a full hour and a half of cooking, however, there still weren't any significant changes in texture or taste, so I declared the experiment a failure and considered my options. If boiling didn't work, I wondered if I would have better luck with frying. I got out one of my older cast-iron pans and added a bit of rapeseed oil, which has very little flavor on its own and is therefore perfect for taste experiments. Once the oil reached frying temperature, I threw in some freshly cut birch cambium. A quick and quite fragrant sizzle later, I held the first golden-brown birch cambium strip in my hand.

Tasting it was a real revelation. Crunchy and brittle, the cambium was actually as easy to eat as a vegetable chip. It had completely lost its salad-green taste and was now sweet and starchy, with the tiniest hint of a quite pleasant bitterness. After I added a bit of salt, I began to see it as a real alternative to the bag of potato chips I buy every once in a while. Only some tiny woody bits randomly dispersed in the cambium (quite similar to those found in pears) felt a bit strange to swallow; however, they were not a real deterrent. If I had harvested the cambium at the right time in spring, the wooden bits would be likely nonexistent.

Seemingly having found the best way to prepare tree cambium, I was eager to also give the others—namely willow, maple, and poplar—a try. However, after having cut some fresh cambium from all three trees and frying them in fresh oil, I would soon find out that they simply weren't up for the task, as they became only chewier and bitterer. (This was probably why the Native Americans hadn't used them in the first place.)

After tasting many different tree barks prepared in a number of ways, I was very surprised to see how diverse they actually were. Yet when trying to think of a shared flavor note, only bitterness came to mind. Now, bitterness isn't normally a desired taste. For us humans, it immediately sets off alarm bells, as many poisonous plants taste bitter.[29] Yet it is not always a negative thing.

This is probably best demonstrated by the worldwide popularity of tonic water, the essential component of every gin and tonic. Originally patented under the rather clunky name "improved aerated tonic liquid" by a Londoner named Erasmus Bond in 1858,[30] its invention goes back to British officers and citizens stationed in India and other tropical outposts of the British Empire. For them, however, it wasn't considered to be a beverage drunk for pleasure but rather a necessary medicine for daily survival. Colonizers in the tropics faced a mortal threat from an unexpected enemy: tiny mosquitoes, or rather the diseases they carried. Chief among these was malaria, much fiercer than the strains encountered in Europe.

Yet the tropics also offered a cure for the dangerous infection: the bark of the cinchona tree. Originally discovered by the indigenous people of what is today called Peru, and therefore called "Peruvian Bark" (or "Jesuit's Bark" after those who first conveyed the bark to Europe in the seventeenth century), it quickly became the most effective drug against malaria. Initially the bark was simply ground up whole, but in the 1820s its active component, called quinine, was isolated and soon after dispersed as white quinine powder to all colonies in the tropics. In the 1840s British soldiers and citizens used 700 metric tons of cinchona bark annually, as it had been discovered not only to cure malaria but also to prevent it. The quinine powder was, however, so bitter that people were soon looking for ways to make it more palatable by mixing it with soda water and sugar. Born was the first rudimentary version of tonic water—and probably also that of the gin and tonic. Both remain hugely popular to this day, proving that the bitterness of tree bark is not an altogether negative thing.[31]

Yet bitterness was just the common flavor connecting all the types of bark. Individually, they had a range of flavors that I described to myself as tasting like rhubarb, Manuka honey, salad greens, or even green potato. That method worked well for my personal records, but what if I had to describe the flavor to someone who had never tasted Manuka honey or green potatoes before? How could he or she possibly know what I was talking about? The straightforward answer is that they wouldn't. The lack of vocabulary to describe flavor in Western society was beginning to pose a large problem for me as I embarked on my quest to identify the flavor of wood.

CHAPTER 2
The Issue of Flavor

The languages of Western cultures (in stark contrast to those of many Asian, African, and South American cultures)[32] are seriously lacking in vocabulary when it comes to matters of taste. We simply have very few words at our disposal to describe the taste and smell of food—or other things, for that matter.

How is this possible? After all, it has been a hundred thousand years since our ancestors developed the necessary anatomical preconditions (a more developed larynx and vocal cords) to voice even complex words like *Worcestershire* or, one of my personal favorites, *squirrel*. How can it be that we don't have the words to adequately describe the flavor of a strawberry, much less the one of tree bark?[33]

Already in classical times, philosophers from Aristotle onward developed a hierarchy of the senses. Senses which can perform at a distance, such as sight and hearing, were admired and regarded as more objective. Those that required closer contact, including taste, touch, and smell, were shunned as being carnal, animalistic, and subjective.[34] This attitude toward taste continued throughout the centuries and had devastating linguistic effects. Taste was considered useless to the progress of knowledge and became associated with gluttony. The result was that no particular popular vocabulary was developed to describe the taste of foods. While scholars like Giorgio Vasari wrote entire books expressing their opinions on visual art[35] or music, no such thing was done for food. Instead, there were books on manners, which stated that it was extremely rude to talk about one's personal preferences (that is, tastes) while sitting at the table.[36]

Perhaps the exception to the rule, one significant historic event does give us several written records of individuals trying to describe the taste of food: European contact with the Americas starting in 1492 and the subsequent exposure to completely novel fruits and vegetables, like corn, cacao, potatoes, and tomatoes. Corn, for example, was first described by Guglielmo Coma, a companion of Christopher Columbus,[37] simply as "good tasting." A second account by another companion, Michele de Cuneo, describes it rather negatively as tasting like "acorns" (generally considered a famine food).[38]

Those records are, however, quite rare, and continued to be so for several centuries, although many New World plant varieties including potatoes, maize, and chili peppers began to blaze a trail of success throughout Europe. Initially imported as treasured rarities for the prestigious gardens of Europe's monarchies, these plants later became staple crops deeply embedded in regional cuisines (e.g., the tomato in Italian food culture).

With so many people coming in contact with completely new food items, it's hard to comprehend that there wasn't more written discourse on their taste. Even when still-life paintings depicting tables and plates heaping with delicious-looking and exotic foods became popular in sixteenth-century Europe, the actual taste of these foods wasn't of much interest. It was all about their aesthetic, geometric, and, most of all, symbolic meaning.[39]

Only toward the end of the sixteenth century did things slowly start to change. In this era, Italian, German, English, Spanish, and, later, even French chefs started to write cookbooks that were targeted at a broader public, featuring prefaces and recipes that included general considerations on taste.[40] Before, cookbooks had been extremely brief, immediately getting to the point without any nonsense like thoughts on taste. After all, they were written by professional chefs for professional chefs. But this approach changed, for example, with the publication of the French cookbook *Le Cuisinier François* by François Pierre La Varenne in 1651.[41] Although his cookbook was still conceived as a guide for professionals, it nevertheless included a preface by both the author and the publisher (who basically tried to explain why he would publish such a mean thing as a lowly cookbook). Furthermore, in a bid to make it more accessible, it had an easily comprehensible structure, an index, and even useful recommendations on where to buy certain ingredients cheaply.[42]

Around the same time that *Le Cuisinier François* was published, the figurative meaning of the word "taste" was invented, and it became important for a true gentleman to become a master of "good taste" in all of life's aspects. Moreover, "taste" began to be used to refer to aesthetic judgment of the fine arts.

Finally, in the eighteenth century the introductory writing of cookbooks was taken over by professional writers, who celebrated the discussion of taste and cuisine to the point of likening them to art and science.[43] However, as there was still no real vocabulary available for doing so, the authors could only use synonyms for good and bad taste, the basic taste terms of sweet, sour, salty, and bitter, or simply comparisons to other food items.[44]

Nowadays, of course, taste is spoken of much more positively, but we, the people who write about food and taste, still have the same fundamental problems as those French authors in the eighteenth century: a lack of broadly accepted vocabulary as well as a prevailing (but thankfully dwindling) disinclination to even talk about taste due to cultural conditioning.

Several other language families show captivating alternatives to the few commonplace terms that describe flavor in the West. There is, for instance, the Lao language (spoken in Laos, northeastern Thailand, and Cambodia), where people use several more basic flavor terms on an everyday basis. In addition to sweet, bitter, umami, sour, and salty, they also have precise words for "not salty (enough), bland," "hot, minty" (e.g., of mint leaves), "biting, tingly" (e.g., a very tart apple), "chalky, dry in the mouth" (e.g., of unripe banana or overly strong tea), "spicy, hot" (e.g., of chili, wasabi, pepper, or strong toothpaste), "causing an itch in the teeth" (as from eating too many sour candies), and "oily, starchy, rich."[45]

Already with these additional basic flavor words, the possibilities for describing taste have more than doubled. They however pale in comparison to the options the Siwu language of Ghana offers. The Siwu language, amongst numerous other African, South American, and Asian languages, relies on a special class of words called ideophones. Almost nonexistent in Indo-European languages, this word class (grammatically distinct from nouns, adjectives, and verbs) is used to precisely characterize sensory experiences like taste.[46] Described as "poetry in ordinary language,"[47] these ideophones create a vivid mental image of sensory experiences. For instance, the word *tìtìrìtìì* means "sticky like a cat's tongue," and *saaa* refers to a "cool sensation" (e.g., from ginger).[48] The closest English equivalents are perhaps the onomatopoetic terms like *splash*, *boing*, and *wham* seen most often in cartoons,[49] but these are by no means as elaborate and ubiquitous in everyday adult language as they are in Siwu. Also, I am pretty certain that using them for more complex sensations simply wouldn't work very well in English. Describing, for example, the taste of the birch cambium chip I made in the previous chapter as an ideophone would result in a crazy word like *crunchstarchbittersweetpleasurechomp*. Fascinating as it might be to come up with sensory image words in English that describe tastes, I probably won't use them out of fear of harming the readability of this book.

Nevertheless, having begun to consider the strong language differences in the realms of taste, I began to wonder if the only English word in existence that has anything remotely to do with the flavor of wood, "woody," even exists in other languages. And if so, was its meaning the same?

To find out, I asked some of my food study colleagues who are spread across the world. Within hours, I had learned that "woody" indeed exists in many languages, although with different principal meanings. In Canadian French, Afrikaans, and Finnish it seems to be mainly used in the world of wine and whisky and is understood as the typical flavor stemming from the (oak) barrel aging process. In South American Spanish, Hungarian, and my mother tongue, German, it contrastingly refers to root vegetables that have become really tough and chewy due to late harvesting. In Hebrew it seems to mainly refer to a somewhat stiff and uptight, maybe even slightly odd, person, while in Italian it refers to clunky movement without grace.

I was surprised to see that in Arabic and Russian it primarily insinuates a certain scent used in cologne. But by far the most unexpected and hilarious use of the word is in Norwegian, where people literally say "I have a wood(y) flavor in my ass!" when they have been sitting on a hard, wooden chair for too long. I can't think of a better demonstration of language differences.

Although it would be nice to bring the vast toolbox of taste vocabulary offered by other languages with me on my quest for the flavor of wood, I am beginning to realize that this lack of vocabulary also offers great freedom. We can pick and choose from the existing English vocabulary, be it for describing music, visual art, feelings, or even people, and recombine them so they fit best for the specific taste we want to express. To be honest, I am actually quite happy that there isn't a single universal standard for taste terminology, beyond the basics, because when one is used, a lot of diversity is lost. Of course, the words we choose can seem somewhat artificial and strange at times, but isn't it also quite fascinating to see how lively and re-combinative a language can become?

PART II
Tasting Trees

CHAPTER 3
Pizza al Faggio

In the spring of 1787 when Johann Wolfgang von Goethe first approached the ancient city of Naples, situated at the base of the then-active Mount Vesuvius, he was filled with cheerful anticipation. In his mind the city was pure paradise (a notion deeply shared by the Neapolitan people), and its appeal was only enhanced by its immediate proximity to the fire-spitting maw of Vesuvius. Naples was a city of stark contrasts, where the immensely beautiful lay right next to the dreadful. Probably to the dismay of many Romans, he, when later comparing the two cities, described his previous destination, Rome, as an ill-placed monastery.[50]

With Goethe's words in mind I looked forward to my trip to Naples, even though today's press coverage of the city paints a much different picture. Despite Naples's rank as Italy's fourth-biggest urban economy and as one of the most important ports of Europe, chaos, corruption, crime, and flat-out danger to life dominated the news coverage of the city. My friends, however, praised the city and its people in much the same way Goethe had—while still recommending that I keep a close eye on my belongings when exploring. Left with the choice between expecting the horrible and the amazing, I chose the latter.

I arrived at Garibaldi train station early in the morning, still sleepy and banged-up from a night in the couchette coach. When I looked out from the train windows and took in the heavy rainclouds hanging over the city's newly developed business center, the horrible stories I'd heard of Naples came flooding back to me—why the hell had I come here?

It all began when some colleagues from work (I was working at the 2015 Milan World EXPO at the time) planned a short trip to the beautiful island of Ischia off the coast of Naples and asked me to join. I was intrigued by the island, and by southern Italy in general, since I had never traveled farther south than Rome. (Plus, the chance to travel with four stunning girls, my colleagues, was anything but a deterrent.) I was so caught up in the excitement of making travel plans that it wasn't until a few days later, when we went to purchase our tickets at the local Trenitalia office, that I realized what a great opportunity this could be for my research. Pizza! This was my chance to finally taste the world-famous, original Neapolitan pizza.

Straightaway I booked a ticket that allowed me to spend almost two full days in Naples before taking the ferry to Ischia together with my colleagues. Determined to find the absolute best pizzeria in Naples, via the university's Facebook group I called upon my fellow gastronomy studies alumni, my go-to source for all matters of food, to advise me. Within hours I had sparked a healthy discussion about whether Da Michele (launched to fame by its portrayal in the film *Eat, Pray, Love* starring Julia Roberts) or Sorbillo was the best pizzeria in town. A classmate native to Naples finally made the convincing argument that Sorbillo simply used the better ingredients, especially the oil and the tomatoes. How could I possibly argue with that? Sorbillo it was!

I hoped to speak with one of the pizzaiolos, or pizza makers, about the importance of the wood-fired oven to Neapolitan pizza, but a colleague familiar with Naples and its ways told me that this would be pretty much impossible. I learned that the pizzaiolos working in Naples' most famous pizzerias have two trademarks: swiftness of service accompanied by a rudeness that compels you to eat and pay for your pizza with an equal, or preferably even greater, swiftness.

Yet I was still determined to speak with an expert about the Neapolitan pizza, so I asked an Italian colleague to track down the number and call Sorbillo on my behalf—my Italian was much too basic for such a sensitive task—and request an interview with the owner, Gino Sorbillo.

To my great surprise we somehow got his cell phone number; a few calls and text messages later, we had actually managed to set up an appointment with one of the city's best pizza makers.

So there I was on the platform of Garibaldi train station in Naples, arriving in the gray, dreary city after enduring a ten-hour train ride. I was surprised when I reached the nearest metro station to find it was very modern and orderly with all its trains running on schedule. All my sources—Goethe, newspapers, and friends—had agreed the city was chaotic. And so the almost violently modern metro station with punctual trains seemed suspiciously out of place. But once I disembarked at the Municipio metro station equidistant from the medieval castle Nuovo (also called Maschio Angioino) and the center of the city and its world-famous harbor, I found the chaos I'd been promised; I was in the heart of Naples now. This metro station was a huge, noisy construction site, surrounded by frenzied traffic coming from all sides, scooters weaving on the sidewalks, and pedestrians walking in the middle of the street. The incessant honking of car horns added to the cacophony, only to be briefly drowned out by the horn of a massive cruise ship announcing its arrival or departure. For a European city it was pure pandemonium, but I loved it—especially once I walked a bit from the rather industrial part of the harbor into the narrow roads, back alleys, and myriad staircases winding through the historic center.

Naples is one of the world's oldest cities, with archeological evidence placing its beginnings in the early Bronze Age, some two thousand years before Christ. All major Mediterranean cultures, from the early Greeks to the Romans, had seen it as a major hub of their seafaring activities, and between 1282 and 1816 it was even its own kingdom.[51] This historic pedigree is something you sense immediately when wandering through the city's constricted streets, which were obviously built to suit not modern cars but rather horse-drawn carts. Those narrow roads lead into even narrower alleyways, which are always comparatively cool even during the sun's zenith. They seem to function as natural cooling ducts; even on the hottest of days there is always a fresh breeze which seems to come directly from the sea. This phenomena is utilized by the neighboring households, which have spanned a spider web-like net of clotheslines across the alleyways. As I wandered through the ancient heart of Naples, a ballet of freshly washed clothes tirelessly performed above my head. However, this performance was suddenly interrupted when I jumped aside to avoid being flattened by a motor scooter driven by a ten-year-old hurtling around the corner at breakneck speed. Two nuns with wafting light gray and white frocks passed by immediately after, so if the accident had occurred I at least would have received the last rites.

Having narrowly cheated death by motor scooter, I managed to find my hotel, store my luggage, and freshen up a bit before continuing to explore the city. As I walked, I repeatedly passed statues of what appeared to be a clown. After coming across several statues of this strange figure, I finally researched one of them on my smartphone. I learned that the statues depicted Pulcinella, a classic character of comic Neapolitan theatre who was meant to represent the Neapolitan soul: dynamic, clever, and always ready to tackle the daily problems of life with irony and a smile.[52] All these characteristics were very much in accordance with the impressions of Goethe, who described people in the street as merry, liberated, energetic, and generally skilled in the art of carefree living.[53]

After exploring ancient underground Naples, I was sure that this wasn't like any other Italian city I knew. In fact, it reminded me more of the Spanish cities Seville or Granada, which had been under a strong Arab influence for centuries. A friend would later suggest that Naples was very similar to Lisbon, Portugal, not only in its location by the sea and topography but also in architecture and even clothesline hanging habits. But—and this is essential—Lisbon doesn't have the traditional Neapolitan Pizza, which I just couldn't get out of my head.

Having toured the city all day, I had worked up an appetite. As it happened I was quite close to the original Pizzeria Sorbillo, which was just about to open for dinner guests, so I headed in that direction. I arrived not five minutes after its opening for dinner, but I barely got a table—a very good sign indeed. I suspected my waiter was very early into his shift, or perhaps new, because he was surprisingly friendly and obliging as he took my order, a *búfala* (pizza with buffalo mozzarella), and even convinced me to start my Sorbillo experience with a traditional *pizza fritta*: a giant ravioli made from pizza dough, filled with fresh ricotta, fiordilatte (a cheese slightly sweeter, less fatty, and more delicate than mozzarella), pepper, and cicoli (dry aged fatty pork bits), which is then deep-fried.

After a rather long wait (which is surprising, as pizzerias in this part of the world are known for their speed) I finally got my *búfala*. It was perfect; the pizza barely fit on its very large plate and its scent was otherworldly. Once I bit into the first slice I finally knew what everyone was talking about when they discussed the indescribable texture and consistency of the Neapolitan pizza dough. It was both crispy and doughy at the same time—a perfect balance, so to say. The tomatoes actually tasted like tomatoes, the likes of which you never get to taste in a northern European country, and the fresh pieces of buffalo mozzarella were still really moist, a sure sign that they were barely a few hours old. Fresh basil leaves completed the bright red, white, and green picture. This was without a doubt the absolute best pizza I had ever had in my life. What was particularly surprising for me was the intensity of the flavors. Since I was practically certain that no artificial flavor enhancers had been used, I started to wonder if this was simply due to the quality and freshness of ingredients—or if the wood oven had something to do with it.

The next day I slept in and, after enjoying an amazing breakfast overlooking Naples atop the hotel roof, prepared my questions for Gino Sorbillo. Since my Italian wasn't the best at the time, I had arranged to meet with a friend of a friend who was from Naples and happened to speak not only perfect English but also German. We were going to meet for lunch at Sorbillo (originally I had planned for this to be my first Sorbillo pizza, but hunger and curiosity got the better of me), and afterwards she would help me with the interview.

I arrived there early and immediately had to duck into the alleyway to cool off in its breeze, having overheated from walking too quickly out of excitement—a grave mistake in thirty-eight-degree weather. Once I regained my composure, I swooped past the line of people waiting in front of Sorbillo and put my name on the list. "Artur, due persone!"—these were the words I now had to wait for.

It wasn't long before Monica, my translator, arrived and we began talking about all things Naples. We were so engrossed in our conversation that we completely missed the Italianized version of my name crackling through the loudspeakers. By the second or maybe even third time an increasingly unnerved voice yelled "Artuuuro!?" into the microphone, we finally heard it and were hastily shown to a table. This time we got the proper Naples pizzeria treatment: The waiter was unfriendly, the yet-again-amazing pizza came almost immediately, and we had barely eaten half of it when waiters started to give us a pointed look, plainly asking whether we were done yet.

However, one thing was noticeably missing: Gino Sorbillo. I had already sent him a text when we sat down but received no reply. So I asked Monica if she could ask the cashier, who reigned over the register on an elevated platform overlooking her subordinates (this category included the paying customer), whether Mr. Sorbillo happened to be around. I stayed at the table while the two were talking, but Monica's slight look of disappointment and the cashier's shaking head told me that something hadn't gone according to plan. According to the cashier, Mr. Sorbillo had a very important meeting with the police, which would keep him from coming to the pizzeria all day.

We paid and left the pizzeria feeling rather disappointed, although I had expected something like this; after all, I'd been warned of the unpredictability of Naples. After unsuccessfully trying to reach Mr. Sorbillo once more, Monica suggested that we go for a *caffè shakerato* (an espresso mixed with sugar and ice cubes in a cocktail shaker and served in a martini glass) at a bar around the corner. As we sat, venting our disappointment, I suddenly received a text with these exact words: *Bussi via [Street Address] Casa della Pizza,* meaning "Knock [Street Address], House of the Pizza." I showed it to Monica. It was Gino Sorbillo's number—but hadn't we just been told that he was unavailable? Perhaps we'd been given the wrong cell number and it was actually the owner of the other Pizzeria Sorbillo, which was practically next door to the original but not as good by a long shot. (A friend from Norway who happened to be in Naples a few days before me and to whom I recommended Sorbillo actually made this mistake and had just told me about it.)

Either way, we were determined to find out, so we quickly paid for our iced coffee, which had been very refreshing indeed on such a sweltering day, and headed for the address in the message. We found ourselves in front of a rather inconspicuous door, whose bell was, sure enough, labeled "Casa della Pizza." We rang and it opened immediately, followed by a voice asking us through the intercom system to come to the second floor. We were received by a quite nice young man who asked what we wanted. We told him about our appointment with Gino Sorbillo, which he knew nothing about, but he let us in anyway, telling us that Mr. Sorbillo—so it was the real Gino Sorbillo!—had a meeting with business owners from the area to discuss the worsening local security situation. He led us into the main room of the apartment, which was filled with elegantly dressed people. They all sat or stood around a huge glass table, at the center of which sat Gino Sorbillo in his double-buttoned white chef's jacket like a judge presiding over court. He listened intently to the heated discussions at his left and right, but never spoke himself. So as not to disturb the proceedings, he communicated with his assistant, the younger man who had let us in, via text message to ask us if we could wait for maybe half an hour (which we obviously could) and offer us coffee while waiting.

It wasn't long until people started to leave and Sorbillo was available to discuss the importance of the wood-fired pizza oven to original Neapolitan pizza. I was particularly curious to know why a wood-fired pizza oven seemed still to be the gold standard in the world of pizza making, as there were several alternatives on the market. I was surprised to learn from him that there actually is a law in Naples mandating that pizza ovens must have a chimney; this means there has to be some kind of a wood fire burning in the oven. However, making and maintaining the perfect fire is not only a lot of work but actually an art in and of itself. For one, you have to know exactly which type of wood to use. Sorbillo uses only beech wood, but the bark must be removed before burning because it contains sap, which creates a lot of smoke and an unpleasant accompanying flavor, much like burning turpentine.

He told me that unlike oak or chestnut, beech wood has a controlled burn. It doesn't spatter and therefore doesn't fling pieces of burned wood onto the pizza. His trusted firewood source is the third-generation family business Formisano, located at the foot of Mount Vesuvius. The firewood they provide specifically for pizza ovens goes through a lengthy process also used to prepare wood for fine furniture making. Beech trunks from the region surrounding Naples, called Campania, are first sawn into rough boards, then dried and aged outside for up to two years. Afterwards, the now very-dry boards are sawn once again into square twenty-inch pieces, carefully avoiding any remaining bark, and then packed in cardboard boxes before being shipped to the best of Neapolitan pizza makers.[54]

Traditionally, the fire is always built on the left side of the pizza oven to allow the heat to circulate along the contour of the dome, heating it as evenly as possible. At Sorbillo they start the fire first with pressed wood briquettes; other pizza makers use spelt, hazelnut shells, or walnut husks; these fuels all burn easily and vigorously and are therefore perfect for igniting the tougher beech wood. Once the fire is started, the pizza oven then must heat to a temperature of more than 752 degrees Fahrenheit. This high heat is a key element for the creation of the perfect texture of the Neapolitan pizza, and produces its signature crust. I asked Sorbillo how this apparent contradiction (crust that is simultaneously crispy and doughy) is possible, and he answered that the first key element is the high heat, which causes the outside of the crust to crisp immediately before the dough has enough time to release all the water inside. The second key element is how the burning chamber is shaped. It must have a very specific dome shape. If the dome is too high, the pizza doesn't rise enough and stays too flat; if the dome is too low, the pizza will simply burn. Getting the shape right is an art only mastered by very few Naples-area kiln engineers, most of which are family-run businesses where the knowledge gets passed down from father to son.

So a perfect Neapolitan pizza is as much down to the kiln engineer and the firewood supplier as it is to the pizzaiolo. However, the kiln engineer has to only build the oven once, and the firewood supplier has to only focus on the task of preparing the wood in the best possible way. The pizzaiolo is the one who brings all those components together within minutes, like the conductor of an orchestra. This not only includes making each pizza by hand and keeping the fire going at just the right temperature, but also monitoring up to four pizzas in the oven at once, and, since the fire is only on the left side of the kiln, frequently turning all four to cook them evenly.

The amount of work necessitated by a traditional wood-fired oven is likely the reason why various pizza makers have devised a way to partly bypass—or let's say interpret—the law mandating a chimney for every pizza oven in Naples: using electrical ovens that have a small smoking chamber. This gives the pizza a desirable, slightly smoky taste but still offers the ease of use of an electric oven. But does this shortcut result in a pizza as good as that of Gino Sorbillo? He, of course, doesn't think so, and neither do I.

Monica and I left the house of the pizza with a wealth of knowledge about the intricate relationships between the real Neapolitan pizza, the pizzaiolo, the kiln engineer, and its firewood, which is much more than just a fuel for the oven. As I still had several hours before I would meet with my colleagues on the ferry to Ischia, Monica showed me some of her favorite spots in the city. We finished with a beer on her apartment's terrace overlooking the roofs of this ancient city. Mount Vesuvius loomed on the horizon, the long-gone sun only remembered through a faint reddish ribbon on the sky's edge, the moon slowly but surely gaining in strength.

Returning to Milan from my trip to Naples and my amazing experience at Sorbillo, followed by a weekend on the idyllic island of Ischia, I had a lot to ponder. While going over my notes of the encounter, I realized that although I now knew everything in theory about wood-oven pizza, one piece was missing: taste. Gino Sorbillo had convinced me that the high heat of a wood-burning oven was crucial to the texture of Neapolitan pizza, but did it impact the taste, too? It was clear that I had to find a way to conduct an experiment comparing pizzas made in two different ovens.

Normally I am all for trying things at home, and I have a very well-equipped kitchen that can accommodate the most complex of food experiments. However, if there was one thing I didn't have, it was an actual wood-fired oven built by professional Neapolitan oven builders with generations of experience.

My first thought was that I could make this experiment in basically any pizzeria with a wood-fired oven. But when I brought it up at my go-to pizzeria, I was made aware of a fatal flaw in my supposedly simple plan: A pizzeria that has a wood-fired oven typically neither needs nor wants an electric pizza oven. (Not any old electric oven would be up for the task of generating heat above and beyond 450 degrees; it had to be one designed [or engineered] specifically for making pizza.)

It would take me several months and moving countries until I was able to find a solution to my oven dilemma. My favorite Viennese pizzeria, Riva, had just opened a new location, and it had the unimaginable: Not one but two electric pizza ovens, right around the corner from a beautiful wood-fired one. The owner, of course, wasn't planning on ever using them for making classical pizzas but rather for making the in-house innovation *crisparelle*, an extremely thin breakfast pizza. However, he agreed to let me use the electric oven for my experiment. So one rainy day in May, his pizzaiolo, Davide, prepared two identical *pizze Margherita* and simultaneously put them into a preheated electrical oven and their beech wood-fired pizza oven.

When he brought them to my table I could instantly spot the difference. While the one from the wood oven looked really appetizing, with its perfectly browned crust and colorful toppings, the one from the electric oven had an uninviting yellowish crust and drab, brownish toppings. Upon first bite, the textural difference couldn't have been clearer. The wood oven had yet again produced a perfectly crunchy yet simultaneously doughy texture, while the electrical oven had made the dough both crunchy and rubbery. Both of these were outcomes I had expected. But what was really surprising was the difference in taste. The electrocuted pizza was not only hard to chew but essentially inedible. The tomato sauce was really sour, the basil leaves were slightly bitter, and the mozzarella had a strong musky taste. Uniting them was a certain wateriness and a lingering lack of balance throughout the dish.

The myriad of positive tastes coming out of the wood-fired oven, though, was a revelation. I, uncharacteristically, noted words like "flavor rainbow" or simply "explosion" in my notebook. First the wood-fired pizza had a slightly smoky sensation paired with the surprising taste of rolled oats and a strong, savory yet sweet, almost wiener sausage–like component. Everything from the tomato sauce to the mozzarella tasted much more balanced. The sourness of the tomatoes had been buffered and turned into a beautiful smoky sweetness, while the mozzarella had lost all of its unpleasant musky character. Even the basil had been transformed into a harmonious, aromatic, almost perfume-like version of itself. Altogether the pizza had a much stronger taste, as if it had been crafted adhering to an ancient secret only available to pizzaioli from Naples.

I knew, however, what this secret was. It was the beech wood that not only delivered the perfect heat and a slightly smoky, rolled oats, milky, and wiener sausage–like taste, but also acted as a buffering agent that balanced the flavor of all toppings while simultaneously lifting their intensity to new heights. Finally, I had found the influence wood has on the taste of the classic Neapolitan pizza.

CHAPTER 4
Postcards from London

Having found the extraordinary tastes of tree barks and discovered how vital beech wood smoke is for the Neapolitan pizza, I became curious about a tree's leaves.

While the trunks and branches of trees provide stability and perseverance over time, their roots and leaves constantly adapt, grow, explore, and connect with the surrounding world. The roots' part in this ever-changing game happens out of our sight, but the leaves' work can be vividly seen and admired. Most visible are undoubtedly their spectacular seasonal color changes, which occur dramatically in deciduous trees but also more subtly in evergreen trees. Arguably, leaves are the most important part of a tree—the functional equivalent to solar panels. Leaves use the sun's energy to produce sugar from carbon dioxide (the gas humans pump into the atmosphere through the burning of fossil fuels) and water. An essential "waste" product of this process is oxygen. Additionally, leaves also function as a natural air conditioner by dispersing water vapor drawn up by the roots from deep in the earth, thereby cooling the surrounding area by up to thirty-seven degrees Fahrenheit.[55] The water also enters the water cycle and produces rainfall in forested areas, sometimes surpassing average rainfall in non-forested areas by 40 percent.[56]

The forests surrounding my house in the hills some twenty minutes outside of Vienna are mostly deciduous, but at the bottom of some cold ravines evergreens still find shelter from the ever-warming climate. Starting in spring, I admire the seemingly endless color palate of green, each tree or even each leaf having its very own hue. By early summer the canopy starts to resemble a perpetually growing light green cumulus cloud formation, looking as soft and cozy as cotton batting. Turning ever darker over summer, the leaves finally begin their colorful transformation in fall before they tumble to the ground, where they will decompose and deliver the nutrients for many repeating cycles.

Sometimes, however, leaves don't follow this primary natural cycle but rather enter a secondary cycle: the one of being eaten. In many cases this is done by animals and insects, but humans also eat tree leaves quite happily. Ancient Europeans used tree leaves for food and medicine alike, and some still do today. Young, bright green and delicate linden and beech leaves, for example, make great salads; young spruce shoots matured in sugar or honey with the help of sunlight make excellent cough syrups. In the Japanese city of Minoh in the Osaka prefecture is a shop which has been selling deep-fried Japanese maple leaves (*Momiji tempura*) for at least a hundred years. The leaves are harvested from the shop's own forest in the fall, when they are bright yellow. They are washed and then preserved in a salt-filled wooden barrel for a year, then dipped in a batter made from wheat flour, sugar, and sesame seeds and deep-fried.[57] A friend from the Shizuoka prefecture also told me that in her region they make tempura from fresh young persimmon leaves. This, however, is not the most fascinating use of persimmon leaves. That designation goes to their use in the city of Osaka, known for its many waterways and rich fishing grounds, where Nigiri sushi made from mackerel has historically been wrapped in persimmon leaves for transport to cities further inland. The persimmon leaves' natural antimicrobial and antifungal properties kept the fish and vinegar-soaked rice from spoiling.[58] Although today's refrigerated transport vehicles make the preservation abilities of the persimmon leaves obsolete, the art of *Kakinoha-zushi* (Persimmon leaf sushi) is still practiced today, as it is valued for its special taste and appearance.[59]

However, neither persimmon leaves nor maple leaves were the

reason that I found myself one misty September morning getting on the train at Wimbledon in the direction of Vauxhall Station in central London. Rather, it was another tree leaf product that most people have tried at least once, if not many more times: tea made from the humble *Camellia sinensis* plant.

The fact that the common tea beverage is actually a tree product might be surprising to many, as most people associate the tea plant with vast, lush gardens covered with bushes no higher than three feet shaped into a tightly clipped box hedge. Yet this shape and size are entirely human-made, to facilitate easy leaf picking. Wild tea trees can reach heights of fifty feet and live for several hundred years.[60]

To get an in-depth insight into the mesmerizing world of tea, where better to travel than the United Kingdom, a country responsible for the success story of tea in the Western world?

My interest was in tea generally, as it is my absolute favorite beverage in the world. Yet more specifically I was interested in the flavors of tea. Given that tea is a tree product, I was curious to see which flavor notes were common in tea leaves and if there were perhaps some that I had previously encountered in my explorations. Also, what influence does the manufacturing process have on flavor? How strong is the flavor difference between green tea (unfermented), oolong tea (partly fermented), black tea (fully fermented), and pu-erh tea (green tea fermented by fungi)?

I was hoping Tim d'Offay, the owner of a small but very renowned tea shop in London called Postcard Teas, would be able to help me with this quest. I had heard about Tim, an important name in the London tea scene, from a friend who got to know him through his consulting work for high-end restaurants and hotels.

My appointment with him was to take place in his small tea shop in the prestigious Mayfair district on Dering Street, a small side alley of New Bond Street just a short walk from Oxford Circus Station. Thanks to very orderly morning commuters, I arrived perfectly on time in front of the store. It looked very inviting from the outside with its warmly lit, large French-style windows that were framed by an all-black piano lacquer border and the store's name written in gold lettering above it. The shop windows were decorated with beautifully handmade Japanese teapots, cups, and tea-making utensils. The left-hand and right-hand walls on the inside were filled with a dazzling selection of teas packaged in cylindrical containers featuring colorful labels, while in the back there was a table with two benches and a small sales counter that also functioned as a tea kitchen. D'Offay and one of his employees were already in the store and gave me a warm welcome, quite literally, by offering me a cup of tea. With so many amazing teas to choose from, I finally decided on a Lapsang Souchong, since I had never gotten around to trying one.

As chance would have it, this type of tea, a particularly aromatic Chinese black tea that is smoked over pinewood fires, first inspired d'Offay to explore the fascinating world of loose-leaf tea after he tried it for the first time at a friend's house. When he finished with university in 1993 and faced a deep economic recession, his father, a well-known modern art collector,[61] recommended that he go to Kyoto, as he had both family and friends there. D'Offay moved and immediately found himself surrounded by tea. From the growers in the mountains that encircled the city on three sides to the schools of Japanese tea ceremony in the city itself, tea was everywhere. Now finally knowing that he wanted to work in tea, but not liking any of the existing tea businesses, d'Offay decided to start one himself. With the small proceeds he got from selling a painting by one of his father's artists, he went on a targeted trip to tea-growing areas for several months, kicking off his importing business.[62]

He opened the shop in 2005 and went on to pioneer the idea of *provenance* in tea. This term is normally used in the art world, whereby a piece of art's history of origin, its changing ownerships and locations over time, and any curious events involving the artwork are meticulously researched and recorded. This record practically defines the value of an artwork, and every serious art dealer prides himself in only selling pieces with an impeccable provenance. Unlike a large part of the worldwide tea market, whose only metrics are volume and price, d'Offay very much sees his teas as a work of art in need of provenance, which means that each of his sixty-plus teas, only made by small producers, bears at minimum the maker's name and the location. More often than not, one can read up on their story on the Postcard Teas website, accompanied by images and notes on flavor. Reading the website is almost as fascinating as sitting directly opposite d'Offay and hearing the story of the Lapsang Souchong tea I was drinking. He told me it was made on Mr. Xiang's five-acre tea farm in the village of Gua Dun, which lies in the misty mountains of Wuyishan, China. Mr. d'Offay had found him through a tea maker he'd befriended, Master Xu, who himself is one of China's most respected tea masters. Mr. Xiang's two-hundred-year-old tea plants in his village are the very plants from which the first Lapsang Souchong was made. Mr. d'Offay told me how, even today, the tea is smoked lightly over fresh pinewood in a traditional wooden house, giving it nice warmth and depth.[63]

These references to wood were the perfect occasion to tell d'Offay about my hunt for its elusive flavor. I was interested in discovering the different flavors found in tea thanks to various production processes. Ever curious, he gave my question a moment's thought and then dived into a discussion on the world of tea flavor, starting with the wonderful Lapsang Souchong tea we were drinking. Due to its smokiness, it was one of the first teas that came to d'Offay's mind when he thought about the flavor of wood. However, when focusing only on untreated teas he immediately connected the concept of a woody or malted flavor with black teas in general and Assam or pu-erh teas in particular. In pu-erh teas, he said, the woody and leafy flavor only develops over time through the aging process; the teas start off with a much brighter and fruitier taste. Another intriguing tea he told me about was KuKicha tea. Made from a blend of tea stems, stalks, and twigs, this Japanese green tea has a strong sweetness mixed with certain resinous elements.

But the flavor variety in tea doesn't end there. The grassy, vegetal, sometimes even nutty flavors of green tea, the floral and fruity flavors of oolong tea, and the rich, leathery, earthy flavors of black and pu-erh teas were just a few of the tea flavors d'Offay introduced. A special one was definitely the *teiguanyin* oolong tea from China, whose almost pungent hyacinth aroma always reminds d'Offay of his late grandmother, who used to love those flowers.

Our conversation would only last the better part of an hour, but within that short time I learned more about tea and its flavors than I could have ever imagined.

After meeting with d'Offay in his London tea shop, I was eager to try my favorite teas at home and see if I was able to discover some of the flavors and differences d'Offay mentioned. Who knows, maybe there were even some new flavor notes I could uncover myself?

Having grown up in a family that fostered a great liking of Indian teas, I had a huge selection of Darjeelings and Assams at my disposal, but I also had stocked up on some interesting new teas after interviewing d'Offay. From this treasure chest I brewed a selection of several teas. Some of the resulting flavor highlights I was able to discover included chestnut aromas, hints of jasmine flowers, hazelnut and caramel notes, grapefruit essences, and, remarkably, a bit of savory saltwater algae with its characteristic iodine flavor.

The hazelnut and caramel aromas from the Darjeeling tea vividly reminded me of when I had first discovered it on a trip to northern India with my family many years before. After flying into New Delhi's hectic airport (crammed with people even at 3:00 AM) and spending the night, we'd taken a flight north into the state of West Bengal, located in the Himalayas. Our destination, Bagdogra Airport, was situated in the fertile floodplains at the foot of the Himalayan mountains, which extend all the way to the state of Assam in the east.

Split in half by the mighty Brahmaputra river, Assam was India's first region to establish tea plantations under British rule to assure the empire's independence; before then, most tea consumed in the UK had been imported from the birthplace of tea culture, China. The introduction of tea plantations into the state of Assam had, however, a rough start. Although a variety of the tea plant was growing wild in the hot and humid jungle of the Brahmaputra valley, the British stubbornly wanted to introduce to the region the Chinese variety they had grown to enjoy. They plotted an audacious smuggling mission into China, which was then closed to foreigners, to bring some tea plants and seeds as well as a handful of Chinese tea manufacturers to Assam. These would, however, fail spectacularly, as the Chinese tea variety *Camellia sinensis* (*sinensis* means "from China"), normally cultivated in cool mountain climates, couldn't cope with Assam's tropical climate and acidic soils.[64] Furthermore, the qualification of the contracted Chinese tea manufacturers was quickly called into question. They seemed to have been selected solely based on the assumption that being Chinese automatically makes one experienced in tea making. It soon became obvious that this wasn't the case.[65]

Thankfully, some aspiring British tea farmers, with the help of locals, had in the meantime located patches of the wild-growing Assam tea plant (*Camellia sinensis assamica*) and had started the laborious task of pruning the plants to encourage new growth, as well as clearing the surrounding jungle. It wasn't long before the first tea was produced from those appropriately named "tea forests" and sold for an incredibly high price at a London tea auction in 1839. The generally well-received strong, woody flavor of the Assam tea, and the public interest that followed, spurred a planting frenzy in Assam and transformed it into the world-renowned tea-growing state it is today.

It would take, however, another fourteen years for India's highest-value tea to appear in the heart of the eastern Himalayas. On a then-unknown hilltop station situated 6700 feet above sea level, some of those tea plants smuggled out of China and propagated in nurseries in the Himalayan foothills started to grow remarkably well. They had been planted on a hunch by the station's superintendent, Dr. Archibald Campbell, an energetic Scottish civil servant in the Indian Medical Service who, with the help of hundreds of Nepalese workers, transformed the sleepy, hard-to-reach hill station of Darjeeling into a busy town with seventy European-style houses, a troop sanatorium, a hotel, a bazaar, and even a jail. Those plants were soon followed by others and resulted in the first commercial tea gardens growing *Camellia sinensis* in the Himalayas. Their excellent tea is now known the world over as Darjeeling tea.[66]

This enclave of fine Chinese tea growing in the Himalayas was exactly where my family and I were heading. We drove north from Bagdogra

Airport. First the road went through the outskirts of Siliguri, northeastern India's biggest city and an important transit point to the neighboring countries Bangladesh, Bhutan, and Nepal. The streets were lined by colorful wooden and concrete huts with corrugated metal roofs, market stalls, car garages, carpenter shops, gas stations, farm equipment shops, and a surprising amount of large deciduous trees. Cows were everywhere, mostly dozing, completely oblivious to the bustling scene around them.

And busy it was indeed. I was extremely happy to have a driver, as traffic was intense. Under a constant umbrella of Indian truck horns, the road was jam-packed with motorcycles laden with up to five people, tractors bouncing along on three wheels, extremely lavishly decorated yet completely overloaded trucks, speeding cars, bicycles loaded with bundles of sugar cane sticking out at least three feet on each side, tuk-tuks (motorized rickshaws), normal rickshaws, people, dogs, monkeys, and, of course, cows. My complete and utter amazement at the driver's ability to navigate through all of this alternated at minute intervals with sheer terror and fear for my life. However, after half an hour of praying for survival, we left the bustling city behind us and I could finally relax enough to enjoy the exotic landscape flying by the car window. We passed the first tea estates with their bright green carpet of tea bushes flanking each side of the road (with a cow's head sticking out every so often), the already harvested rice fields, and teak plantations. Then for the first time I saw the massive wall of mountains rising ahead, growing taller by the minute. I asked the driver if these were the famous 29,000-feet-plus Himalayas. He started laughing and assured me that these were just the small foothills. At thirteen to nineteen thousand feet high, any one of them was higher than the highest mountain in Austria. It's all about perspective!

Soon we left the floodplains and headed into the Himalayan mountains. Steadily climbing, the road became smaller and more winding as the vistas became grander. The driving speed dropped considerably due to the many bottlenecks in the road, which required careful maneuvering, often taking us uncomfortably close to the road's edge and the long drop beneath. As we gained in altitude, so did the humidity. The temperature, in contrast, was dropping, living up to the region's name of "India's misty mountains." No wonder the Chinese tea plants had felt right at home here, in a climate so similar to one of their proposed original homes in the mountains of Southern China and the Southwest Yunnan Province.[67]

The higher-altitude mountainsides were covered predominantly in tea bushes interchanging with small pockets of forests, harkening the days when wild orchids, rhododendron, tree fern, tigers, bears, and zillions of birds once dominated the slopes. In the early afternoon it was finally time for lunch at a roadside restaurant perched atop a cliff whose panorama windows allowed brief peeks on vibrantly green mountain valleys through the ever-changing, almost dancing mist. The food was excellent—steamed, vegetable-filled dumplings called *momos* with a hot chili sauce—but the real treat was dessert: freshly brewed, amber-colored Darjeeling tea.

After lunch the precarious driving conditions absorbed my attention once again. We began to share the already very narrow street with a swaying, bright-blue steam train, whose bumpy tracks crisscrossed the road at unpredictable intervals. The road was as chaotic as it had been in town, but was now much narrower, with a several-thousand-foot drop to one side and a very old, slightly unstable steam train to the other. Perhaps unsurprisingly, the quantity of prayer flags on or across the road increased dramatically the higher the drop down the mountainside became.

An intense hour and a 3000-foot ascent later, we had finally arrived in rainy Darjeeling. The once-tiny hill station atop a small mountain (by Himalayan standards at least) had now grown into a sprawling town with more than a hundred thousand inhabitants. Yet the tall, colorful houses fit surprisingly well into the landscape, framed by a large number of soaring, dark green cypress trees.

With daylight fading by the minute, we deposited our luggage at the hotel and rushed to the center of town, following a hand-drawn map. Our target was just a seven-minute walk downhill from the hotel, yet we managed to pass it twice before we finally found the destination of our travels: Nathmulls of Darjeeling, Darjeeling's oldest and most reputable tea shop.

Opening the door, a warm and intensely aromatic wave of tea aromas washed over us. On the inside the shop was buzzing with people busily selling, buying, brewing, tasting, smelling, weighing, and repacking teas. The store had ceiling-high shelving on two sides, packed to the brim with labeled tea packages and accessories, and one side was completely covered with stacked wooden tea chests. In the front of the shop was a large sales counter atop which a long row of jars stood, filled with all varieties of tea available for tasting in the store. Quite overwhelmed by it all, we told one of the patiently waiting employees that we were looking to first try and then buy some Darjeeling and Assams. He readily produced a list of several pages featuring their stocked teas; however, this only added to our confusion, as we weren't very experienced in tea at the time. Seeing our puzzled faces, he started laughing kindheartedly and suggested several teas to try. Most of them were already brewed, so he gave us a small teacup of each. Based on our liking and disliking of those tasted, we then together narrowed it down to several packages of tea, later sent directly to our Austrian home in a large wooden tea chest, which still has a proud place in the living room. Slightly over-caffeinated, we returned very happy to our hotel room. The next day, we woke early. With cups of Darjeeling in hand, we enjoyed an unhindered view of Mount Kanchenjunga at sunrise, which turned the snow-covered peaks a glowing red that melted away into bright orange clouds.

Our northern Indian adventure would continue later into Sikkim, past almost kitschy-looking bright green tea gardens dotted with pink flowering cherry trees, 13,000-feet-high mountain passes, cloud forests with gray langurs, and finally even into Bhutan. This trip will always be one of my most precious adventures, not only because of its numerous breathtaking experiences but also because it ignited my passion for tea.

In the following years I learned a lot about tea and probably drank even more. Yet it was talking with d'Offay that opened my eyes to the extremely wide variety of tastes tea can have, not only depending on where and how they grow but also how and by whom they are processed. It was fascinating to find yet another tree product that offered so many tastes, including everything from hazelnut, caramel, chestnut, and iodine aromas to grapefruit, jasmine, and even hyacinth flower essences. I was beginning to realize that the flavor of wood wasn't something all tree products had in common but rather seemed to define itself through its diversity. Only the flavor note "woody" seemed to have been a reoccurring theme, particularly in the description of Assam teas. Easily recognizable and yet hard to describe, the best I could compare it to is the sensation of an old bookstore. This dusty, slightly sweet but very dry and a bit astringent sensation was for me the first sign of the presence of a woody flavor note.

However, I was soon to learn that another food relying on wood opened up an even wider world of complex flavors.

CHAPTER 5

A Mellow Scotsman

Reinvigorated in my quest by all the new flavor discoveries I had made in the world of tea, I would very soon start to look closer at wood's impact on the flavor of another world-renowned product: whisky. I had always wanted to look further into whisky, as it seemed to be the first food product that people clearly associated with wood. Wine was a close second, but still not as univocal as its fiery distant cousin. However, what really got me started was a comment Tim d'Offay had made almost in passing. He told me of a surprising connection between tea and whisky, which he had heard about from one of the present-day blenders of Johnnie Walker whisky, the dominant leader in today's blended whisky market.[68] As it turns out, Johnnie Walker had started his career in 1820 as a very young grocery store owner in the small Scottish town of Kilmarnock,[69] where he soon made a name for himself as an excellent blender of teas and spices. At that time many Scottish groceries bought unaged whiskies from farm distilleries in the area and transferred them into their own secondhand barrels. These barrels had been previously filled with everything from wine to sherry and soon bestowed their characteristic flavor notes upon the newly transferred whisky. This perhaps unexpected result caught the interest of several grocers, who then started to experiment with blending the different types of whisky.[70] According to d'Offay's source, a blender himself, one of those grocers was Johnnie Walker, whose blends of slightly smoky whiskies may very well have been strongly influenced by his experience as a tea blender. This is by no means a stretch of the imagination, as many of the imported teas were smoked at the time to make them last longer during transport.

I couldn't have asked for a better connection between two tree products. On my flight back from London, already I was trying to figure out why whisky seemed to be so connected with people's conception of a woody flavor. Was it really that whisky tasted woodier than other foods or was it rather due to many years of highly successful advertising by the whisky industry? If that was the case, why focus so strongly on this aspect? It was time to explore the world of whisky, starting, maybe surprisingly to some, in Austria.

Austria's first whisky distillery can be found in Roggenreith, a tiny quintessential farming village in the country's northern highlands bordering the Czech Republic. Perhaps fittingly, this region is known as the Waldviertel, or "wooded district." At nearly 3000 feet above sea level, Roggenreith offers beautiful vistas into the surrounding countryside, which is, true to the area's name, covered in forest interrupted only by small strips of fields hardly wider than a tractor's turning radius.

When I drove through the region with an international group of former classmates from my master's program in gastronomy, they told me that now they finally understood why I kept on talking about forests and trees. As most of them lived in cities, the region must have seemed in their eyes an utmost wilderness. Luckily, it wasn't so remote that innovations from the outside world couldn't arrive here, as the founding of a successful whisky distillery in 1995 clearly shows.

No one knows exactly when the first whisky was made. When it was first mentioned in written history in a 1494 business document detailing the supply of whisky to the court of King James IV in Edenborough by a Benedictine monastery in Lindores, Scotland, distilling was already well established all over Europe. However it wasn't called whisky yet.[71] In Latin, distilled spirits were called *aqua vitae*, or "water of life," and several European countries translated this term into their own language. The

French called it "Eau de Vie," the Scandinavians "Aquavit," and the Gaelic-speaking Scots "Uisge-Beatha," which over time was abbreviated to "whisky" or "whiskey" with an "e", as whiskies made in the United States and Ireland are spelled. Additionally, each country adapted the basic formula for whisky to incorporate its local, botanical components by using different basic ingredients that were readily available, such as grapes in France and barley in Scandinavia and Scotland.[72] Today one differentiates strictly between malt whisky, made only from malted barley without any other grains added, and grain whisky, made from a variety of grains and malts thereof; this wasn't the case back then, as grains and their malts were used and mixed according to availability.

As "aqua vitae" were generally regarded as a tonic with great medicinal, almost mythical, properties, distillate recipes and their production were entrusted to religious institutions like monasteries.[73] However, it wasn't long before farmers would discover the merits of distillation, which allowed them to transform excess crops into a vermin-proof spirit that had all kinds of positive side effects, at least temporarily.

At its inception, whisky was consumed as white spirit; it was clear because it was not yet being aged in wooden barrels.[74] There is no written record of when white whisky was first matured in a wooden barrel, but common belief is that it happened purely by chance sometime in the eighteenth century.[75] In those times wooden barrels were the universal storage and transport containers, so it is easy to imagine that a farmer forgot some of his white whisky in a barrel and found it several years later, only to discover that the spirit within had been completely transformed. How he scrounged up the courage to actually try it then is a little harder to imagine, but someone must have done it.

Contrary to what one might think, though, this discovery did not change anything for another hundred and fifty years, as whisky continued to be mostly drunk as a clear spirit. Aged whisky remained the exception. In 1915, however, the British government, lobbied by the temperance movement, passed the immature spirits act, which decreed that all whisky had to be stored in barrels for three years and one day. The purpose of this act was to squeeze distillers out of business, because it was believed that no business could survive those three years without sales. But several distilleries somehow did manage to survive, and this marked the beginning of a new era in whisky.[76] Aging added a completely new layer of complexity and color to this fine spirit and created a product so successful that whisky has become one of the most consumed spirits worldwide.[77]

But what does aging in wooden barrels actually do? Does it only add color, or does it also add flavor? The answer to this question, or so I hoped, was just another ten minutes of driving ahead of me at the Waldviertler Roggenhof whisky distillery in Roggenreith.

Although the art of whisky making is a relatively new arrival to this small village, the practice of distilling has a very long tradition in the country. The first written record of Austrian distilling actually dates back to the fourteenth century. Since Austria has always been a country rich in fruit trees, most of its distillates were schnapps made from fruits, contrary to the "schnapps" sold in the United States, a grain-based alcohol that is later mixed with artificial fruit flavorings.[78]

Today, the enterprising Johann Haider, owner and founder of Waldviertler Roggenhof, is using neither fruits nor the traditional barley for his whisky. Instead he is using rye in parts grown on his farm, a much hardier grain that is perfectly adapted to the rather poor soil and colder winters in northern Austria. In fact, the village's name, Roggenreith, literally means "rye forest clearing."

Haider started the distillery in 1995 when he realized that his family farm desperately needed an additional economic base to provide for his family. True to his can-do attitude, he founded a distillery without ever having learned the art of distilling, but he nevertheless mastered the craft through books, trial and error, courses, and travels to established distilleries in other countries. In 1998 his first whisky was finally ready and immediately struck a chord with the Austrian media. Their extensive reporting on "Austria's first whisky distillery" launched him to instant fame, and busloads of people who wanted to tour his distillery and buy his product arrived by the hundreds. Twenty years later, his whisky has won many awards including from the renowned International

Wine & Spirits Competition (IWSC), and has been regularly featured and praised by the likes of Jim Murray, author of *Jim Murray's Whisky Bible*, and Michael Jackson, famed author of *Michael Jackson's Malt Whisky Companion*. His farm has in the meantime been transformed into a "Whisky Adventure World" receiving more than seventy thousand visitors per year.[79]

I arrived at the distillery a little late, but thankfully Haider had to run some errands and had been behind schedule as well. He welcomed me with a curious look on his face; I think he wasn't sure what to make of me and my interest in the flavor of wood. Once I explained a little more about my quest, he happily showed me around his distillery and introduced me to the world of rye whisky. We started at the distillery's heart, the two high-performance stills made in Germany, which glistened in the spotlight. An intricate system consisting of two stainless steel vats with two copper refractory towers on top, an additional tower sitting in the middle, and a vast quantity of different fittings, dials, displays, and pipes, it had the look and feel of a satellite being prepared for its imminent launch to outer space.

But this space-like apparatus was actually based on a pretty simple physical principle. Distillation takes advantage of the different points at which various liquid substances change from the liquid to the gaseous phase; the so called "boiling point." Most will know it from boiling water in the kitchen, which happens at 212 degrees Fahrenheit. Ethanol (alcohol) on the other hand has a lower boiling point at 173.1°F. So if one wants to separate ethanol from water all one needs is a simple distillation apparatus consisting of a heat source, a vat (a pot with an airtight lid) and a cooling element (usually in the form of a water-cooled spiral) connected to it. Once such an apparatus is procured the next step is to heat the liquid in the vat of the still to around 173.1°F. This will evaporate ethanol, but not water. Finally, that ethanol vapor has to be cooled below its boiling point in the stills cooling spiral and voila, liquid ethanol.[80]

Of course, this is only in principle, as in reality a bit of water and further substances present in the base liquid (called flavorful organic compounds) will always evaporate alongside. The less complex a distilling apparatus is the more substances other than ethanol will be in the final distillate.

Leaving the still room, we continued into an exhibition room containing the grain that actually goes into a Roggenhof whisky. By showing me the differently prepared grains, Haider introduced me to a hugely important procedure in the preparation of whisky that allows for one of the biggest taste conversions to occur: the process of malting. Malting encourages the grain to germinate by immersing it in warm water and then drying it to stop it from actually sprouting. Germination transforms the starch within a grain into sugar, which is then available for yeast fungi to ingest and convert into ethanol and carbon dioxide. Depending on the level of heat and the duration of drying, the malt develops different roasting aromas. Additionally, it's possible to scent the malt through smoking. At the Roggenhof distillery, for example, they use peat, harvested carefully and in small quantities from a nearby moor, to smoke some of their malt, which in turn imparts its flavor on these particular whiskies.

Most of the grain and malt used by Haider is from the area, and so is the water that comes from a nearby forest spring, specifically selected for its aroma and softness. His penchant for utilizing local production was most apparent, however, in the warehouse. Boasting a notable square footage, the warehouse was filled floor-to-ceiling with huge wooden shelves with perfectly square openings, each of which held a sixty-gallon barrique barrel filled with whisky. Standing in front of this wall of barrels I instantly understood why people made the connection between whisky and wood. None of the other products I had discovered thus far came even close to this visual embodiment of the use of wood in food manufacturing.

But what about the taste? When I asked Haider, he strongly affirmed the presence of wood flavors in whisky and began to tell me the fascinating flavor journey he undertook with his barrels.

In the beginning, Haider simply followed what everyone else in the whisky industry was doing, which was using barrels made from either French or American white oak. The industry generally seems to prefer those two types of oak wood, as they give a very pleasant and universally liked vanilla or chocolate aroma to the whisky, from the American and

French oak, respectively. One day, though, it dawned on him that his region of Austria was covered with oak forest. Why should he buy expensive barrels from thousands of miles away, he asked himself, so he decided to give the local oak a try. Working with a forester and the Austrian cooperage Schneckenleitner, he produced a few trial barrels and filled them with his rye whisky. The resulting flavors had more in common with the vanilla of American white oak than with the chocolate of French limousine oak, but with a less aggressive, more rounded effect. He was so impressed with the result that the distillery now exclusively uses Austrian oak for its rye whiskies.

When I sampled some of his whiskies, there were no Scottish whiskies available against which to compare the notes of vanilla in its taste. However, Haider had something even better: white whisky. This unaged whisky directly from the still provided a marvelous opportunity for me to actually see and taste the difference wood makes in whisky. A strong change in color was obvious, from the completely clear and colorless white whisky to the beautifully translucent deep copper that morphed, depending on the light, into an almost opaque treacle color of the barrel-aged whisky. But what was really interesting to discover were the differences in taste. The white whisky, made from 100 percent rye malt, initially had a very mild honey note that was soon overpowered by the burning sensation of the 41 percent alcohol. But after having been stored in an Austrian oak barrel for three to four years, the aged whisky revealed a much more harmonious, full-bodied flavor that, of course, included vanilla but also a more pronounced note of honey, faint coconut aromas, and even a hint of smoky cinnamon. Curiously, the burning effect of the alcohol also seemed much less noticeable, even enjoyable.

After the tasting, I'd realized I'd spent more than two and a half hours at the distillery and hadn't even noticed. I thanked Haider for his extreme generosity, both in sharing his time and knowledge, and drove back to my parents' place. My head was filled with information on whisky and the influence wood has on it. But I knew that I had barely scratched the surface.

How much more there was to know, I would only fully realize several weeks later, when I had a fascinating conversation with Annabel Meikle, a renowned whisky expert who, after working first for the Scotch Malt Whisky Society and later as global brand ambassador for the Glenmorangie Distillery, was now both the director of her own consultancy, The Whisky Bell, and of the highly exclusive Keepers of the Quaich Society, an invitation-only Scotch whisky appreciation society founded by the leading distillers in the industry.

I got in contact with her through a mutual friend and was blown away by both her genuine kindness and her wealth of knowledge of flavors in whisky. The flavors I have already mentioned, like vanilla, coconut, and chocolate, can be detected by most people, but Annabel has a much more discerning palate than others. Interestingly, she detects an actual taste of wood in many if not all whiskies, and for her there is not just a single "woody" flavor. She says that the woody taste can vary hugely, from green, sappy wood to the rather more exotic sandalwood. She also noted that a whisky can also be overly woody. There are many reasons for an overly woody flavor, she explained, like using fresh, previously unused barrels, or when the whisky is overaged and the wood dominates the taste. I was surprised to learn that longer barrel aging is not automatically better. But the most surprising data she revealed was her estimate that more than 70 percent of the whisky's final flavor, as well as all of its color, can come from the barrel itself. (If it is a new, previously unfilled barrel.)

Although I had known that wood had a strong influence on whisky, 70 percent was a much higher number than I had expected. People's perceived connection between whisky and wood was most definitely founded in reality: Wood is more important to whisky than all the other ingredients, techniques, and processes combined.

CHAPTER 6
Vienna Speakeasy

According to an old German saying, "April—April does what it wants." Indeed, one April day as I was traveling back to Vienna from my parents' home in northern Austria, I witnessed bright, warm sunshine change to a thick snowfall within ten minutes, fundamentally transforming the look of the landscape. A mellow springtime blazing in all shades of green, dotted with white, flowering plum trees and earth-colored freshly harrowed fields, topped with a bright blue sky suddenly transformed into a grayish landscape of muted greens and browns. This, in turn, slowly disappeared behind a curtain of snow and rain. Ten minutes further into my journey, the same spectacle occurred in reverse; the mud and snow of the previous few miles gave way to a verdant landscape. Disembarking the train would be a gamble. Would I arrive in the midst of a snowstorm, or would I get the full springtime treatment?

Either way, I had two appointments awaiting me in the city. The first one was with someone who'd listed a piece of artwork on an online classifieds platform. I had arranged a meeting in order to see the painting in real life. It was by a rather unknown and therefore still very affordable Austrian artist who lived around the turn of the last century and intriguingly combined the techniques of traditional Japanese woodcarving with European and Eastern landscapes. Together they form a truly fascinating combination.

The seller's address was just a few hundred feet from the train station—fortunate, as I had spectacularly lost in the weather lottery. As I arrived, glazed in ice, I could see men busily carrying boxes out of an old house and loading them into a van. Every time one of them passed by me, a waft of what I only can describe as an "old bookstore smell" came with them. Following the origin of the smell, I suddenly found myself in the middle of an old Viennese villa that was fully and most beautifully furnished with light Biedermeier and dark Empire furniture. The slightly creaking herringbone parquet floor was covered in Persian silk rugs, and the walls were adorned with all types of paintings in heavy, golden, baroque frames. In the background, I could hear men running up and down stairs. One of them came my way. It was the person I had talked to on the phone. He knew who I was right away and started to look for the painting amongst the piles of artwork lying in the corners of each room.

It became apparent that this beautiful building had been owned by an avid art collector who had recently passed away. His children sold the house immediately, saddling an antiques dealer with the task of removing and selling everything within. He was the man who was now busily—or, more accurately, frantically—searching for my painting of interest. His obviously high level of stress was the result of a call he had just gotten informing him of the arrival of a demolition crew the very next day. This beautiful building was going to be replaced with yet another concrete building that would probably need replacement in less than fifty years. What a great shame.

After a while it became clear that he had already sold the painting to someone else. However, he invited me to have a look around. It was a dream come true for me, and so I spent more than an hour carefully sorting through all the paintings and drawings. After just a few minutes I found a small bluish painting, signed in orange with "Chagall." My heart stopped. Had I just stumbled across an actual painting by Chagall, the famous Russian-French early modernist? I did a quick online search. Did the painting show some similarities to his *Creation of Man* series? Maybe it was more like *The Sacrifice of Isaac*. But the simplicity of the depicted figures and the colors used most resembled *Noah's Ark*.[81] The longer I looked, the more I began to notice different abstract aspects of the painting, which cast doubt at the painting's authenticity. While it was exceptionally beautiful, it surely must be a fake—a very well-made one at that.

I put it aside and continued the treasure hunt. During the next hour, I found two paintings by the artist I had come for in the first place and managed to negotiate a very good price for them. The antiques dealer even threw in the fake Chagall. I was over the moon, as I really liked it, fake or not.

During my search, I was so focused that I almost missed several texts arriving from the subject of my next appointment, asking me if I would be available slightly earlier. Fortunately, I saw them just in time to tear myself away from the late art collector's house and make my way to the appointment with Reinhard Pohorec.

Reinhard is somewhat of an institution in Vienna's bar scene, and this at the age of only twenty-seven. I first met him through a friend who told me about a new bar that had opened in the city with a very interesting concept. It was called Tür 7, or Door 7, a so-called *speakeasy* inspired by the illegal bars operated during Prohibition in the United States, where people met in covert locations, mostly private apartments, and consumed illegally acquired alcohol. Guests were encouraged to keep as quiet as possible ("speak easy") in order to avoid detection by the authorities.[82]

Though it has its required liquor license, this is the exact experience of Tür 7. To get in, you have to know the bar's address and their phone number to make a reservation by text message, both of which you would usually get from a friend of a friend; or at least, that's how I got them. Once you arrive at the unmarked door in a quiet side alley, you ring a bell for someone to open. Inside, the bar is furnished like a posh, plush apartment. You are welcomed by the bartenders, your hosts, who hang your coat and even offer you slippers. The idea is to feel like you're over at a friend's place, and it almost does.

Reinhard is one of the key persons involved in the creation of this unique place, which is where I met him for the first time. We have kept in contact ever since, and he was one of the first people I thought of speaking with regarding the flavor of wood in the world of spirits.

On this April day we met at the location of one of his newest projects, the Park Hyatt Vienna. As a consultant, he had completely transformed their bar concept and was about to do the same for the hotel's sister locations in Milan and Moscow. We met in the hotel's lounge just around teatime, so we both ordered a tea and started talking all things wood and spirits.

Right at the start of our conversation, Reinhard assured me that wood is an enormously interesting topic for him personally and for the world of alcoholic drinks (mixed and unmixed) in general. But he also added that it is very important to distinguish between two different aspects of flavor when talking about wood: maturity and wood flavor. These are often thought of as one in the same, but according to Reinhard, maturity of a spirit doesn't necessarily mean that it has been noticeably influenced by wood. This is due to the wooden barrel's unique, twofold ability to influence the liquid it contains: one is the transferring of flavor-giving compounds from the wood itself and the other is allowing contact with oxygen through minute pores. To explain further Reinhard gave some examples.

The first was the "no age statement" movement in Scottish whiskies, whereby distilleries have started to blend differently aged single-malt whiskies and therefore can't put a single, definitive age on a given bottle. As a rule of thumb, the longer aged a whisky, the better the product; the NAS movement allowed distilleries to somewhat break free of this rule and promoted experimentation.[83] While it was itself a great idea, some producers unfortunately tried to mimic the flavors of long-aged whiskies by using "green," previously unused barrels. As these barrels had never before been in contact with any spirit, their wood was still full of tannins and other secondary substances. Filling those barrels enabled them to quickly get as much wood extract as possible into their product, thereby mimicking a very long-aged whisky (to a degree). However, due to the speed of the process, while the strong wood flavor might have been there, the maturity of the spirit's flavor that can only develop over time and in contact with oxygen through the barrel's wood was not. This resulted in improperly aged spirits entering the market.

To give a perfect example of a beverage where maturity is everything, Reinhard brought up sherry, a type of barrel-aged, fortified wine that is produced mainly in the southern Spanish region of Andalucía. In the world of sherry, a barrel is only deemed worthy for aging after it has been used in winemaking for at least fifty years. Some of the barrels in the cellars of Jerez are two to three hundred years old and hardly give off any wood flavor anymore, yet they are still essential in maturing the drink. The key process here is, once again, microoxidation, which is only possible through the naturally porous material of wood.

Wood pores in general are a fascinating topic as they do much more than just allow minute amounts of oxygen to reach the liquid within a barrel. They are also the pathways that allow the liquid to enter the barrel's walls and extract substances from the wood. One tree's pores are not like that of another. Some pores are large in diameter; others are very fine. Even in a single tree, wood from the bottom or the top show differences in pore diameter.[84] While there can be great variation in the size of wood pores, they all exist on a miniscule scale; the largest pores have about the diameter of a human hair.[85]

The difference depends not only on the tree species but also on the growing conditions of a tree. If the tree has a lot of space to grow quickly, it develops large pores. Limited space, however, results in slow growth and small pores. This difference is most apparent in cognac, as Reinhard explains next.

A variety of brandy, or distilled wine, cognac can only be produced in the southwestern French town of Cognac and its surrounding area by definition, and it must be aged in French oak barrels either from the nearby forests of Limousin or Tronçais in central France. The Limousin forest is dominated by the oak species *Quercus robur*, whose wood is slightly softer and more porous than the *Quercus sessilis* oak species growing predominantly in the forests of Tronçais.[86] Additionally, trees in the Limousin forest are much younger and more widely spaced,[87] which results in even larger pores. The Tronçais forest is an old, relatively dense, uniformly aged oak forest,[88] resulting in finer pores in its trees. This lends a more tannic, woody, and overall stronger taste to the Limousin oak and a finer, more aromatic taste for the Tronçais oak. Each cognac producer uses the type of oak wood that they think fits best with their product and the house's tradition.

Honoring tradition in general seems to be a trait shared by many of the centuries-old spirit producers, be it cognac, sherry, whisky, etc. Talking with Reinhard, it became clear that he has a great admiration for what he sees not only as tradition but as vast experience. This experience, in his view, must be acknowledged and trusted by bartenders. Unsurprisingly, he is therefore rather careful in utilizing what has become somewhat of a trend in the bar scene: barrel aging of cocktails. Under this method, cocktails are prepared, poured into small wooden barrels (unfortunately not always of the best quality), and left for several days or even weeks to age right at the bar.

Reinhard's problem is not with the practice itself but rather the base alcohols used for the cocktails. He feels it makes no sense whatsoever to take a carefully barrel-aged cognac or whisky, mix it with some other elements, and then age it once again in a wooden barrel. This completely annihilates the flavor of the often-valuable originals and replaces it with a bland and uniform barrel taste. He much prefers to age white spirits for his cocktails, such as in his creative interpretation of the famous Hanky-Panky—gin, red wine, and cocktail cherries, all aged in an oak barrel and then served at room temperature with a dash of water— or his barrel-aged interpretation of the classic Angel Face cocktail made with equal amounts of white whisky (instead of gin), apricot brandy, and Calvados.

It was particularly intriguing for me to hear that in his personal experiments he uses many different parts of the tree, like twigs, leaves, and bark, fresh wood, and aged wood, in producing alcohol-based wood extracts. This results in an amazing variety of colors and flavors, some of which become intensely bitter over time. These experiments have made him realize that there are many flavors out there beyond those of oak. Overall Reinhard is absolutely convinced that choosing and sourcing the best barrels possible for your product and then balancing their flavor profiles accordingly is essential for any wine producer, distiller, brewer, or even barkeeper wishing to age and refine their product in wooden barrels.

When I returned to the Tür 7 bar some time later, I asked Reinhard if he could create a dry, cognac-based drink for me. Moments later he handed me a shallow, intricately decorated crystal glass filled with a translucent, medium-dark amber-colored cocktail. He wouldn't, however, tell me what was in it until I had tasted it. In any Hollywood spy movie, this would be a worrisome sign of a possible assassination attempt, but at Tür 7 it is an absolutely exciting proposition. I tried a sip from the chilled drink and immediately tasted the slightly sweet note of distilled wine. It was, however, accompanied by an unfamiliar freshness. After a while the two primary flavor notes were joined by a familiar vanilla flavor from the oak barrels that was somehow different from a typical cognac. When I took another sip, a distinct mandarin flavor came to the surface. The next one revealed a smoky note in the nose that was then complemented by a hint of red grape juice.

Much like the fake Chagall painting I had stumbled across earlier, this cocktail kept on revealing a new layers; every sip changed my perception of the whole. I had absolutely no clue what was in the cocktail, but I knew that I really enjoyed it. Reinhard would later tell me that besides cognac, it contained a dash of *Beerenauslese* (a very sweet and rich-tasting Austrian/German dessert wine made from grapes affected by the noble rot *Botrytis cinerea*), a hint of whisky, some lavender extract, and elderberry syrup. Taken individually, the ingredient profiles bore very little resemblance to the flavors I previously had perceived in the cocktail.

This was the true genius of an artist, be it in painting or in the making of cocktails: to recombine existing base materials into something far greater than the simple sum of their parts. For this genius to be able to thrive, an artist needs a vast knowledge of what base materials are available, their individual qualities, and how they interact with each other. Now I really understood what Reinhard meant when he emphasized the importance of tradition, experience, and knowledge in the making of a great aged spirit. So far, I had always believed that simply combining a high-quality clear spirit with an equally high-quality barrel and leaving those two to work it out amongst themselves for an extended period of time would automatically result in an amazing spirit. Reinhard taught me that by no stretch of the imagination was it that simple.

CHAPTER 7
Rum Run to Genoa

After my eye-opening cocktail tasting session with Reinhard Pohorec, I realized that I had merely glimpsed (or tasted, in my case) the tip of the iceberg when it came to the importance of wood in the world of spirits. So far, I had personally explored the world of whisky, and Reinhard had given me some fascinating insights into the world of sherry, cognac, and barrel-aged cocktails. But what about the many other spirits out there? Surely others must be influenced by wood. But how? If mature spirits didn't necessarily taste of wood, what did barrel aging really accomplish? Also, could a fresh spirit be mature without having ever seen the inside of a wooden barrel? I had so many questions.

I decided to contact my Italian friend Marco Callegari, with whom I had undertaken many wild experiments with spirits. When we met, he had already finished his undergraduate degree at the University of Gastronomic Sciences and was working for the university's communication office, while I had just started my master's program. We crossed paths due to our mutual interest in all things related to spirits, and we had stayed in close contact ever since. Marco's incredible passion and knowledge about spirits soon drew attention from many in the Italian spirits scene. One day he received a phone call from Luca Gargano, the owner of Velier, Italy's most distinguished spirits importer. Luca offered him a job looking after their select list of small spirits producers at Velier's headquarters in Genoa, one of Italy's principal port cities. Of course, Marco accepted without hesitation and moved a few months later to the Ligurian capital.

When I first contacted him about the possibility of a visit to Velier, he was traveling in southwestern France looking for small-scale cognac producers, and therefore unable to facilitate a tour. However, once he got back to Genoa he not only managed to get me into the Velier office and its world-renowned tasting room but, incredibly, managed to set up an appointment, or perhaps I should say an audience, with Luca Gargano, the grand master of imported spirits himself.

Conveniently, Marco managed to arrange the meeting just a few days after Easter, when my girlfriend Carmen and I would be visiting her family in the undulating Tuscan hills to the southeast of Florence. From there, Genoa should have been just an easy four-hour train ride away.

But as it turned out, Italy's public railway company Trenitalia, or rather its keen customers, had something different in mind. I looked at the schedule online a few days in advance and saw there were hourly trains from Florence to Genoa. But when I arrived at Florence's Santa Maria Novella train station on a Tuesday afternoon, for some incomprehensible reason the next three trains were all fully booked. I would have to wait for several hours in Florence.

Now, there are worse things that can happen to a person than being stranded in *the* Renaissance city, but, sadly, exploration was out of the question, as it had started pouring. Fortunately, since Carmen was a Florence native and I'd traveled with her before, I'd already seen a fair bit of this breathtaking city and had some knowledge of the area. This local intel included the whereabouts of a cozy little café that serves excellent tea (a rarity in Italy!) just around the corner from the train station.

Arriving there soaking wet, I ordered some hot tea and a piece of chocolate cake and began my research on Velier in general and Luca Gargano in particular. I learned that Velier was founded in 1947 by the economic attaché of the French embassy in Genoa, mainly to import small quantities of wine and liqueurs as well as champagne, tea, and cacao beans, which the company distributed all over northern Italy. It would do so until 1983, when the twenty-seven-year-old Luca Gargano, at the time already head of marketing at Italy's biggest spirit importer, bought a controlling share in the company and began expanding the import portfolio to include high-quality wines from the New World, rare white spirits like cachaça, mescal, and pisco from Latin America, world-famous Cuban cigars, real absinthe, excellent single-malt scotches, a careful selection of wines without chemical preservatives called "natural wines," and, most importantly, the best Caribbean rums.

Velier quickly became renowned for the rums it imported, thanks mainly to the passion Gargano had for the sometimes-underappreciated spirit. Having traveled all over the Caribbean at a very young age as a brand ambassador for St. James Rum from Martinique, he had fallen in love not only with this beautiful part of the world but also with its fiery liquor. So, it was no wonder that with his takeover of Velier he soon began to exclusively import some previously unknown, yet excellent, rums into the Italian market, which was at the time beginning to go wild for the Caribbean spirit.

His biggest success would come from a visit to the renowned Damoiseau distillery in Guadeloupe, where he found a batch of 1980s rum that had been set aside as unsellable because it didn't fulfill the requirements of the National French Institute of Origin and Quality (INAO), which awards the Protected Designation of Origin (PDO) certificate. This PDO certificate, like a trademark connected to a specific geographical place, protects selected food products with long traditions in a certain place from being reproduced anywhere else in the European Union. The INAO requires rum from Guadeloupe to be made only from pure sugar cane juice, yet the batch Gargano found contained a small percentage of residual sugars from molasses, a byproduct of the sugar refining process. Out of curiosity he tasted it anyway and was so impressed by its quality that he decided then and there to buy it and sell it full proof (undiluted) at 60.3%. Although scientifically still not completely understood, spirits are often diluted with water as it seems to modify their flavor by facilitating the release of certain flavor compounds while masking others.[89] This is however a process frowned upon by purists like Gargano. Releasing a spirit undiluted was a notion completely unheard of in the world of rum, yet the result was eagerly accepted and soon cherished by rum aficionados worldwide. The release of Velier Rhum Damoiseau 1980 Full Proof in 2002 catapulted Luca Gargano, together with Velier, into the rum hall of fame. Many exceptional spirit releases have followed since.[90]

I was so engrossed in reading about Luca Gargano and Velier that the hours passed almost too quickly. I had to rush back through the pouring rain to the train station, which was guarded like an army base on all sides by heavily armed soldiers; after several horrendous terrorist attacks, Europe was on high alert. Thankfully they let me pass, and I caught the regional train that would bring me to Pisa, where I would transfer to the high-speed train heading for Genoa.

I only realized after a while that the train had reached the spectacular Ligurian coast. As nightfall loomed, a continuous string of tunnels allowed for only short, intermittent glimpses of a storm-gray sea from the windows, interchanging with dimly lit, picturesque seaside towns and the blinking light of ships on the horizon.

When I finally arrived in Genoa, twenty minutes late, Marco was waiting in front of the train station with his trusty Vespa. We scooted back in true Italian fashion to his roomy apartment. There we met Paola, his colleague at Velier, and his roommate, a ship engineer. This seemed outlandishly cool to me as I always considered shipbuilding equaling rocket science in complexity. It is however quite normal for the city of Genoa, which is home to several large shipyards. Over dinner—a delicious traditional Ligurian *farinata*, a pancake-like dish made from chickpea flour, salt, olive oil, rosemary, and water—we had a lively conversation about spirits, punctuated with my awed questions on ship engineering. After dinner, we settled in the living room. To my great excitement Marco was beginning to put small sample bottles on the table. I could read handwritten labels bearing the names of distilleries and whisky makers[91] like Clynelish, Karuizawa, Ezra Brooks, Compass Box, Bowmore, and Glendronach. Though I was hardly a spirit expert like Marco, I had heard some of those names before, pronounced in reverential whispers. Here they were, neatly lined up in front of us, and behind them, a row of empty scotch glasses just waiting to be filled.

The glasses trembled with excitement—or was it me who did the trembling? Probably it was all of us, even Marco, although he had obviously tried them before. Before he poured a small sample from each bottle, he told us the often incredible background stories, not only of the whiskies themselves but of how they had gotten into his possession. The appropriately named Spice Tree Extravaganza blended whisky from Compass Box, with its well-balanced chocolate taste stemming from strongly charred barrels, was exceptional. Another highlight was the equally rare single-malt Asama from the now-closed Japanese Karuizawa distillery, with its incomparable rubbery, dark sugar qualities that for me brought up memories of old teak wood furniture.

But none was more fascinating than the 1971 Bowmore from one of the oldest Scotch distilleries and the first on Islay. It was an amazing cellar find of a friend of his, who called on Marco's expertise to evaluate the bottle. Filled by the now-defunct independent Italian bottler Sestante, a café owner in the province of Emilia-Romagna who in the sixties and seventies bought Scotch whisky casks directly and bottled his own selections, it was so rare that one cannot even Google any tasting notes on it. In perfect condition such a bottle would have been worth many thousands of dollars, but the one Marco's friend had in his possession had already lost some liquid through natural evaporation and would therefore have sold for a mere several hundred dollars. They had nevertheless decided to break it open, give most of it to a mutual whisky collector friend, and reserve a small part of it for tasting themselves. The half-empty small bottle in front of us was Marco's share, and, unbelievably, he wanted to share it with us.

Reverently sipping only tiny amounts from our glasses, we in unison used the word "fireworks" to describe it's outrageous taste characteristics, which kept on developing even ten minutes later. Its complexity stemmed from being aged in extremely high-quality sherry casks, the likes of which were only available in the 1950s in combination with malt made from the premium *marisota* barley variety, rarely used anymore today, and the characteristic peat of the Islay distilleries. Flavors that ranged from peat, butter, spice, and tobacco to fruit, ginger ale, coconut, and even seaweed and oyster were perfectly choreographed in each sip. Was this whisky the answer to my question of what maturity tastes like? I'd like to think so. A 1971 Bowmore, aged for fourteen years in sherry casks and bottled undiluted at 57.7%, was the very essence of a mature taste—and, of course, it was only done with the support of wood. All extremely content and much drunker on excitement than on the alcohol (we each took minute, very attentive sips), we went to bed. Marco had even prepared a private guestroom for me.

The next day I got up early and washed the dishes, feeling I should repay at least a tiny little bit of his incredible hospitality. Once everyone was up, we had a typical, sweet Italian breakfast of *cornetto* (the Italian take on the French *croissant*) and espresso. As my appointment with Gargano wasn't until noon, Marco headed off to work alone, and I seized the opportunity to explore the historic center of Genoa, just a few bus stops away. After disembarking in front of the impressive fountain at Piazza de Ferrari, I headed straight for Genoa's historic harbor, as this was the landmark that had shaped the city like no other.

The city's exact founding date and story are a little vague (it might have been founded by the Etruscans, by the independent Celtic Ligurians, or by some combination of the two), but archeological evidence places it with some degree of certainty at the beginning of the sixth century BC.[92] In comparison with other very renowned Italian cities it was, historically speaking, a very late bloomer. It remained a little village for centuries, albeit with a tremendous natural harbor. Genoa's harbor not only offered a rare large safe haven along Liguria's rugged coastline but was also easy for sailing ships to enter and exit, due to weak southwestern coastal currents as well as constant favorable winds from the northwest. Why, given such favorable conditions, wasn't the city immediately snapped up and developed into a major seafaring hub by the Phoenicians, the Greeks, or even the Romans, the latter of whom only really used it as a way station toward more interesting provinces in the west (Provence and Spain) and north (Lombardy, Milan, and Pavia)?

The answer to this question lies in the simple fact that Genoa didn't have anything else to offer besides a good natural harbor. Due to its location right at the bottom of rugged, steep mountains, there wasn't any good agricultural land that could support a larger city's population. Also, high forests, vital for the construction of ships, weren't in the vicinity, and the ones farther away weren't connected to the city by a sufficiently deep river to enable lumber transport via waterways. Even the fishing grounds in front of the city left a lot to be desired, as the sea floor abruptly drops right off the coast, creating unfavorable conditions for large fish populations. Also, minerals or valuable metals weren't found nearby. Altogether, Genoa had a stifling lack of resources. That the lack of any standing freshwater would hinder a mosquito population, and therefore leave the area relatively unaffected by malaria, was the solitary small positive for the city against a massive list of negatives.[93] But, against all odds, the city did prosper thanks to the renowned toughness of the Ligurians, who survived everything from a century of Byzantine rule (537-642 AD) to a massive Muslim raid by the navy of the North African Fatimid Caliphate in 934-935 AD that destroyed all but a few historic records. Evidence suggests that after the raid the city might have been completely abandoned for several years but was rebuilt before long and even took part in several attacks in Sardinia against the caliphate, which controlled a large part of the island in 1016 AD. Skirmishes with the caliphate's navy, together with the nearby and formidable sea power Pisa, would intensify in the following years and later culminate in a joint raid on Mahdia, a strategically important military settlement of the caliphate on the territory of today's Tunisia.

The raids, together with trading activities, captured silver mines in Sardinia, and a bit of piracy, slowly but surely increased Genoa's wealth and size. It was the city's participation in the first Crusades at the end of the eleventh century, however, that placed Genoa once and for all on the world map as a naval and trading force to be reckoned with.[94] With maritime commerce now the dominant activity, Genoa played a leading role in the commercial revolution of Europe in the twelfth and thirteenth centuries. Trading everything from eastern spices, dyes, and medicines to textiles, wool, corals, and gold, Genoa acquired enough capital to fuel a flourishing shipbuilding, banking, and textile industry within the city's perimeters and a vast network of self-governing colonies all around the Mediterranean coast and, later, even the Black Sea. An overwhelming victory over Pisa, the other great Italian naval force and a former ally, marked the zenith of Genoa's rise.

The next few centuries would consist of a lot of up and downs. The city endured several periods of foreign rule (notably by the French), gradually lost all its colonies, and in 1861 lost its independence completely and became part of Italy.[95] Nevertheless, to this day it remains one of the Mediterranean's most important ports and a hub of innovation. Fascinatingly, a seventeenth-century master painter, unidentified to date, depicted Genoa's working class as wearing clothing that looks identical both in structure and color to today's denim. Dubbed "The Master of the Blue Jean," his paintings are the first solid evidence that links the origin of the garment to Genoa, with some suggesting its very name may be derived from the French name for the city, *Genes*.[96]

With the northwesterly wind blowing strongly in my face, I had by now reached one of Genoa's landmarks called *Il Bigo,* a spiderlike white crane structure placed in the harbor's corner. *Il Bigo* had been conceived as a viewing platform by one of Genoa's native stars, the architect Renzo Piano. It was flanked by the world-famous aquarium on the one side and a long row of private yachts in all shapes and sizes on the other. Together with a few cruise ships and ferries, these were the only remaining users of Genoa's historic port, the new industrial version of which had been moved a bit farther up the coast.

As it was still a bit early for shops to open—I definitely wanted to see Genoa's Eataly, a globally successful shopping and dining concept that makes purchasing high-quality Italian food an experience for all the senses—and the very intense wind made exploring rather unpleasant, I returned to the slightly less windy side alleys. My audible steps were accompanied by the almost rhythmic emptying of espresso machines' portafilters and the subtle clinking of sugar spoons against espresso cups. I followed these emblematic awakening sounds of an Italian city back to one of the open café doors on every corner, walked up to the counter, and ordered a tea, affording myself a brief reprisal from the wind before continuing my journey.

Once I departed the café, and its respite from the weather, I passed the ancestral home of another household name with strong Genoese roots, Christopher Columbus, whose tiny family home (now besieged by tourists and parked motor scooters) I passed on my way to Velier's office situated on a hill above the city. Occupying the whole first floor of a nineteenth-century aristocratic villa, its windows offered a breathtaking view over Genoa.

Marco was awaiting my arrival at the office's reception area, and we had an espresso together while Gargano finished a meeting with natural wine producers. Before long, Marco ushered me into his light-flooded corner office, which was dominated by a gigantic wooden table made from a single slab of ancient Kauri wood. The modern artwork on the white walls, the space in between the art covered in seemingly random handwritten graffiti, a white sofa, and several bars overflowing with spirit and wine bottles from all corners of the world in various stages of openness, rounded off the art gallery feel of the office.

With the ever-strong wind drumming against the windows, we began a conversation that would profoundly impact and diversify my view on the influence wood has on spirits. After I gave Gargano a short introduction on the topic of my research, he immediately assured me that wood was deeply important to the world of spirits and began to differentiate between three processes that he thought needed to be looked at separately. One was the interaction of living food products with the living tree (e.g., truffles growing on its roots), one was the interaction of animate, living foodstuffs with dead wood (e.g., fermentation in wooden vats), and one was the interaction of inanimate food with dead wood (e.g., the aging of spirits). I had frankly never thought of categorizing the interactions between food and trees before, but it was logical, for each categorized process had, of course, its individual characteristics and tastes. Gargano was particularly interested in the second and third categories, fermentation and barrel aging.

Referring to the process of fermentation as "transmutation," he brought up one fascinating example after another where wood was not only useful but far superior to its metalloplastic competitors. In Cape Verde, he compared the same must—freshly pressed sugar cane juice undergoing the process of fermenting for the use of making moonshine rum—in wooden and stainless-steel vats side by side. Intriguingly, the must in the wooden vat looked different, much more alive, if you will. Also, for years Gargano had been importing *Clairin,* a traditional Haitian distillate made from fermented wild sugar cane juice, and he could taste a big difference in quality depending on whether the fresh sugar cane juice had been fermented in wooden vats (made, intriguingly, from mango wood) or metalloplastic ones. Generally, he had found that, in the Caribbean, transmutation facilitated by wild, location-specific yeast was only ever fully successful in small wooden vats, as larger vats and vats made from different materials somehow seemed to inhibit a full fermentation. This discovery was also the reason that back in Haiti he had begun to have small mango-wood vats made for his small-scale suppliers, to even further enhance the *Clairin*'s unusual flavor characteristics.[97] His company was also undertaking its first experiments with barrel aging, albeit in traditional oak barrels.

This brought us to his third defined category, the interaction of inanimate food with dead wood: barrel aging. This categorization alone was already a surprise to me, but it still didn't prepare me for his next classification of barrel aging as a cultural process, whereby humans teach the wild soul of the white spirit to become an adult; to become complex, via the barrel. He wasn't necessarily sure that this education was always a good thing. This was something I had never really considered. Could the barrel be understood as a form of school for wild, untamed spirits?

To elaborate, Gargano used the example of the metaphorical master distiller, a true virtuoso in his craft, who is able to capture the very quintessence or soul of fresh raw materials, be it apples, pears, sugar cane, or some other plant. If you were to taste his product, you could easily recognize the base. Yet if you then transfer this distillate into a wooden barrel and age it for an extended period of time, it becomes something very different. You have transformed it profoundly. It can even become difficult to recognize its base, particularly if it is aged for a very long time. Did it start as cognac made from grapes? Or rather as whisky made from barley? Maybe it was rum made from sugar cane? Or something altogether different? It is simply hard to tell, as its main flavor is the one of the barrel: wood. In some cases, Gargano assured me, the influence of the barrel on the flavor can be more than 80 percent—nearly pure wood essence.

When I asked him whether he personally preferred aged or unaged spirits, he, after a bit of thinking, opted for the wild, uneducated, and unaged ones. They simply had more soul.

Finally, I fully understood his great passion for *Clairin*, the moonshine rum made in small batches from wild sugar cane that has never seen chemical fertilizer or pesticides, in stark contrast to cane that is industrially grown. It was wild, in every step of its making. Suddenly, I realized that my search for the flavor of wood had become political; the impulse to take all these wild, variable ingredients and tame them by confining them in an artifact of human culture to yield predictable results was a conservative notion. The barrel was the embodiment of conservatism or tradition in spirits. Yet why does tradition have to be so conservative when it comes to the choice of wood?

When I ask Gargano about the overwhelming dominance of oak in barrel making, he thought that it might have to do with the environmental realities in the regions where most of today's leading spirits had been developed. There were simply a lot of oak trees available, and they proved to be excellent for barrel making. So, people got in the habit of using them, and it became a tradition.

To emphasize his point further, he brought up Brazil, home of cachaça, another sugar cane–based spirit that was the essential base alcohol of Brazil's hit cocktail, the Caipirinha. Made from half a Key lime and two teaspoons white sugar, mashed together before the glass is filled with ice and 1.7 fluid ounces of cachaça is added, its refreshing taste is strongly dominated by the lime, yet sugary and fruity notes are also present. Given that Brazil is home to the hugely diverse Amazon rain forest, there was historically a seemingly infinite supply of different tree species suitable for barrel making. (Today, that is unfortunately not the case.) For this reason, cachaça is aged in a mindboggling number of wood varieties, from Amburana, Cabreúva, and Canarywood to Amedoim, Jequitibá, and West Indian Satin wood. Each gives the fiery spirit its own flavor and education.[98] I resolved to try each barrel variety, and outside the context of a Caipirinha.

Our conversation lasted almost two captivating hours before Gargano had another appointment. I was only beginning to process all these new leads and inputs, but Marco had one last surprise for me.

Besides being very famous for exotic rums and other high-quality spirits, Velier was also known for its large, open-bar tasting room, which had every spirit imaginable ready for sampling. The master of what amounts to one of the world's most exclusive libraries of spirits was Angelo Canessa, the mixology manager of Velier. It's Angelo's duty to experiment with all the newly imported spirits, test their individual qualities exhaustively, see how they interact with each other, and then pass on his knowledge to Velier's professional customers. And Marco had arranged a surprise appointment with him in the middle of what was a spirit enthusiast's dream room.

While Marco was busily pulling bottle after bottle from the vast collection and placing them on the bar in front of us, I took the chance to get Angelo's opinion on barrel aging in general and for cocktails in particular. Much like Gargano and Reinhard, Angelo had a rather careful approach to the subject. He told me that there was no shortcut to using spirits that, firstly, have been made from fantastic raw materials and, secondarily, haven't been too strongly distilled. Preferable are less efficient stills, which extract not only the alcohol but also a lot of congeners (another word for the flavorful organic compounds found in spirits besides ethanol and water). Those congeners give not only a diverse bouquet of tastes to a spirit but also provide the distillate with enough flavorful strength to stand up to the barrel's own strong flavors. In this context, the flavors lent by the barrel support the spirit's taste rather than essentially replacing it. Additionally, it is fundamental that the freshly distilled white spirit be left to rest in a large container, ideally made of nonreactive glass, for several days before it is transferred into any barrel. This allows the different parts of the spirit (alcohol, congeners, and water) to settle and blend on a molecular level following the very real stresses of the distillation process. Rum, for instance, has a particularly high congener content. If not rested properly, it has a tendency to split in one's mouth, resulting in an unappealingly strong, oily sensation after drinking.

To explain his stance against wood-barrel aging cocktails, Angelo used a great example: the classic Manhattan cocktail. Rye whisky, the base alcohol, has many congeners. The cocktail's second ingredient, sweet red vermouth, brings its own aromas to the mix, topped only by the flavor in the final dash of Angostura bitters. Blending those three strong flavors well is already a challenge; aging them in a fresh wooden barrel would add a fourth flavor dimension, making it exponentially more difficult to reach the proper balance in the blend. Angelo prefers to use a glass container for aging some of his cocktails. Much like the mandatory resting period after distillation, this lets a myriad of aromas present in a cocktail blend well without their flavor being additionally influenced by their container. When he does use wooden containers, he prefers ones that have been used many times before and thus have much more subtle flavoring properties.

Naively, I expected this would be the end of our absorbing conversation on barrel aging cocktails, but Angelo suddenly began to differentiate between barrel aging a cocktail and finishing a cocktail in a barrel. As it turns out, aging a cocktail in a barrel means keeping it in there for six months or more. Finishing, on the other hand, is a matter of days or weeks. For finishing some of his cocktails he likes to use wooden barrels, even fresh ones—provided, of course, they are of excellent quality. A short stay in the barrel lends just a small hint of additional flavor, much as a pinch of salt rounds off a dish.

So, what would you need to do to make the perfect Manhattan, then? According to Angelo, first mix it in the right proportions, subsequently age it in a glass container for several months, and then, finally, put it in an oak barrel for several days to give it that perfect finish. If only there were one ready and available for me to sample!

But Marco and Angelo had something entirely different planned for me in the tasting room, as was evident by the long row of bottles set out before us. They had quietly selected some of the most remarkable wood-influenced spirits on this planet for me to try.

We started off with a notable bright-green herb liqueur from France, Chartreuse VEP, whose ten-year aging period in large oak barrels is without equal. Its sweet, aromatic, spicy smell reminded me of an Indian spice market or exotic incense, while its long-lasting, vegetal taste—initially slightly tingly on the tongue—reminded me of a room filled with drying herbs hanging from the rafters. Its remarkable smoothness, unparalleled by any other liquor I have ever tried before, I attributed to the effects of the wooden barrel.

Next was a very rare heavy rum (55%) from Trinidad, whose maker, the Caroni distillery, had unfortunately closed in 2002. The one I sampled was made in 1996 and then aged for twelve years in the tropics in oak before it was bottled by Velier. The moment Angelo poured the dark, amber-colored drink into the glass, a very intense whiff of sweet, ripe tropical fruits paired with a leathery, tobacco-y scent hit my nose. A slight trace of vanilla from the oak barrel lingered in the air. The taste was extraordinarily long-lasting, starting off as very spicy and, contrary to the smell's suggestions, not at all sweet, before it began to reveal strong hints of dark chocolate, leather, tobacco, and the oak's vanilla, finally giving way to the surprising taste of ripe banana.

Speaking of tropical, Angelo and Gargano had let me in on the secret behind Velier's remarkable selection of rums. Unlike any other importer, they let all of their rums age in the tropics, where the hot temperatures lead to an angel's share (the industry's rather poetic term for natural evaporation that occurs through the porous wooden barrel) of up to 10 percent per year. This means after ten years of aging, some 80-percent-plus of the initial rum is gone! Most other importers ship their rum to Europe for aging, where the climate leads to an angel's share of less than 2 percent per year. But Velier's approach gives the rum incomparable condensed aromas, for which they can claim a high premium. As they say, quality over quantity!

Meanwhile, two other drinks had found their way in front of me, having been poured somewhat secretively in a corner of the room out of view into two black wine glasses. I recognized those opaque glasses immediately from blind tastings in sensory class, back at the university. They were used to mask the drinks' color, which has a remarkable influence on the tastes we perceive. A bright green olive oil, for example, always tastes much fresher and grassier, the desired tastes in olive oil, than a bright yellow one, even if it is the same oil artificially colored without the taster's knowledge.

Curious, I sampled first the glass on the right, whose sweet perfume of ripe tropical fruits and a hint of vanilla gave it away as rum, though with less intense aromas then the *Caroni* before. However, it was very fiery in the mouth, leaving a tingly sensation on my tongue that only later revealed a strong spiciness and the taste of very dark chocolate and almonds. In short, it was the very opposite of the smoothness normally achieved through extended aging in a wooden barrel. Was it unaged rum? I mused aloud. Maybe wild, untamed *clairin*?

Now, the glass on the left. It exuded a very delicate, buttery scent that reminded me of toffee. The taste further revealed soft, yet still aromatic chocolate and vanilla components paired with a white fruit variety, maybe apricot . . . an aged rum, perhaps? It was definitely much smoother than the first mystery spirit. The slight vanilla note surely must be from a barrel. But why was it so faint? Perhaps the distiller had used an old barrel, the kind which would be perfect for aging cocktails?

With each rumination I shared with Angelo, his smile grew brighter and brighter. Finally he couldn't hold back anymore and revealed the two bottles. The first drink I had tried was rum all right, but that's where my correct assumptions ended. It was a Versailles 2002, from El Dorado Distillery in Guyana, aged for twelve years in a bourbon barrel cask— the very opposite of a wild, untamed, and unaged *clairin*. The other one, meanwhile, was a very rare Port Morand White, an unaged Guyana single rum bottled by Velier in 2015, hardly the rum aged in an old wooden barrel I was expecting. The unaged rum tasted smoother and more balanced than the aged one. Angelo thus elegantly proved his and Gargano's point: It all came down to the quality of the white spirit and the right concentration of flavors through careful distillation. An aged spirit is by no means necessarily better than an unaged one.

Still very much impressed by this "small joke," as Angelo called it, we moved on to the next bottle. I'd had my eye on this one since the beginning: a Brazilian cachaça from Caetanos aged in Amburana wood. Finally, something that wasn't aged in oak!

The spirit's yellow color was already very distinctive, but that proved to be nothing compared to its taste. Initially, it smelled slightly sweet but soon developed the scent of fresh propolis (a bee building material consisting of wax and plant-based saps tasting slightly bitter) with a hint of sour beer. The taste itself was initially sour, mixed with the flavor of Manuka honey, again propolis, and those granules of edible bee-collected pollen. A final, certain sweetness developed only afterward. "My god, that's different!" I explained after sampling it. But I could envision enjoying it on a hot summer day with ice, just like a fruity or herbal drinking vinegar.[99]

Finally there was one more exotic spirit on the table: an Amruth single-malt whisky from India, aged first in a mix of ex-bourbon and virgin oak casks and then in ex-sherry casks before it was yet again transferred into ex-bourbon casks. This astonishing mix of barrels, paired with the tropical savanna climate at the distillery's location in Bangalore in southern India, promised an interesting result, and I expected something truly unique. Initially, the whisky only revealed the typical sweet sherry, red fruit, and vanilla aromas you would expect of any whisky matured in sherry casks. But soon a certain exotic spice note joined the party. The dry and sweet taste very soon revealed a strong turmeric note paired with vanilla and a hint of incense. Curiously, there were some slight parallels to the chartreuse liqueur I had tried at the beginning of this boozy trip around the world in a tasting room.

With my notebook full with new wood-facilitated flavors and a differentiated view on their benefits, I said goodbye to Marco, Angelo, and Paola (not without saying thank you many more times) and headed down from the Velier villa to the Genova Brignole train station. My train back to Florence happily was on time.

When recapping everything about wood and spirits that I had learned on this once-in-a-lifetime trip, one of Angelo's sentences soon came to mind: "Barrel aging should just be an added value, not the main deal." In one sentence, he had condensed all that I had realized thanks to the people at Velier. In order to get the most exciting spirit, every distiller should ask himself: Am I really improving this by aging it in a barrel? If the answer is yes, a whole new quest starts: finding the perfect barrel.

CHAPTER 8
From Tree to Spirit

After having realized how important wood was in the transformation and taming of spirits, including everything from whisky, sherry, and rum to complex cocktails, I was enthusiastic to see how the life history of a tree diffused into the liquor it contains as a barrel.

This meant I had to start in the forest. As chance would have it, some of the wood used for the other clients of Haider's barrel maker came from an oak forest that I walk by several times a week. Growing on the south-facing slopes of the Wienerwald (a national park forest in Vienna), those oak forests offer a remarkably beautiful setting, as they are spaced quite far apart, letting in lots of sunlight to flood the forest floor. Ample sunlight allows grass and other ground-covering plants to grow, which makes it a very comfortable spot for picnics.

In the wintertime, however, this idyllic scene is transformed into something that resembles a battlefield, as woodcutters carefully, but still forcefully, cut several of the eighty- to a hundred-year-old trees and winch the fallen giants toward higher ground, where they are sorted and piled by thickness. If you walk by those piles of freshly cut oak trees on a windy day, the characteristic vanilla aroma is almost overpowering. After a few days, a timber truck arrives to pick up the piles of oak wood. Only the straightest and least knotted are suitable for barrel making and are transported to the cooperage.

Historically the wooden barrel has been the world's most important shipping container, only comparable to today's large iron shipping containers, the holding vessels of our globalized consumer society. Like the shipping container, the wooden barrel has been used to transport an extremely wide variety of commodities, ranging from apples, gunpowder, salted meat, cement, coins, flour, fish, molasses and pickles to tobacco, linens, tar, seeds, vinegar, potatoes, oysters and, of course, beer, wine, and whisky, the transport of which they are still used for today. The barrels' shape meant that they could be easily rolled and maneuvered, even by a single person, and their solid yet comparatively lightweight structure was very durable. This proved to be an unbeatable advantage over the amphora (a ceramic vessel with a large oval body, narrow cylindrical neck and two handles), which was, at the time of the barrels' first documentation in 350 BC, the dominant transportation container in and around the Mediterranean.

The barrel's origin goes back to the Celtic regions of northern Europe and their vast, mixed forests. Already excellent woodworkers, the Celts had also mastered the art of smelting iron and welding steel to the edges of iron tools, which was essential for machining hardwood. Although there is no solid evidence available, most historians believe that the barrel is an evolution of the wooden bucket, or better, two wooden buckets theoretically joined at the opening.

Today, this Celtic innovation would be immediately labeled with the title "disruptive." It completely displaced the amphora within a few centuries, which interestingly, but unconnectedly, occurred in tandem with the demise of the Roman Empire. As European trade increased, the barrel came into its own during the Age of Discovery. Christopher Columbus's discovery of the Americas, Vasco da Gama's successful exploration of India, and Ferdinand Magellan's circumnavigation of the world would all have been quite difficult without a durable storage container that held food, water, and other essential commodities safely. Throughout the following centuries barrel production continued booming until it reached its peak as a mass-produced commodity that held the first yields of the budding oil industry. The universal measuring unit for crude oil, "barrels" still recalls the barrel's last hurrah as oil receptacle before it was replaced by large steel tanks. Other industries quickly followed; even the wine, beer, and spirits industry made the switch. Yet they never fully abandoned the wooden barrel, since for them it was more than just a holding vessel. It had become an essential part of their products.[100] How much so, I was determined to find out.

Driving through the center of Waidhofen an der Ybbs in Lower Austria feels like taking a trip back in time. Marvelously restored medieval buildings sit adjacent to gothic courtyards and arcades, which in turn connect houses with facades from the Biedermaier, neo-Renaissance, and neo-Baroque periods. I was still admiring the sheer abundance of beautiful buildings when my GPS insisted I drive down a narrow and increasingly steep road at which end the Cooperage Schneckenleitner supposedly was located. Still unsure and rather alarmed by the ever-narrowing road right next to the river, suddenly I was confronted by a scene right out of a medieval play. Partly situated under the arcs of a tall stone bridge was, indeed, a cooperage. I saw rows of wooden barrels, piles of staves, and people hammering iron rings around half-finished barrels. I knew I had arrived at the right place to continue my quest into the life history of a barrel.

Absorbed by the scene, I parked my car right in the middle of the narrow access road, thereby blocking it completely; a mistake I would be soon alerted to by the tooting horn of the arriving postman. Once properly re-parked, however, I was finally ready to find the cooperage's young manager, Paul Schneckenleitner, Jr., with whom I had spoken on the phone the day before.

The postman had, meanwhile, disappeared into one of the many workshop doors, so I followed him, trusting that he must have been here before. Indeed, he came back followed by Schneckenleitner, whom I recognized from a photo on his website. He signaled me that he quickly had to sign some delivery documents but would be with me in a minute. This gave me time to have a proper look around the cooperage.

Built on a terrace about halfway between the intensely turquoise waters of the river Ybbs and the average altitude above sea level of the city, the cooperage consisted of several roughly plastered stone buildings with narrow doors and windows, all connected by a projecting roof resting on wooden stilts. The whole of the area underneath the roof was covered in piles of roughly sawn boards, or staves, waiting for their transformation into barrels. The central passageway connecting all the buildings was neatly lined with oak barrels, their metal hoops sparkling beneath spots of sunlight. Presumably they were awaiting their delivery to the customer. Any minute I expected to hear the noisy clip-clopping, creaking, and rolling sounds of a horse-drawn carriage on cobblestones arriving to pick up the barrels for a monastery's winery. The only indication of the modern era was a blue metal wheelbarrow with rubber tires, and the noise of machinery coming from the back.

The sound of arriving footsteps brought me back to the present. Schneckenleitner had finished his dealings with the postman and welcomed me enthusiastically to his family's cooperage. Quite proudly he told me that it had been in the family since 1880, which meant that he was now the fifth generation running it. In fact, he had only recently taken the reins at the cooperage from his uncle and father, who still worked in the company. Their many years of experience were still in high demand.

Amazingly, the cooperage itself had existed since 1628, having been founded right in the middle of the Thirty Years' War raging all over Europe at the time. Today, their business is divided over two locations, with the much more space-intensive sawmill and lumberyard situated some fifteen minutes outside of the city. This location is hugely important in the making of their barrels, as it is their mission to complete every step of production, from the sawing or splitting of the wood, its proper air drying, to its shaping and final assembly into a barrel in-house. This ensures the highest level of control over the quality of their barrels. The outside location would also be the place where the oak trees from "my" forest would be delivered.

However, contrary to my belief that the arrival of the tree trunks was the starting point of Schneckenleitner's work, I was curious to learn that the barrel-making process starts with the tree still standing in the forest, when the experienced cooper chooses the right trees for his barrels. Schneckenleitner still relies on his father and uncle for this sensitive task; they travel personally from woodlot to woodlot selecting suitable trees in Austria, Germany, and even France.

Schneckenleitner continues to tell me that the trees must be felled during the cold winter months, when the tree sap has retreated deep into the roots and the wood pores are therefore closed. Once it arrives at the sawmill, the wood destined for smaller barrels is hydraulically split (avoiding damage to the natural wood fiber structure), and that for bigger barrels is quarter-sawn into staves; the trunk is first sawn into quarters and then each quarter is sawn into boards, with the saw blade parallel to the centerline of the quarter. Immediately afterwards, the boards are stacked outside to dry, sometimes for years. Schneckenleitner's rule of thumb for drying is one year of aging per each centimeter (1cm = 0.4inch) of the stave's thickness. For a standard-sized barrel holding sixty gallons (called a *barrique*), the stave aging period takes therefore up to three years.

I was fascinated to hear that the location specific elements have a hugely important role in the production of a good quality barrel. Rain, wind, ice, snow, scorching heat, and heavy fog wash out the wood's harsh tannins and transform the flavor characteristics. Additionally, location-specific bacteria and fungi break down chemical compounds in the wood, therefore making them soluble to alcoholic liquids.[101] This means that a barrel's flavor notes not only depend on how and where the tree was grown, at which time of the year it was cut, and how the wood was dried, but also on the specific weather patterns, bacteria, and fungi populations of a place. This meant, unmistakably, that a barrel has *terroir*, a term mostly used in the wine world to describe the specific environmental conditions (soil, topography and climate) that produce its unique taste.

As we spoke we had walked in the direction of the mechanical din in the back of the cooperage, which had by then morphed into a rhythmic hammering, and stopped in front of a neatly stacked pile of staves. Upon closer inspection, all of them bore clear signs of scarring by the elements, most visibly the naturally toasted grey surface, courtesy of the sun, that at times even darkened to black. Clear signs of water, with its characteristic run marks, and the tiniest spots of fungi growth were also visible.

Schneckenleitner further explained how from this rough state the staves are first passed through a planer that forms the horizontal curvature and are then cut to length with a circular saw. Finally, a shaper forms the vertical curvature and taper. Unfortunately, on the day of my visit the cooperage wasn't assembling any barrels, a fact Schneckenleitner really regretted as it was supposedly truly spectacular when the pre-assembled barrels are bent into their final shape with the help of fire and water.

He tells me that at his family's cooperage every barrel is made to order, which means that customers can choose between several standardized sizes and, most importantly, select an intensity for the char layer on the inside of the barrel. Thereby the barrel is left for a certain amount of time over a fire that forms a char layer on the inside. This so-called toasting process has a strong influence on the flavor characteristics of the barrel, the most obvious one being a smoky note. Once the heads of the barrel are fitted the final step is to test the barrel's water tightness by filling it with water. Delivering a leaking or otherwise faulty barrel is out of question for Schneckenleitner, as his business relies on reputation and the word of mouth it generates. He seems to do pretty well in this respect, as he not only supplies numerous Austrian winemakers and distillers but recently even has begun delivering barrels to South Africa and Australia.

Having seen the whole production process, I was keen to ask something that has nagged me since I began my quest. Why is the world of barrel making and ultimately the whole wine and spirits sphere so dominated by the oak? Unquestionably, the oak is a beautiful tree with particularly strong wood. Yet one would think that amongst the estimated 80,000 to 100,000 different tree species in the world,[102] there would be other suitable trees for barrel making.

According to Schneckenleitner, it simply comes down to demand. No one really seems to be asking for barrels made from other wood, although there are some wineries that still order small amounts of acacia wood barrels, favored for their very light, fruity taste. There are certain limitations on which kind of wood can be used, as it must have rather tight pores and shouldn't be too soft or brittle in order to survive the duress it undergoes during the barrel-making process. Fascinatingly, though, he remembered that his father once made barrels from larch, which is relatively durable but much softer than oak.

Encouraged by the discovery that barrels can be made from a wide variety of woods, I was keen to look into an alternative to the all-dominating oak. The general consumer and producer might be content with the quite recognizable oak barrel flavor profile, but I was not.

But before I could start to search for alternatives, I had to analyze what the flavor profile of an oak barrel exactly was, beyond its signature vanilla note.

I soon realized that there were many different components that influenced the unique flavor profile of a barrel and even more so when it came to the spirit itself. Let's take whisky as an example. Some studies actually identified up to four thousand nonvolatile (nongaseous) compounds in oak-barrel-aged whisky,[103] whereby each different chemical part of the wood plays an important role. Bearing a striking resemblance to a sponge when viewed under a microscope, the wood structure consists of parallel strands of cellulose (long chains of complex sugar molecules that make up the main component of the very paper these lines are written on), which are wrapped in a mash of hemicellulose (variably organized complex sugar molecules), which in turn is interwoven with lignin strands (a highly complex polymer that binds cells together and is, for example, responsible for the crunch in vegetables[104]). In between this extremely strong, yet flexible structure, varying amounts of proteins and extractive substances are deposited.[105]

The hemicellulose contributes wood sugars, which are important for the body of the whisky. During the toasting process of barrel production, they are caramelized, which contributes strongly to the whisky's unique amber color.[106] Lignin gets broken down by the ethanol in spirits into important flavor compounds like vanillin, which adds to spirits the very notable vanilla flavor, the oak's signature taste.[107] Furthermore, it also contributes to the color. Extractive substances like tannins and lipids introduce a certain amount of astringency and remove notable off-notes, like the sensation of a rubbery taste sometimes present in a fresh distillate. American white oak barrels additionally have a high amount of lactones, which are derived from lipids in the wood. Lactones give the whisky a somewhat woody flavor (old bookstore sensation) and a hint of coconut.

Overall the charring of the barrel plays a very significant role, as it not only breaks up hemicellulose, lignin, and lipid structures, which later react more readily with the ethanol, but also removes off-notes by essentially creating a layer of active carbon (used in many filters). Moreover, some parts of the char layer are themselves dissolved, which gives a certain smokiness to the whisky.[108]

With the different influences of the wood chemical components in mind, I set out to find some intriguing wood species whose taste I wanted to explore. The first one that came to mind was the Austrian native larch mentioned by Schneckenleitner. The next was a wood I had a love/hate relationship with, starting from my days as a cabinetmaker's apprentice. While learning how to build a sizable media cabinet (this was in the good old days of bulky tube TVs), I chose, for some irreproducible reason, mahogany from a plantation in the Americas, not taking into consideration its brittleness. Although this did not present a real problem for straight parts of the cabinet, it was indeed a huge problem for the edge band that had to be bent and glued all around the round tabletop. As you might imagine, brittleness and bending don't go well together. It took me two full days and countless mahogany edge bands until I finally got one that wouldn't break during bending. Back then I swore never, ever to do anything with mahogany again, but time seems to heal all wounds. So, mahogany was my second choice. To keep a balance between exotic and local wood species, I decided to use locally grown black alder and imported Australian eucalyptus as my third and fourth selections.

Selecting four different wood species in theory was one thing, but actually procuring the wood samples was quite another. Having found larch, black alder, and mahogany quite easily (luckily, I still had several of the broken edge bands), it would take me the better part of two days to find a sample of eucalyptus. The problem wasn't availability but quantity. All the specialized wood dealers I called assured me immediately that they had large quantities of the Australian hardwood available, but this assurance was always followed by the question of how many board feet I wanted. My reply that I would only need board inches—ten, to be exact—somehow didn't impress them at all. Their voice immediately took on a rather patronizing tone as they informed me that they simply couldn't sell anything below thirty board feet. Since I didn't need new eucalyptus flooring in my kitchen, I declined their bids, even when offered a discount, and finally called my local cabinetmaker, something I should have done right away. We knew each other from previous dealings, so he was likely no longer surprised by my strange inquiries. Within an hour he had found a small piece of eucalyptus from an old project. When I picked it up the next day, he even gave me the piece for free.

With all four types of wood now in my possession, I set out to test their flavoring potential as barrel wood based on a home-developed, wood-flavor extraction process (which always has people and pets alike flee my kitchen as it involves copious amounts of steam, burning wood chips, smoke, and ample four-letter words on my side).

Once it was safe again for people and pets to return to the kitchen I had discovered a remarkable variety of amazing wood flavors. The Australian eucalyptus had an extremely gratifying taste of caramel or sweet toffee that was very long-lasting, while the mahogany reminded me of green tea with a hint of smokiness, like a pine-smoked Lapsang Souchong made from green tea, rather than black. As the flavor profile developed in the mouth, however, it became more and more astringent, a problem that could be most likely fixed by properly exposing the staves to the elements and thereby washing out the harsh tannins. A strong, sweet, long-lasting taste of marshmallow was the flavor surprise the larch had in store for me, while the alder initially tasted like a first flush Darjeeling tea but very soon developed a perfect raspberry flavor.

I was speechless; four more or less randomly selected woods had resulted in four completely different flavors, from sweet toffee to smoky green tea and from raspberry to a marshmallow. With 80,000 to 100,000 tree species in the world, what a galaxy of flavors there was still to discover. It doesn't require much imagination to envision the profound influence all those wood types could have on the flavor of spirits. When knowledgably combined with the terroir of a barrel, there could be so many more flavors than the old oak's vanilla and coconut. But if I were to convince anyone in the spirits industry to change their ways after decades, I had to fully understand the flavor of wood in all its complexity, part of which has to be the scent of wood.

CHAPTER 9
Vietnam's Forest Essence

Our perception of food changes profoundly when you start to concentrate more on its exact flavors. Suddenly, food items that simply used to taste "good" or "bad" start to become much more nuanced as their more subtle flavors emerge. For me this transformation started with my first cooking experiences, when I realized that one dish needed a bit of salt while others were a little too acidic and longed for a bit of sweetness.

Strictly speaking, "taste" only describes the signals received through our taste buds, which can only distinguish five basic qualities: sour, bitter, salty, sweet, and *umami*, or savory. (Evidence for a sixth taste receptor for fatty substances is also mounting).[109] So what about the rest of the flavors we perceive—those subtle buttery, floral, or fruity nuances?

The bouquet of myriad other flavors that compose what we usually call "taste" relies on sensations from the olfactory receptors in our nose, which are connected to the mouth through the nasal passage. Furthermore, studies show that our perception of flavor can even be influenced by sound, from the crunch of potato chips to background music at a restaurant.

Have you ever wondered why airplane food tastes so bland? The plane's low humidity and cabin pressure dull the sensitivity of our taste buds and olfactory receptors; the constant drone of the airplane engines also plays a role.[110] Our eyes also play tricks on our taste buds, as the aforementioned example of the fresher tasting, artificially colored olive oil shows.

Tasting includes our mouth, our nose, our eyes, and our ears, with the nose actually being the primary organ of taste as well as smell. With its six million olfactory receptors, it is capable of detecting the tiniest trace amounts of airborne substances as well as influencing our emotions, our perceptions of other people, our ability to concentrate, and even our choice of romantic partners. Our olfactory receptors are directly connected to the deepest part of our brain, the limbic system. This means that fragrances can trigger a deep-seated emotional response even before they reach our cortex, where cognitive recognition occurs.[111] The tastelessness of food one experiences during a cold is probably the best example of the importance of the nose for the perception of flavors.[112]

This meant if I were to explore the flavor of wood, I had to understand the scent of wood as well. Since I had always been interested in perfumes, especially naturally derived, non-synthetic ones, I knew immediately that this was the perfect area to start.

My journey into the peculiar world of woody perfumes unexpectedly began one January morning just before dawn, after many hours of sleeplessness. I had found a somewhat successful cure for my insomnia many years ago: reading all the interesting online articles I can find. That way I could at least feel like the time isn't being wasted, since I would be actually learning new things, and the process of reading would make me tired over time. However, if I stumbled upon something *too* interesting, I would fall mind-first into a sleepless exploration of the far reaches of the internet, no return guaranteed. This is exactly what happened that particular night in early January while strong winds howled around the house and I, restless once again, resorted to my nightly reading routine in search of sleepiness.

As I scrolled through the *Frankfurter Allgemeine Zeitung,* a headline caught my eye: "The Scent of the Wilderness." The article was about a man, Laurent Severac, originally from the French Bordeaux region who had been so gripped by his first trip to Vietnam that he moved there, earning his income by exploring the immense, wild scents of the Asian jungle, taking samples of every plant that piqued his interest and then capturing their scents through distillation. He used to sell those extracted wild scents to French perfume makers in the region of Grasse; however, for the past several years he'd instead been focusing on creating his own perfumes in a small laboratory in Hanoi.[113]

While reading the journalist's accounts of his travels with Severac, I knew that I had to find a way to speak with him, not only because of my great interest in the art of natural perfume making but also to gain an insight into wood-derived perfumes and their qualities. Severac seemed to be the perfect source of information, and so I set out to find a way of contacting him.

Within a few days I managed to get ahold of Severac, and he generously agreed to answer some of my questions via e-mail. I expected to learn a lot, but nothing could have prepared me for the treasure trove of information that arrived several days later.

I was amazed to learn that scents derived from wood are for many reasons very important in the perfume industry. For one, they are used as fixatives for other volatile scents, like the ones derived from citrus fruits, flowers, and herbs. By drawing all the different components of a perfume together and combining them into a whole, they basically act like an unwrapped block of butter in the refrigerator, which absorbs all the food flavors around it all while retaining its own subtle, buttery note.[114]

Similarly, woody scents give an intense and long-lasting note to the perfume. But not only wood, in the technical sense, is used for its scent in perfume. The leaves of eucalyptus, tea, cinnamon, and pine trees are favored for their light and airy notes, which offer a complete olfactory contrast to the very wood from which the leaves arise.

Yet another element of the tree used in perfumes is the resins, some of which have the most intriguing and mysterious names. Peru balm is one such resin. Belonging to the balsam tree family and native to Central and South America, it has balsamic, sweet, spicy, and vanilla notes which, when diluted, smell like hyacinth.[115] Another much better-known resin is frankincense, which is deeply intertwined with religious and medical history. Its smell of fresh turpentine mixed with green lemon and unripe apple[116] has been the defining scent of churches and temples for thousands of years. Recently it additionally became of great interest to medical research, as it seems to have the ability to prevent the spread of or even kill cancer cells.[117]

Historically, frankincense was one of the most valuable substances known to humanity, right next to gold and myrrh, which is probably why, according to the Bible, those were the gifts given to baby Jesus by the three wise men. But the history of frankincense goes back much further than that. Records of its production in Wadi Dawkah, a UNESCO world heritage site in what is now southern Oman, date as far back as 7000 BC. From there it was shipped via camel caravan to Egypt and forwarded by sea to Europe. Persia, India, and China, on the other hand, obtained it via an intricate system of shipping routes through the Arabian Sea. Under the rule of Augustus, the Roman Empire tried to gain control over its production by sending tens of thousands of troops to find its legendary source somewhere in the southern Arabian Peninsula. However, the intense heat and aridity of the desert drove them back, and so both the immense expense for the Roman Empire and frankincense's shroud of mystery remained.[118]

Today, of course, a simple internet search reveals frankincense as the resin of a rather unimpressive, scraggly-looking bush from the Boswellia family of trees, perfectly adapted to the arid climate. In a procedure unchanged for thousands of years, the trunk of this bush is scored with a knife and soon produces small droplets of sap, which very quickly dry in the searing desert sun. The dried sap from the first score isn't used for the perfume, as it is full of impurities and doesn't exude the desired scent associated with frankincense. Only the dried sap droplets from the second and third scores have the desired quality and can be sold around the world. The first potential buyer that comes to mind today is the Catholic Church, yet they actually don't buy Wadi Dawkah frankincense. Their product of choice comes from Somalia, where it is much cheaper.[119]

During our e-mail conversation Severac listed several other resin-based scents, like the well-known myrrh or, completely new to me, styrax benzoin, a balsamic resin obtained from the yan tree which is native to southeastern Asia.[120]

In his daily practice as a perfume maker he not only values resins for the woody, sweet and warm notes they give to a perfume but also for the sustainable way they can be sourced. If harvested correctly, resin can be obtained from trees without damaging them permanently. This is a prime example of how forests can support entire communities without having to be cut down. Unfortunately, the same cannot be said for all perfume making. Today's perfumers favor the very identifiable and sticky scents of sandalwood and rosewood, both of which are heavily endangered species. The only way to obtain the trees' scent is by cutting them down, grinding them into small pieces, fermenting them, and finally vapor-distilling them, an unsustainable practice that has been happening in the forests of Vietnam for ages.

Interestingly, Severac doesn't think that there is a profile all wood-derived scents have in common. He agrees that there is a woody note but says it is multifaceted, like everything else in nature. Even some leaves picked from herbs can exude light notes that remind him of wood when blended; however, in no way can they be compared to typical, very intense tree-derived scents like sandal, rosewood, or agarwood.

Agarwood, which is, as Severac tells me, his favorite scent, has a particularly fascinating history to tell. It is derived from the wood of some individual trees of the *Aquilaria* tree species, which is native to the high-altitude forests of southeastern Asia. Although much rarer, they are as indispensable in the east as the oak trees are in the west, not only due to their sometimes perfumed wood but also because of their bark, which can be used as paper or for making string.[121, 122] Curiously, not every tree of the *Aquilaria* genus has this fragrant wood; only those which have been wounded develop special resins and oils in the affected areas as a defense mechanism. Those substances then turn the normally yellowish-colored wood dark and exude one of the most complex olfactory chords known to perfumers. It is described as having the combined notes of oriental-woody and very soft fruity-floral fragrances and is particularly valued by the Buddhists' tantric movement, where it is used as incense for liturgical and meditative practices. It is believed that oil from agarwood was used by the ancient Egyptians to embalm their dead.[123]

Over millennia, legendary stories and myths concerning its enigmatic origin and production spread all over Asia and Arabia, fueling the demand for it.[124] Traders and explorers searched for it in the vast, untouched forests of Asia. The tree itself is rare, so finding those that have been wounded in a particular way is like finding the proverbial needle in a haystack. Agarwood oil was sold for fortunes via an intricate trade route system called the "Incense Road of Antiquity" linking the Mediterranean world with eastern and southern sources of incense, spices, and other rare goods.[125] As a result, agarwood oil, also named *oodh*, became culturally embedded in Asia and Arabia and remains so to this day. At the present time the scent is still so immensely valuable—commonly earning USD $1,000 per kilogram of wood—that people spend their lives searching for the trees and thereby continue to decimate their numbers. Periods of particular demand have been recorded that pushed the tree close to extinction.[126] But in a strange twist of history, the Vietnam War actually had a positive impact on the formation of agarwood in the country, when bullets, bomb fragments, and other exploding objects damaged numerous *Aquilaria* trees and thereby induced the trees' fragrant immune defense.[127]

Around 1990, people from East India to Papua New Guinea[128] started to cultivate *Aquilaria* plantations and experimented with crude methods of wounding the trees and thereby encouraging agarwood production. Over the years methods were improved, and today it's possible to produce medium- to high-grade *oodh* oil by these methods. The nongovernmental organization called "The Rainforest Project," operating out of Ho Chi Minh City, has created a method that has a near-perfect success rate and produces a very fine *oodh* oil.[129] The highest quality still hasn't been attained from cultivated trees, but the technology is advancing.[130] Together with a longtime friend, Severac is also involved in an *Aquilaria* plantation high in the cloud forests of neighboring Laos. On a fifty-thousand-acre plot they are experimenting with several ways of damaging the trees to induce the desired immune reaction and have already had some success.[131]

We finished our e-mail conversation with a discussion about the sense of smell and its importance for perceiving the flavor of the food we eat. Only a few weeks before our e-mail exchange he had been at a friend's place for dinner, and they opened a bottle of a very expensive wine, Haut Brion Grand Cru 2001. After spending ten minutes just smelling the fantastic nose of truffles, forest soil, and minerals the wine exuded, he was utterly disappointed by its flat taste when he finally took a sip. For him, 99 percent of the value of this great wine was its nose. I wondered if this was also true for the flavor of wood. Is it actually a smell?

To find out, I spoke to Pratap Chahal, a London-based chef who, after cooking for years in many of the city's best Michelin-starred restaurants, set out to create his own branded products and a supper club that hosts spectacular perfume-inspired dinners. Titled "Perfume: The Edible Scent," the dinners feature fantastic dishes like grilled sandalwood monkfish, atlas cedar wood soda bread, and chocolate and black pepper mousse with frankincense shortbread and pine needle ice cream.[132]

Chahal's fascination with perfumes began with a book from the American author Mandy Aftel titled *Fragrant: The Secret Life of Scent*, wherein he read that in the past it was actually quite common to use perfumes like frankincense to flavor food. He set out through months of trial and error to rediscover this forgotten ancient art. Like Severac, he thinks that tree-derived scents are very distinct from each other and therefore uses them for different dishes. His two favorite perfumes are frankincense and agarwood (*oodh*); frankincense, with its warm, rich, balsamic, and slightly sweet notes, is perfect for desserts, while he uses the intensely rich, smoky, yet slightly sweet notes of *oodh* for savory dishes.

Chahal is convinced that tree-derived scents are much more perceptible by taste than by smell. Especially with the small amounts he uses in his dishes, the strong smell of the main ingredients, be it lamb or chocolate, overpowers the faint smell of the perfumes. Only when people taste the dishes does the perfume reveal itself in the most spectacular way. Diners are positively puzzled by this unknown sensation. Although people quite often recognize many exotic smells from the perfumes used around them, they have never before tasted them. This complete lack of reference points puzzles our brain and creates the sensation of surprise and novelty—the Holy Grail of desired sensations chefs around the world aim to attain.

Pratap Chahal's revelations were extremely valuable for my quest, suggesting that even wood-derived essences are different in smell and taste, which meant the flavor of wood could very well be more than just a smell.

To find the definitive answer, I set out to explore the world of wood-derived scents for myself. Armed with my trusty tabletop still, I began to look for a wood whose scent intrigued me. It wasn't long before I thought of teak, a tropical hardwood species that is one of the world's most desired lumbers due to its combination of easy workability, high stability, beautiful golden-brown color, and extremely strong rot resistance. It is often used in contexts where it is exposed to the elements, such as in building ships, garden furniture, and decking.[133] In India it is grown in huge plantations and therefore can be fairly sustainably harvested. Out of pure coincidence, a loyal, untreated teak garden chair at my parents' house had recently collapsed after years of service, which meant that I could turn one of its broken legs into fine woodchips without my mom's objecting.

To produce the teak wood essence, I decided on using the same method Severac uses in his perfume making: steam extraction. So I filled my tabletop still with some distilled water, placed the teak chips on a mash structure slightly above the water level, and started to heat the system. Within an hour small, clear drops of a strong-smelling essence began to drip out of the end of the copper cooling spiral.

I started to brainstorm an experiment that I could conduct at home to assess whether the "flavor" of wood was actually more than a smell. It wasn't long before I came up with a simple experiment that would at least give me a hint. I bought one of the blandest-tasting products I could think of—rice cakes—and sprayed some of the teak essence on one. To extend the experiment beyond the pure essence of teak, I spread on a second rice cake a thin paste consisting of very fine teak dust mixed with distilled water, which I had previously prepared in my unfortunate blender. In theory, this would allow me to actually taste the teak wood.

So there I was, sitting at my kitchen table with one plain rice cake, one sprayed with teak essence, and one covered with a rather grim-looking teak wood paste in front of me, a notebook to my side.

I first smelled and later tried the plain rice cake to develop a smell and taste baseline. It exuded a very faint paper or cardboard-like note with a hint of roasted wheat and slight sweetness. Then I smelled and tasted the rice cake with the teak wood essence. What a difference! The cardboard smell was completely replaced by a quite strong leathery and almost fresh aroma. When tasted, it was actually quite pleasant, with the flavor combination of bergamot, tobacco, black tea, and leather. Probably due to the bergamot notes, I immediately had the mental image of drinking Earl Grey tea while sitting on a freshly polished leather sofa.

Next was the teak paste. Its scent was very strong; the leather smell was almost overpowering. Then it was time to actually try it. I managed to chew it several times before the intense dryness and overpowering flavor made me cough profusely. Once my eyes stopped watering and the cramp in my shocked tongue finally loosened, it was nevertheless curious to note that the flavors were in most parts the same as the leather smell, if a lot stronger and skewing toward an almost chemically enhanced sensation. A few flavor notes were notably different, though. One new flavor, that of natural rubber or "caoutchouc," stuck out. Additionally, the teak paste was extremely astringent and had a very dry texture, although it was completely soaked in water. Together those flavors formed the mental image of a powdered latex medical glove sticking out its index finger as if to say: "Wait a minute: there is more to the flavor of wood than just smell!"

The glove was completely right. Although in the particular case of teak wood the smell and taste of the essence were most definitely more pleasant than the raw wood, they clearly demonstrated that taste would always reveal more than smell alone. It was now clear to me that the flavor of wood could not be simply condensed into an olfactory sensation. It was more than just a smell.

CHAPTER 10

Mountain Pine Cuisine

South Tyrol, officially a province of Italy, historically a part of Austria, and realistically a blend of both, has for years successfully marketed itself as a place with a very high quality of life. Indeed, a recent ranking of the happiest municipalities in Italy showed that the top three spots are occupied by South Tyrolean towns.[134] This result is probably not overly surprising for anyone who has had the chance to experience the beautiful landscape of Italy's most northern province, which includes charming villages built in the attractive "Überetscher" style (think alpine farmhouse meets Tuscan castle[135]), winding roads, crystal clear lakes, and towering, snow-covered mountain ranges.

I was always particularly stunned by the stark contrast between the seemingly untamed wild mountain reaches and the intensely cultured landscapes in the valleys beneath. On the one hand there are mountaintops with such harsh climates that trees can't grow on them; on the other hand, every square centimeter in the valleys is filled with vineyards and apple orchards—not to mention palm trees! All of this grows in a linear distance of less than a few miles, due to very favorable climatic conditions.

This contrast not only makes for an intensely beautiful countryside to travel through but also seems to produce interesting people—one of whom I was on my way to visit in the fall of 2015, while making a trip to the area around the city of Bolzano. His name is Georg Wenter, and he is commonly known as the "Mountain Pine Chef."

I had first heard of him, or better to say about one of his products, when visiting the wine estate Manincor, not far from Bolzano, for the first time a few months earlier. While touring the estate, I'd seen a flyer announcing a partnership between the wine estate and a local South Tyrolean cosmetics company called Trehs. The partnership had been formed around a surprising byproduct of their vineyards: the colorless vine sap that exudes in spring from cuts made while pruning the vines in late fall. Plinus Secundus, an ancient Roman author (23-79 AD), named this most natural, non-alcoholic product "Aqua vitis" (not to confuse with aqua vitae, the clear white spirit) and credited it with several positive effects on human health.[136] Manincor and Trehs had revived it as a line of interesting cosmetics. "Aqua vinea nobilis," based on the vine sap, was the newest of many products launched by Trehs; their most successful was the product line "Sarner Latsche," which was based on essential oils obtained from mountain pines growing in the Sarn Valley, thirty minutes outside of the city of Bolzano. I'd been immediately intrigued, especially once I'd learned that the creative mastermind behind the cosmetics line, Georg Wenter, was a well-known chef who cooks with mountain pine. On a subsequent visit to Manincor, its owner Count Goess-Enzenberg kindly connected me with Wenter, and I secured an almost immediate appointment.

Entering the Sarn Valley coming from Bolzano is a visual feast in itself, with increasingly steep, tree-covered slopes on both sides ending abruptly in plateaus. One side is covered with vineyards, and the other side is the site of the medieval castle Runkelstein.[137] This castle was of great importance in the Middle Ages, when the road going through the Sarn Valley was the main northern trade route connecting Venice, the Western world's trade capital at the time, with Germany.[138] Bolzano's position right along this all-important trade route brought respectable wealth to the city and gave rise to some very affluent and influential patrician families,[139] one of which later bought the castle and transformed it into a fresco-covered palace. In fact, it is the home of the largest collection of secular frescos in the world today.[140]

As I traveled farther up the road for my appointment with Wenter, against the flow of the Talvera river, I passed through a series of steep tunnels that obstructed the view, except for the few gaps in the tunnels through which the vista could be glimpsed. Once out of the tunnel, though, it was possible to soak in the beautiful scenery comprised of the nearly vertical stone walls covered in gravity-defying fall-colored trees, ragged clouds, the last traces of morning fog, and the green, undulating meadows in the valley bottom. Right in the middle of it all was Wenter's "wellness hotel," Bad Schörgau. Built in a style similar to an alpine farmhouse and accented with exposed wood and stones, its entrance revealed a comfortable interior, cozy with the warmth only a wooden fireplace can provide.

The story of Wenter's mountain pine cuisine, unfortunately, started with a tragedy. His family had first rented the hotel before purchasing it some years later. Eventually, the hotel grew to be so successful that his parents decided to enlarge it by building a wooden extension. When his father suddenly died in the middle of the expansion, however, the task of overseeing hotel operations and the restaurant fell to Wenter; before, all the cooking had been done by his father, himself a well-known chef, but now all was down to Wenter, who was at the time a successful chef on Italian television.

It was clear to him that they had to develop a new concept for the hotel's restaurant, and, after brainstorming with his mother and two sisters, the family decided on mountain pine, which has always been a common household remedy in the Sarn Valley. The mountain pine growing in the Sarn Valley is quite different from all other mountain pine varieties, as it grows on a volcanic, slightly acidic soil and mostly in south-facing locations. (All other varieties of mountain pine grow on alkaline, chalky soil.) This difference in soil and growing orientation not only makes the Sarn Valley pine grow twice as fast but also produces premium versions of two Mediterranean-flavored essential oils, *limonene* and *citronella* (also present in lemon balm plants). Both seem to have a stronger ability to stimulate the self-regulating functions of the user's body than other comparable mountain pine oils, even at a much lesser concentration; this meant that they could be used in a lower dosage in both Wenter's cosmetics line and mountain pine–based dishes.

However, the essential oils from the mountain pine are not the only part of this robust tree that can be used for cooking. In fact, Wenter and his head chef, Egon Heiss, have developed several techniques to use virtually all parts of the tree, even solid wood, in the restaurant's dishes year-round. In spring, the freshly sprouted needles are used in a delicious pesto by being first immersed in olive oil, then frozen, and finally ground and seasoned. According to Wenter, freezing has several advantages. From a purely technical point of view, it's much easier to grind something that's been frozen solid. But the main reason is that, during mechanical grinding, the generation of a certain amount of heat is unavoidable, which would denature many of the valuable chemical compounds of the needles and result in a bitter taste.

However, if you grind the needles once they're frozen, they will never reach temperatures of eighty degrees or higher, therefore keeping intact most of the treasured compounds and preserving the pesto's fine taste. Curiously, it is important to maintain an even higher level of hygiene than usual in a commercial kitchen when making the mountain pine pesto, as the needle puree seems to be particularly attractive to yeast fungi. Wenter learned this the hard way when several of his first containers of pine pesto suddenly blew up in the middle of the kitchen due to carbon dioxide buildup, a byproduct of yeast-facilitated fermentation.

Learning how to best grind parts of the mountain pine and avoid pine pesto explosions in the kitchen was just one of the many processes Wenter had to develop and perfect over the years to make his dishes taste as good as they do now. Bad Schörgau is open all year long, and they always have a mountain pine dish on the menu; after all, it is their signature ingredient. Yet the tree itself is heavily influenced by the seasons. In spring the needles are very fine and delicate-tasting, while in summer, fall, and winter they are very tough and full of tannic sap. The same is true for the cones that develop from soft and delicate to rock-hard and pungent in taste. So, Wenter and his chefs couldn't simply develop one recipe, but had to develop many iterations that took the changing characteristics of their mountain pine–based ingredients into account. While the young and aromatic pine cones are perfectly suited to infuse delicate meats, the old and tough ones are ground into a very fine powder that is then added in small quantities to cream-based dressings. Outside of the kitchen, the pine cone powder is also used in their cosmetic line for face peels. One part of the tree that doesn't change drastically over the year, though, is its solid wood. At the Bad Schörgau kitchen it is mostly used in the form of chips to carefully smoke a variety of fish.

After listening to Wenter describe all the innovative dishes, I told him that they all sounded extremely delicious, and, after a pause, he agreed, although he added that it had taken him more than ten years to reach the point where he was able to cautiously agree with such a state-ment. This hasn't always been the case. He told me that, in retrospect, the mountain pine dishes he served at the beginning of his experiments were more than appalling—in his words, gross and inedible. However, the media loved his idea of a mountain pine–based kitchen so much that they kept on supporting him through favorable reports and TV segments in the starting years. This leap of faith would soon pay off, as his cre-ations became not only tolerably edible, but downright tasty the more he experimented with the exotic ingredient. Nowadays he can create dishes like trout filets infused with green pine cones, gin and tonics served in a pine-needle-smoked glass, and, of course, his famous mountain pine risotto. All of these rely on a carefully honed mountain pine cooking in-tuition, which gives him a feeling for how dishes will be influenced by the unusual ingredient.

Something that really fascinated me was how his idea not only pos-itively influenced his hotel business but also revived the whole valley eco-nomically. The Sarn Valley mountain pine is now a protected species with its own botanical name, *Pinus sarentensis*. Essential oils extracted only from these certified-sustainable trees are world-renowned and have given rise to a thriving business for essential oil distilleries in the valley. Wenter was also on the forefront of creating a tourism campaign for the valley based solely on its smell. Called the "Perfume of the (Sarn) Valley," it was the only tourism campaign focusing on a destination's smell other than that of the Bretagne in France. A perfume, amongst other things, he said, was the next logical step in his cosmetics line. But besides these innovations with grapevine sap and mountain pine needle, Wenter still had an entire hotel to run. It was this reason he had to leave rather abruptly once we were finished with our conversation, as he had to guide a small group of guests through the valley.

After our interview concluded, a friendly receptionist gave me a tour of the hotel's many spa amenities and richly decorated rooms, all of which had one common, very cozy theme: wood. Rather disappointingly though, I couldn't taste the dishes previously described by Wenter, as it would have meant waiting several hours for the kitchen to open for lunch and my time was most unfortunately limited.

However, on my drive back through the wild Sarn Valley I was somewhat visually compensated, as the sun had come out and was shooting scattered beams of bright light through the turbulent cloud cover. For one brief moment, it illuminated a huge maple tree standing alone in the valley bottom in front of a dark spruce forest, completely covered in bright yellow fall plumage, surrounded by a golden, shimmering carpet of previously fallen leaves, with a thin band of sparkling mist floating right above it. It was one of the most beautiful tree moments I had ever experienced.

Inspired by Wenter's large assortment of ingenious ideas for cooking with trees, I had already come up with several experiments to try when I returned to Milan, where I was living at the time. The one that most intrigued me was the young mountain pine shoots pesto, since a simple pasta dish with fresh pesto is one of my all-time favorite meals. However, according to Wenter, to make a pesto that's delicious—or edible at all—the shoots had to be really young, as they are only in spring. This was a slight problem, since it was fall at the time, and a trip to the southern hemisphere just to gather young tree shoots was out of the question.

So there was nothing I could do besides wait impatiently through a full winter until the spring sun slowly but steadily brought warmth into the soil, first animating a myriad of spring flowers to display their spectacular blossoms and finally also persuading the trees to show their first young leaves. By this time, I had moved back to Austria and was spending the weekend at my parents' place in the northern part of the country. On an early Saturday morning dog walk I was passing by a large stand of larch trees backlit by the still low sun when I suddenly remembered that Wenter had mentioned that their spring shoots were also extremely delicious. A closer look revealed small buds on every branch, out of which a vital tuft of bright green needles was growing, closely resembling a minuscule shaving brush. Curiously, every once in a while the miniature row of shaving brushes was interrupted by a much larger, beautiful bright pink bud that was shaped like a bottlebrush. Later research would confirm my suspicion that this was the female flower.[141]

I carefully stripped only a few side branches per tree (in order not to damage it in any substantial way), placed them into a zip-lock bag (I try to always bring one when on walks, because you never know), and immediately returned home to immerse them in copious amounts of olive oil, thereby avoiding any oxidization that would denature the valuable flavor compounds in the buds. As I had only picked a small amount, which could be blended within seconds without the hand-held blender becoming even slightly warm, I figured that I didn't need to freeze them to avoid heat damage to the natural flavor compounds.

After soaking the young needles in the olive oil for several hours, I cooked a small portion of fusilli pasta, which I prepared *al dente*, then tossed in the freshly pureed pesto. Since I had not only taken the bright green young shoots but also the little, bark-covered round buds, the pesto was not only bright green but also had several brownish specks. Its taste was, however, unexpectedly delicate, with a greenish, sappy note that had many similarities with citrus fruits. Also, the consistency was surprisingly smooth and reminded me of nut butter. The only clear sign that it was a tree product was a certain amount of astringency, which was, however, anything but unpleasant. Encouraged by this first sample, I went on to make a full-blown pesto out of it by adding a handful of walnuts and a generous amount of freshly grated parmesan, topped off with yet more olive oil. The result was a beautiful beige creamy pesto that tasted extremely good when combined with another serving of hearty whole-grain pasta. Curiously, in this combination the taste reminded me of very good, fresh tahini.

Waiting for a whole winter for this tree delicacy that Wenter had introduced me to had been totally worth it. Not only that, it had proven yet again that the flavor of wood was varied and unexpected. I couldn't wait for the flavors still to come.

CHAPTER 11
Pokot's Ash

Waking up to the sound of my alarm clock one very early September morning in 2015, I was immediately excited for the day ahead. A skywards look out of the window confirmed the sunny weather forecast for the day, and quick shower to follow revitalized my still-sleepy brain. Getting swiftly dressed, I grabbed my car keys, walked briskly to the parking lot, and began the drive toward Bra and a very special cheese fair I had been waiting to attend for almost three years.

Slow Cheese in the small Piemontese town of Bra is described by many as the biggest gathering of high-quality cheese producers in Italy. Organized by Slow Food, an international movement for the promotion of good, clean, and fair food that was founded during protests against the opening of a McDonald's fast-food joint by the Spanish Steps in Rome, it transforms the center of Bra every two years into a massive cheese fair. Producers from all parts of the world come to showcase their often strong-scented, mouth-watering cheese products—all of which are the products of an ancient way of preserving milk, in which bacteria transform the liquids into a solid form—to the visiting public. For three September days, the whole city is wrapped in the cheesy cloud of fragrance exuded by hundreds of stands alongside all major streets and squares.

Having planned to visit the fair for several years, I'd unfortunately always had to change my plans at the last minute. In 2015, however, I finally found myself free during the days of the fair, and since I was living in Milan at the time, just a two-and-a-half-hour drive from Bra, I drove there first thing in the morning. I know Bra very well, as I had lived in this small and picturesque Piemontese town during my graduate studies at the nearby University of Gastronomic Sciences. (Most unfortunately, my time at the university took place in the space between two cheese fairs.) Just some forty minutes to the south of Turin, amidst the rises of Piedmont, Bra is perched on a projecting hill overlooking the fertile Tanaro river valley, a tributary to the mighty Po River. Accessible from the agriculturally occupied valley by two winding and relatively steep roads on either side of the hill, the city itself is one of the major examples of Piemontese Baroque architecture.[142] With its many intricately decorated, yet not overly pompous palazzos and churches that line squares, narrow cobbled roads, and alleyways, it is an exceptionally beautiful city that is not only attractive to look at but also tremendously comfortable to live in. Unlike many other towns in the area, which are at a near-standstill during the tourist off-season due to rural depopulation, Bra is a very lively town year-round, with many shops, cafés, bars, and restaurants, and two biweekly markets, all within comfortable walking distance. (The center of Bra is less than a mile in diameter.)

Particularly close to my heart are Café Converso in the city center, which offers the best hot chocolate I have ever tasted (extremely thick, a bit bitter, and topped with dense, freshly handmade whipped cream) and Giolito's cheese shop, which is hidden away in a side alley and offers an unbelievable cheese selection, including an in-house innovation of strong Gorgonzola mixed with creamy Mascarpone called *Manicomio* (which directly translates to "loony bin," suggesting it's insanely delicious) and a very flavorful hard cheese called *Occelli al Malto d'orzo e Whisky* that is aged for a very long time and finally coated with malted barley and whisky.

Since the University of Gastronomic Sciences is just a fifteen-minute bus ride away, almost all students live in Bra, which gives the small town an international flair. Wherever you go you meet someone you know from university, and because everybody is both passionate and knowledgeable about food, you always have something to discuss. Living in this town and studying at the nearby university is one of my dearest memories, so I was looking forward to returning, particularly with the cheese festival going on.

Although I arrived relatively early in the morning, the city was already bustling even more than usual. Everywhere people were erecting conical-roofed white tents and noisily carting in car- and truckloads of cheese from all corners of the world. Still in the car, I managed to navigate through the goings-on and drive to the other side of town. As I returned by foot from a rare parking spot some distance away, the ineffable smell of cheese grew ever more intense. It momentarily reminded me that I had skipped breakfast, fearing morning traffic jams on the highway. Luckily Giulia, a very good friend and former classmate as well as flatmate of mine, had remained in Bra after university and was running one of Slow Food's newest projects, Local, a mixed shop and bar concept that sold only the highest of quality food products from the region. Giulia had told me several times about their amazing cappuccino made with fresh, local buffalo milk, and now was the time to finally try it. Although I am a publicly declared tea drinker, I can enjoy a good coffee occasionally, mostly for research purposes. It would, however, take me twenty minutes or so to reach Giulia and try the indeed excellent cappuccino, due to the line already snaking outside of the shop. (Fortunately, the line included some familiar faces, so waiting wasn't too bad.) Barely able to talk with each other due to the noisiness of the coffee bar, and Giulia's having to work, we postponed catching up until the afternoon. Thanks to the caffeine and a complimentary cornetto, my blood sugar levels were soon at the point where I felt ready to enter the cheese fray I had waited for so long to experience.

The stands were organized by region (of Italy) and by country. Everyone was here, from Sicily to Switzerland, from Lazio to Iceland, from Emiglia Romana to Spain, and from Piedmont to Kenya. Every stand had an unbelievable variety of cheeses and an accompanying symphony of aromas on offer. Some of the highlights included a hard *Bagòss* cow's milk cheese from Lombardy wrapped and aged in green walnut leaves and, similarly, a hard *Testun* cow's milk cheese from Piedmont wrapped and aged in sweet chestnut leaves. This time-honored tradition not only protects the cheese within but also gives it a distinctive flavor. The fresh walnut leaves infused the outer layers of the *Bagòss* with a greenish, herbaceous taste that was complemented by a slightly bitter note, while the *Testun* got a remarkably sweet, caramel-like note with a hint of marzipan from the chestnut leaves. Additionally, of course, the leaf wrappings gave them a wonderfully elegant look.

A few stands farther down the road I got to sample real Icelandic skyr, which, I learned, is classified as a cheese rather than yoghurt. Just around the corner from that I tried the unique Norwegian brown cheese, where the milk sugars are caramelized through a long cooking process, resulting in a wonderfully sweet and slightly crumbly cheese. A definite comical highlight was a French cheese stand with such incredibly stinky cheese that people recoiled when they approached it unprepared. Its position in the middle of the festival must have been, however, strategic, as it attracted all flies away from the other stands. Genius!

Browsing and tasting my way through the immense variety of cheese on offer, after a while I came across the Kenyan stand. First I couldn't see what they were showcasing due to a big crowd of people in front of the stand, signaling the possibility of something exciting (or something free). After a little bit of squeezing I saw that they were pouring a gray-blue liquid into cups and handing it out to people. So, there was something exciting *and* free at the same time. No wonder there was a crowd! I learned from a sign at the back of the tent that it was a special Kenyan yoghurt made from some kind of an ash. Curious, I asked one of the Italian translators working there alongside the Kenyans what kind of ash it was, thinking of generic charcoal, whose use as a surface protectant is quite common in cheese making.[143] Instead he told me that it was ash from a very specific tree only growing in Kenya's West Pokot region. As you can imagine, I was immediately intrigued. Had I found yet another food product whose flavor was influenced by wood?

It took a bit more squeezing through the crowd to reach the other side of the stand, where I had spotted Samson, a familiar Kenyan student from university. Straightaway, Samson gave me a sample of the blue yoghurt and told me the history of its place of origin, the Kenyan region of West Pokot.

Lying in the most western part of Kenya, alongside the border to Uganda, West Pokot is divided into a somewhat fertile highland region and a very dry, savanna-like lowland region. Both regions are influenced by seasonal weather extremes, with the lowland being affected the most. Particularly in the lowlands, the dry season tests the endurance of every living being, and is quite suddenly replaced by the violent extremes of the rainy season. The soil, baked hard by the unforgiving sun and only broken up by stones, termite hills, and rare acacia tress, can't absorb the streams of water falling from the sky. The results are ferocious, earth-colored floods that blaze their uncompromising trail through the landscape, taking with them everything and everyone not fast enough to escape. Pokot's people compare the bravest among them to this mighty, devastating spectacle: "To be brave like a flood," they say. But following the floods of the rainy season, the moisture that was forcefully pressed into the compacted soil unexpectedly resurfaces in the form of a sea of yellow flowers. Acacia trees put on their best white flower crowns for the occasion, and the vigorous growth of verdant green grass follows shortly after.[144]

This is what Pokot's people, and their herds of Zebu cattle and goats, have been longing for throughout the dry season. Females quickly fatten up on the herbal bounty, and soon the first calves are born, bringing with them streams of nurturing milk. The herds, tended by men and children, roam the countryside, while their excess milk is collected by the women in calabash containers, which have seemingly evolved for this purpose; calabash, a vine plant from the same family as cucumber, pumpkin, and zucchini, are naturally hollow, pumpkin-like gourds sporting a long neck that can safely hold any and all liquids. The Pokot people still use them today to hold their all-important lifeblood, milk, which everyone in the village consumes.[145] However, what happens when all the calves are weaned and the withering grass marks the arrival of yet another dry season? Even the frugal Zebu cow can't provide milk throughout these harsh conditions.

This is where the blue yoghurt I was holding in my hand comes into play. In the absence of any cheese-making tradition, the Pokot people invented their own ingenious method to preserve milk long into the dry season. By using ash made from the wood of the *cromwo* tree (later research would identify it as *Ozoroa insignis*, the "currant resin tree"), milk can, incredibly, be preserved for up to six months.

After receiving such an in-depth introduction to the region and its yoghurt, I was looking forward to giving it a try. Its smell resembled that of Greek-style yoghurt, with none of the acidity of regular yoghurt. The taste itself was also similar to a Greek-style yoghurt, yet with a much more liquid texture and a mineral, slightly smoky aroma. Besides tasting excellent and being full of protein, I could immediately see this being a valuable nutritional additive full of essential minerals like calcium, potassium, and magnesium.

Samson had to leave to give a talk on the curious yoghurt, and we didn't meet each other again during Slow Cheese. However, we stayed in contact via Skype in the following months, and I was extremely delighted when he told me that he would be coming back to Italy together with one of the main producers of blue ash yoghurt for yet another Slow Food event, the *Salone del Gusto*, one of Europe's biggest artisanal food fairs held every two years in Turin.

So exactly one year later we met each other again amidst the beautiful and flavorful chaos of *Salone*, which was for the first time held out in the open in Turin's grand *Parco del Valentino* alongside the Po river. Samson introduced me to Dickson, the highland farmer who, together with his family, was one of the last producers of the ancient blue yoghurt that had already served the Pokots' nomadic forefathers as an invaluable energy source during dry season. Dickson and his wife, Mama Sharon—children are so important for the Pokot that the mother takes the name of the firstborn—have five children, all of whom grew up on a diet rich in blue yoghurt. The production process is comparatively easy. First the fresh milk, either from cows or goats (but not a mixture of the two), is brought to two full boils, in between which it is allowed to fully cool. In the meantime, a branch from the cromwo tree, which has been completely debarked and dried in the sun for at least three weeks, is placed in a fire until the end is charred. This charred layer is then coarsely scrubbed off the stick and ground into a fine powder between two stones before it is transferred into a waiting calabash. Finally, the cooled milk is poured into the vessel, with the floating layer of cream held back by a fork, and the calabash is closed. After three days, the milk has turned into yoghurt and is ready for consumption.[146] The lighter cow's milk yoghurt is consumed by the men, while the richer (in nutrients and fat) and more flavorful goat's milk yoghurt is reserved for women and children.

Sometime later I was able to contact Lonah Chemtai, the West Pokot–born marathon runner who ran for Israel in the 2016 Summer Olympics. She confirmed that not only she herself grew up with cromwo yoghurt but that many Kenyan runners she knew swore by it as an after-workout drink. Forget about probiotic drinks, then—blue ash yoghurt is the next big thing!

While telling me about the yoghurt-making process, Samson used a cromwo stick they had brought from Kenya to demonstrate the production process. After a while I couldn't resist asking him if I could possibly have a piece of the wood, thinking that I could use it for an experiment. Very unexpectedly, he not only agreed to let me have a piece but promised me the whole stick once they didn't need it anymore for demonstration purposes after the event. Extremely happy, I thanked them repeatedly for all the information and their time and joyfully traveled back to Vienna with my extremely valuable (to me, at least) wooden stick in my hand luggage, for which I received more than one strange look from the airport security guy sitting at the x-ray machine.

Back home I was tremendously curious to test if the cromwo wood was really the only one that could be used for the making of yoghurt. Samson had suggested that in a different part of Kenya he had seen people use a different type of wood, and several literature sources I had found had also, very carefully, suggested the possibility.

To find out for myself, I devised the following experiment. I'd prepare raw milk (which was surprisingly easy to come by in a Viennese organic supermarket) in the same way as Dickson and his family did, in two jars. The first held the fine ash of burned beech wood from my wood-fired oven and the second, the very fine, uncharred cromwo wood dust. The idea was to see if the wood itself had the magic yoghurt-making ingredients or if it had to be charcoal. If it had to be charcoal, would only the cromwo charcoal work? Or would beech wood charcoal, and therefore most other charcoal types, do the job?

The results were very surprising indeed. After several days of waiting, the double-boiled milk in the jar with cromwo wood dust didn't change at all. Besides a very fine layer of coagulated fat floating at the top, there was no difference from what I had poured in four days before. The jar with the powdered beech wood charcoal, on the other hand, was a totally different story. Almost all of the milk inside had coagulated, with only very little excess liquid left. Upon opening, a whiff of aged cheese smell, like Parmesan, hit my nose. Once I inspected the quite solid form inside, I saw that it resembled fresh cheese, similar to the Indian paneer (a fresh, unprocessed cheese coagulated with the help of lime juice). The whole outside surface was slick and shiny, with many medium-sized air holes, contrary to yoghurt's matte and creamy texture, which doesn't allow for any visible air holes. Its taste was much more acidic than the original Pokot ash yoghurt, although quite enjoyable and refreshing.

My experiment's results really baffled me, since I didn't know what I had made. Was it cheese or yoghurt? The only thing that was clear to me was that cromwo wood dust alone was not enough to induce any reaction whatsoever in milk. It had to be charcoal, and since beech wood charcoal had induced a quite strong reaction, seemingly any kind of charcoal was fine. Why the focus on cromwo wood, then?

Before I could make any further speculations based on my one-time experiment, I clearly had to talk to someone who knew their way around cheese and yoghurt. I had to identify my shiny white, yet smelly and gelatinous result. Fortunately, I knew the perfect person to ask: Robert Paget, an Austrian cheese-making legend who has his own small herd of buffalos and is particularly renowned for his excellent buffalo milk mozzarella. After leaving several voicemails that went unreturned, I wrote him an e-mail explaining my dilemma. Thankfully he got back to me within hours inviting me to meet once he was back in Austria, as he was currently working in India. So, several weeks later we met at the location of one of his latest consulting projects, Vienna's first cheese dairy.

As I explained the strange results of my experiment, some part of me hoped he would exclaim, "Eureka! You have stumbled across a genius new way of making cheese with only tree ash!" Yet he gently but surely brought me back down to earth. Most likely there had been some kind of contamination in the beech wood charcoal jar that induced the forming of a rogue soft cheese. Also, the Pokots' ability to make yoghurt with cromwo tree ash was in all likelihood due to a culture of wild yoghurt bacteria living in the calabash containers. So, the Pokots' blue yoghurt formed despite the presence of charcoal and not because of it. However, he was nevertheless intrigued by my experiment and offered to redo a similar one in the confines of his professionally equipped and rogue-bacteria-free dairy. He was particularly interested in the supposed properties of the cromwo tree ash.

So, a week later we met again in Vienna, and I supplied him with two jars, one loaded with a tablespoon of freshly made cromwo charcoal powder (made in minutes with a blowtorch) and another with a tablespoon of beech wood charcoal powder. He then prepared raw milk with two precise heating and cooling cycles, inoculated it with a standard yoghurt culture, and poured the mixture into both jars. I then took them home and placed them in my fridge, where they stayed for a month.

Then it was finally time for the first tasting. I was really excited, first and foremost, to see whether there was any difference in taste. But the longevity of the products was also an exciting question. Had they gone bad? Was one wood a better preservative than the other?

The appearance of the jars didn't offer any clues. Similar layers had formed in both, with the bigger charcoal pieces sinking to the bottom and the creamy white yoghurt substance swimming above. But when I shook the glasses, I was surprised to see that both were more liquid than firm. When I opened them, both released minute amounts of gas, but really nothing worrisome or smelly. The jar with the cromwo ash smelled quite invitingly like Greek yoghurt, while the one with beech wood ash smelled more acidic, like soured milk. Tasting confirmed the smells astoundingly: The cromwo yoghurt tasted pleasingly like liquid Greek yoghurt, with a slight smokiness, while the beech wood yoghurt was very acidic, much like lemon juice, and had no smokiness whatsoever.

Based on this one-time experiment, I took away two preliminary conclusions: First, wood ash in general slows bacterial activity in milk, making it hard for the cultures to form a firm yoghurt. Second, and most interestingly, the cromwo ash seems to go beyond that basic quality of charcoal and additionally protects the milk from going sour over an extended period of time (in this case, one month and counting). This was probably also the reason why in my earlier experiment the milk with cromwo wood dust hadn't shown any reaction while the one with beech wood ash had fallen prey to rogue soft-cheese-making bacteria.

I couldn't have been happier with this result, as it meant that certain types of wood (cromwo), can act as highly effective milk preservatives and at the same time also lend a pleasant mineral, smoky flavor to the product—an example for a food product influenced by wood that I couldn't have possibly imagined when I started my hunt for its flavor.

poplar   willow   maple (red)   birch (paper)

The beaver's favorite tree barks, stripped for tasting

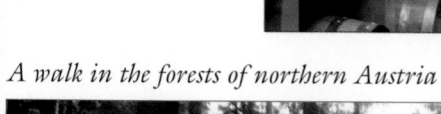

J. Haider's whisky warehouse—the visual embodiment of wood in food

A walk in the forests of northern Austria

Neapolitan pizza from the wood-fired
ovens of Pizzeria Sorbillo

With Gino Sorbillo,
owner of Pizzeria Sorbillo,
at Casa della Pizza

A superb oak barrel in the making
at cooperage Schneckenleitner

*Postcard Teas's
inviting storefront . . .
a treasures await inside!*

*A glimpse of
Postcard Teas's
dazzling selection*

Paddling through the enchanted Spreewald, home of supreme pickled gherkins

A morning walk along the mesmerizing Ligurian coastline on my way to Piedmont

Inside Velier's incredible tasting room high above Genoa

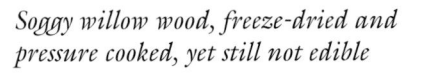

Soggy willow wood, freeze-dried and pressure cooked, yet still not edible

Freshly foraged larch needle tufts about to be soaked in olive oil

Sampling Pokot ash yoghurt poured from a traditional calabash container

Tasting my way through Vienna's annual craft beer festival

Tasting Modenese "black gold,"
the Traditional Aceto Balsamico
di Modena

(Photo credit: Caterina Montorsi)

With my classmate Cate at Acetaia di Giorgio,
Modenese Balsamic Vinegar manufactory

(Photo credit: Carmen Ferraro)

Cooking planked salmon by the waterside in Nova Scotia
(Photo credit: Carmen Ferraro)

Exploring the picturesque landscape of South Tyrol

Fourteen shades of maple syrup at Sugar Moon Farm

Marco Varaldo, the truffle hunter, in search of the white truffles of Alba

Willi Schmid's delicious soft cheeses aging on spruce boards

A tasting menu of wood flavors, made for my friends to celebrate the conclusion of my wooden flavor hunt and the fascinating things I'd discovered

Actual edible wood from Yacaratiá Delicatessen in Argentina

CHAPTER 12
Eastern Germany's Gherkins

Paddling out one fall morning into the branching canals, dikes, and rivers of the misty Spree forest reminded me of a similar trip I had made more than a year before, on Canada's east coast. There were a lot of atmospheric parallels, with the early sunlight still not quite strong enough to power through the thick mist cover, the water's surface as smooth as glass, and brilliantly colored leaves every so often landing gently on its surface. The low autumn temperature and the very type of boat I was paddling in had some similarities, yet the preconditions leading up to the two canoe trips couldn't have been more different. While my visit to Canada was dedicated to clearing my head and only quite unexpectedly resulted in the first promising lead in my hunt for the flavor of wood, the trip to the German *Spreewald,* or Spree forest, had been one of the earliest destinations I had envisioned once I made the conscious decision to write a book about the interconnection between trees and our food. I had read an interesting article in the Swiss newspaper *Neue Zürcher Zeitung* about a very unexpected product coming from the river Spree's alluvial forests: Spreewald gherkins. Traditionally lacto-fermented in large wooden barrels, they are particularly famous in the former territory of Eastern Germany but increasingly appreciated all over Germany and beyond.[147]

In all likelihood their origins in the Spreewald went back to the migration period in late antiquity (spanning the third to eighth centuries), during which West-Slavic tribes from the regions of today's Poland and the Czech Republic moved into the area and brought cucumber seeds with them. A minority group named the Sorbs, with their own language and culture, initially utilized the Spreewald's rich fish and hunting grounds before cultivating large parts of it for vegetable production and animal breeding.[148]

It wasn't until much later, however, that the cucumbers reached their heyday when a different group of people moved into the area, contracted by the then ruler of the Spreewald Count Joachim II von der Schulenburg (1522–1594),[149] who admired the linen-weaving industry while on a trip to Holland and decided to introduce it to the Spreewald. He recruited several Dutch cloth manufacturers to resettle into the area. They brought with them not only flax seeds for the production of linen fibers but also Dutch varieties of cucumber seeds, which they soon realized grew much better on the fertile, wet soils of the Spreewald than flax. Today the cucumber industry is an important economic factor for the region, although most of the production occurs on large, easily accessible fields adjoining the Spreewald, which is now a UNESCO biosphere reserve and therefore off-limits to large-scale agricultural production.[150]

When I read about the Spreewald gherkins in the *Neue Zürcher Zeitung,* it was the aging process in large wooden barrels that immediately grabbed my attention. At the time I had always connected the use of barrels as food storage containers exclusively with liquid alcoholic products. I was pleasantly surprised to learn that one of my favorite foods (I absolutely love pickled gherkins) had been originally aged in wooden barrels—and maybe still were today.

As chance would have it, I'd already scheduled a business appointment in Berlin for the fall, so I simply had to move my return flight by a few days and book a rental car that would allow me to make the roughly one-hour southward trip into the Spreewald.

I took a very early bus from my hotel in the center of Berlin to the airport, picked up my rental car, and headed for the German Autobahn. Driving alongside the Mercedes, Porsches, BMWs, and Audis in their quintessential element in my underpowered Dacia was a frightful experience, but thankfully it was only a short trip.

The closer I came to the alluvial Spreewood forest, the more prevalent the windfarms, and the more intense the mist, became. With the low-lying fog completely obscuring the windmills' bases, the slow-moving rotors appeared to float untethered in the clear space between the mist below and the clouds above like giant airships.

By now I had exited the Autobahn and was driving through picturesque half-timbered towns (a building style typical for this part of Germany) barely visible through the mist, approaching the town of Lehde right on the edge of the forests, where I would stay overnight.

It was only 9:00 AM when I arrived at my hotel and because very few guests were staying at the hotel at the end of the tourist season I could check in quickly. I inquired about the possibility of canoe rentals at the reception desk, and fortuitously, there was a rental place right next to the hotel, which would open at 10:00 AM. To pass the time, I started to explore the area on foot. Every so often I came across large wooden barrels arranged for decorative purposes on the grounds of the hotel. Certainly, these barrels had been used for the production of pickles; after all, the hotel was situated at the epicenter of the region's gherkin history. Established by Karl-Heinz Starick after the fall of the Berlin Wall in 1989, the hotel grounds boasted Germany's only gherkin museum, which hosts a yearly gherkin festival that culminates in the crowning of a Gherkin Queen, who is selected based on both her knowledge of gherkins and a tasting of her homemade pickled gherkins.

To my luck, I spied some movement within the boat rental shop, though it hadn't yet opened. I fetched my photo gear from the car and rented a small, agile canoe, finding myself on the water even before official opening hours. Following both a map and the often-amusing markers on the channel's edge (one was named "Suez Canal"), I very quickly realized why the village of Lehde was called "Venice of the Sorbs." The whole village had no solid roads but rather relied on waterways, which divided it into many small islands, each with its own house built in the Sorbs' traditional wooden block construction. Much like in Venice, all houses were additionally connected by footpaths that regularly crossed the channels with beautifully constructed wooden arch bridges.

Surrounded by extensive gardens and lawns that extended to the channel's edge (some purely for decorative purposes and others with actual productive gardens), many houses were entwined up to their pitched roofs in charmingly fall-colored ivy. Particularly remarkable to me was that every house also had a driveway, or rather a dock, in which to tie up all the residents' boats. Some were heavily laden with freshly cut, slightly sweet-smelling alder tree trunks, which must have been cut the day before in the reserve's high forest. Since it was relatively early in the day and the end of the tourist season, there weren't any people to see around the houses or on the water. Only some wild ducks searched for a breakfast snack near the private docks, and they were plainly unbothered by my presence; I realized, based on their disinterest in my paddling, that a lot of people must come through this beautiful sunken forest during tourist season.

After I'd paddled along the "Suez Canal" for a while and had grown comfortable with the handling of the boat, I reached a T-intersection, with the left-hand side leading further into the forest and the right-hand side to what looked like a clearing off in the distance. By now the heavy morning fog had given way to the ever-stronger sun and sank back into the channels, damp forest floors, and wet meadows. The beaming sun turned the vague clearing on the right into a shining island of light, and I directed my canoe toward it. Upon coming closer, I saw that the entrance to the clearing was guarded by several towering elm trees growing directly on the water's edge, each at least five feet in diameter. As I turned around the final bend, my eyes still adapting to the bright sunlight, I could finally take in the beauty of the clearing. Enclosed on two sides by channels, the triangular-shaped clearing and its vividly green central meadow were seemingly floating in the air, surrounded by radiant morning fog. On the narrow end of the clearing, hay had been piled in the Sorbs' traditional way, around a central pole resembling upside-down cotton candy on a stick.

After gliding past the cotton-candy haystacks I took the next channel to the left back into the bright forest. The trees were frequently punctuated by small fields and meadows, some still with late harvest vegetables growing on them. I marveled at the sheer productivity of this alluvial forest agricultural system. The rich, saturated soils produced copious amounts of vegetables, while intermittently planted fruit trees produced abundantly every fall for the same reason. Combined with animal husbandry (no fences needed, thanks to the ever-present canals), hunting, fishing, and forestry, such a system would produce everything possibly needed and more. I would later read that the comparatively small Spreewald region was nearly the sole supplier of vegetables for all of sprawling Berlin up until a century ago.

Pondering the possibilities of such a productive agricultural system, every once in a while I would come across free-roaming farm animals, like goats or small pot-bellied pigs, as well as wild birds, muskrats, and possibly even a flitting otter. Fall-colored trees lined the water's edge, sometimes standing several rows deep, each with its own shade of yellow, red, green, or brown. The result was a breathtaking mosaic of colors. Constantly changing form and composition through the interplay of sunlight, clouds, and wind, it was delightfully reflected in the channel's serene waters. But as I was paddling below a remarkably tall, fully yellow oak tree leaning halfway over the channel, a sudden strong gust of wind interrupted my otherwise peaceful reverie. Ripe acorns barely hanging on to the tree were all at once lodged free by the gust, releasing a drum roll of mildly painful nuts all over the canoe—and my head. Thankfully I had already passed under the large chestnut trees, whose nuts were now loudly plonking and splashing into the waters behind me. This would remain, however, the only mildly unpleasant surprise on my many-hour canoe trip through the channels of the Spreewald.

Heading home in the setting sunlight, with the mist already returning from its daytime hiding places, I could have sworn I heard the distant song of the cranes preparing for their long trip to their southern wintering grounds. As I concluded the day in the hotel's restaurant with a delicious appetizer of assorted pickled gherkins and a main course of freshly caught catfish, I began to look forward to the next day's interview with the hotel's owner, Karl-Heinz Starick, who not only created Germany's only gherkin museum but was also the initiator behind the Spreewood gherkin festival. No one knew pickled gherkins better than him, and so I was very eager to ask him about the influence of wood on this wonderfully tart product.

The next day, after breakfast, I packed my small carry-on and loaded it into my rental car, as I was leaving for the airport right after the interview. I would have loved to check out the canoe once again and spent the day on the canals, many of which I hadn't explored yet, but my schedule wouldn't allow it. Thankfully, Starick arrived slightly early to our meeting point in the hotel's lobby, which meant I wouldn't miss my flight, though we talked for quite a long time.

We began our appointment with a tour of the gherkin museum right in front of the hotel. The museum's walls were made from old, large gherkin barrels and still gave off a slightly acidic smell when heated by the sun. As we walked about the museum, Starick told me of how he came to become a gherkin expert. Born into a farmer's family and raised in Lehde, Starick's contact with the Spreewood gherkins was practically hereditary. He can vividly remember seeing the wooden boats full of freshly harvested gherkins arriving in Lübenau, the region's market city, where they were bought by the gherkin picklers. His personal gherkin passion would start during his vocational training as a chef in 1968 in the then German Democratic Republic, when he began to collect gherkin recipes.

Starick tells me that in "the old times"—a phrase that worried me, hinting the production methods had since changed—gherkins were pickled in large, three-and-a-half-ton oak or beech wood barrels, which had only one small opening on the side. He quizzed me as to why the opening had to be particularly small. After I warranted several wrong guesses, he told me that it was essential for the cleaning and sterilization of the barrels. They were first filled with a bit of water, and then several red-hot iron balls were thrown in through the small opening, which in turn was sealed up. The barrels were rolled up and down on a flat surface, which allowed the by-now-boiling water to sterilize the inside surface. The small opening was therefore essential: a larger one simply wouldn't have been able to withstand the abuse. Either way, it must have been quite a spectacle to see the barrels rumbling like steamrollers across the picklers' yards, heralding a new pickling season.

Unfortunately, Mr. Starick confirmed my strong suspicion that the pickles were no longer made in large wooden barrels. Although the barrels were still used at the time of his training as a chef, concrete, plastic, or stainless steel vats soon replaced them. He told me that there might still be some individuals that used small wooden barrels for pickling, but he didn't know any. This was disappointing news for me, as I had been hoping that much like in the wine and spirits sector, at least the small-scale, high-quality producers still used wooden barrels to distinguish themselves from the mass-produced products.

However, as this was my chance to finally learn more about the production process of one of my favorite food items, the food I missed most while living abroad, I eagerly listened to Mr. Starick explaining how it was made in the old days—a process that hasn't changed much today.

The story of the gherkins began in the field on the peaty and wet soil of the Spreewald forest, where vegetables in general and the cucumber in particular grow very well. The gherkin was harvested when it reached hand length. (Contrastingly, thumb thickness is the rule today.) It was then transferred as quickly as possible, while being shaded from the sun in wooden boats, via the vast network of canals to the bi-weekly gherkin market in Lübenau, where the picklers waited anxiously for their delicate green cargo. Immediately after striking a deal with the grower, the picklers transferred the gherkins to their production site, where they were washed with cold water, then transferred to the awaiting sterilized wooden barrels. Finally, they were mixed with dill and submersed in the so-called "egg brine", ingeniously named to describe the brine's proper water-to-salt ratio by its ability to float an uncooked egg. Starick tells me that a full and uninterrupted submersion of the gherkins is thereby instrumental in them retaining their "*knackigkeit*," a German word for which the English translation of "crunchiness" doesn't do justice;

"firm to bite" or even "snappiness" is closer.

Achieving this "snappiness" was however not the main concern of the early gherkin picklers. This form of pickling was not yet fully understood, but rather a mysterious occurrence that made the industry a highly financially risky and stressful business. For example, after being submersed in the brine for some time, many gherkins suddenly exploded, making them unsellable. Only later a Spreewald forest native and merchant, Schulz from Lübenau, found the cause of the spontaneous explosions when he realized that during the lactic fermentation process gherkins often started to rot on the inside, resulting in a gas buildup. His solution of piercing the skin, called *sticheln* in German, to allow for the gherkin's interior lactic acid buildup to escape and the brine to enter was what revolutionized the gherkin industry in 1856. With the dangers of possible mass gherkin explosions averted, the picklers could focus on other things like the gherkins' "snappiness."

"Snappiness" is the overarching quality the Spreewood gherkins are famous for today across all their many varieties, including every flavor from sweet and sour, chili, and pepper to mustard and thyme gherkins. Those varieties, however, describe only the main flavor-giving ingredients in the pickled gherkins. Curiously I learned that there are also several other ingredients that contribute to the gherkins' premier taste depending on which of the existing recipes is used—121 in fact. When asked about his confidence in such a specific number, Starick laughed and explained that there were exactly 121 family farms that used to be operated in the Spreewald, and each had its very own recipe. Some added pepperwort and laurel while others added fennel, cloves, or horseradish.

The one that excited me most was the recipe utilizing cherry leaves, which are used in many recipes due to the "fine" flavor note they add to the gherkins. Starick also named another tree leaf recipe, using the walnut leaf. Its use was very fascinating indeed: Late into the harvesting period, cucumbers tend to get quite bitter due to the absence of optimal growing conditions and even the occasional frost. The substance responsible for the bitterness is called *cucurbitacins* and is known to have a harmful effect on humans.[151] This wasn't a deterrent for the crafty people of the

Spreewood, though. They discovered that walnut leaves, when added for a certain period of time to the fermenting cucumbers, seem to absorb all the bitterness and make them as sweet-tasting as ever. So, tree leaves not only add flavor but also seem to have the power to remove certain unwanted flavors from a food product. Much like in spirits, where the wooden barrels' char layer absorbs off-notes, the walnut leaves seems to absorb or neutralize the cucumbers' bitter *cucurbitacins*.

Starick continued to guide me through the museum and told me many curious stories from his hunting adventures into the enchanted Spreewald, and of his replantation efforts of the Spreewald's original elm and oak trees, which had been almost completely replaced some 150 years before with industrially more useful alder trees. We had a great conversation going until, in a moment of our mirror-neurons working in overdrive, we simultaneously checked our watches—we'd been speaking for nearly two hours, much longer than we'd scheduled! We both hurriedly said our goodbyes and made to catch our next appointments, his with a hunting party and mine with my airplane.

On my drive to the airport, as I squeezed every last bit out of the Dacia's estimated two-horsepower engine, I was trying to imagine what the "fine" flavor of the cherry leaf could possibly be. The supposed anti-bitterness powers of the walnut leaves intrigued me, as it seemed to defy common sense. They themselves were full of bitter substances. Do they somehow chemically interact with the cucumbers' *cucurbitacin* and neutralize it?

As it was already fall and both the cherry and the walnut leaves had changed in color and could therefore not be tasted, I had to wait yet again for the following spring for them to return.

Finally, months later on a rainy but warm day in May, the leaves of both trees were finally fully out, and I could head into my garden and pick them. Straightaway, I tried them fresh from the tree. The cherry leaf, still quite delicate, had an unsurprisingly grassy, slightly sweet taste without any bitter aftertaste whatsoever. It took me a while to connect its very fine flavor to anything I had tasted before, but after a while I recognized it as similar to a daisy flower. (Yes, I have tried one, and it makes for great salads!)

The walnut tree standing right next to it teased me a bit with its very high branches, but a quick flick with a stick detached two bunches of tender leaves from its shiny grey twigs. Slightly reddish green in color, their taste was much stronger and very fragrant. Tongue-tinglingly acidic, it consisted of a fantastic flavor cocktail of lemon balm, ripe red grapes, green mango, and an artificial watermelon bubble-gum flavor with a clear hint of walnut in the end. Even after several minutes my tongue was still tingling, much as if I had a strong spirit in my mouth.

Now I obviously had to come up with an experiment that would first test the influence the cherry leaf has on the gherkin's taste and then, of course, Starick's claim of the walnut leaves' de-bittering powers. After some thinking and a quick trip to Vienna's *Naschmarkt*, or "Nibble market," home to a great variety of curious ingredients, I found myself in the kitchen with a pile of fresh, thumb-thick gherkins as well as two bitter gherkins and a pile of tree leaves. The idea was to pickle two jars of each, one with the leaves and one without, so I could compare tastes. The normal cucumbers would be pickled with the cherry leaves, while the bitter gherkin would be pickled with the walnut leaves. The bitter gherkin was my solution to the problem of the unavailability of bitter-tasting normal cucumbers at the market. The worried face of the Indian vegetable stall owner, when he told me about the extreme bitterness of the bitter gherkins, troubled me slightly. However, at least it would be a great test for the walnut leaves' supposed superpower.

No sooner said than done, I quickly had four glasses of experimental pickles, suspended only in a brine of salt and white vinegar to avoid any extra flavor influences, sitting on a shelf in a dark and relatively cool spot of my apartment. I would have to wait for a minimum of four days before I could test the results.

On the fourth day, right after breakfast—and to the dismay of my girlfriend, who absolutely hates pickled gherkins—I retrieved all four glasses from their cool and dark hiding place and positioned them on the kitchen table. To establish a baseline for taste, I started with sampling a gherkin from the normal cucumber jar without the added leaves. They had a very watery, green cucumber taste, with a slight salinity and a surprising lack of acidity considering the amount of vinegar I had previously added. Now to the glass with the cherry leaves. It not only looked quite different (the cucumbers were less bright green but more brownish-green) but also had the pleasant smell of a smoked, slightly resinous, green tea. When I bit into one I immediately had a very different perception to the baseline gherkin: *snap!* It was really firm to the bite! But how?

In terms of taste, the brine flavor was not only much more pronounced, mainly salty and acidic, but there was a fresh cucumber taste accompanied by a literal match for its smell. This was most definitely a much "finer" or refined taste.

Next, the bitter gherkins. Would I discover the de-bittering powers of the walnut leave really existed?

This time I started with the jar to which the walnut leaves had been added, out of fear that the baseline samples' presumed bitterness would prevent me from any further taste experiments. After only trying a small piece, I was surprised by the absence of any bitterness whatsoever. A slight astringency was notable after a while, but that was it. Now to the baseline sample of the bitter gherkins, without the walnut leaves. Would it be bitter?

This time I tried an even smaller piece, out of fear for my taste buds. I was, however, soon relieved: the gherkins were a little bitter, but not exceedingly so. The astringency, on the other hand, was now completely missing. Although I had wished this test to be conclusive, the very slightly difference in bitterness unfortunately doesn't warrant it. It seemed like the brine had done most of the de-bittering work, while the walnut leaves had mostly added some astringency.

Overall, however, I was extremely pleased with the result, as I not only had discovered the "fine" taste of the cherry leaves, which turned out to be smoked, slightly resinous green tea, but also that the addition of the leaves seemed to make the gherkins snappier. My later research discovered a reference to the historical addition of vine leaves, whose tannins inhibit an enzyme that breaks down the pectin cell structure and therefore protects the gherkins' firmness.[152] Scientifically this meant that tannins are one of the keys to the gherkins' snappiness. Since wood is full of tannins, one can only imagine how snappy gherkins aged in fresh wooden barrels could be . . .

CHAPTER 13

Wheat Beer and Larch Trees

The Bavarian city of Regensburg, situated between the bends of the Danube, is a beautiful medieval city with a cultured and vibrant flair. World-renowned for its, in my opinion, almost too impressive, enormous, St. Peter's cathedral in the center of the city, its fortunes were strongly shaped by an architectural masterpiece of a stone bridge across the Danube that was, in medieval times, the only point of crossing for hundreds of miles.

Regensburg had already been an immensely important harbor on the Danube, and the bridge solidified its importance as a trade city, as the many beautifully built storehouses in and around the historic center also attest.[153] Today, Regensburg is unmistakably a student city, as is evident not only by the sheer number of young people everywhere but also by the abundance of French, Italian, and Starbucks-influenced coffeehouses and bars in all shapes and sizes. The streets are lined with tea stores, French restaurants, and spice shops that sit right next to typical Bavarian restaurants, brewhouses, and cheese mongers. Impressive lithic Romanesque churches alternate with richly decorated merchant villas built alongside narrow medieval alleyways, and quite suddenly open to spacious squares, shopping streets, and most importantly the Danube. Names like "Weinlände," meaning "wine landing," or "Holzlände," meaning "wood landing," still precisely describe what used to be unloaded at the most northerly harbor on this mighty river. And beside the river, a few feet downstream from the stone bridge, lies a building that remains highly significant to this day: the oldest sausage stand in the world. Originally built as a site office during the construction of the bridge, it was transformed into a cook shop catering to the hungry harbor workers and dome builders after the bridge was completed in 1146.

Hungry from several hours of sightseeing one cold December day a few days shy of Christmas, I was also attracted by the delicacies this ancient takeaway stand promised to provide. After managing to get one of the few precious tables inside this rustic tourism magnet, I soon had a steaming serving of small homemade sausages with sauerkraut and a glass of rhubarb lemonade in front of me. The small sausages, made 100 percent with meat from a pig's muscular hindquarters, were particularly tasty not only because they were extremely fresh but also because they were grilled above an open charcoal fire, imbuing them with a pleasurable smokiness. Also, the sauerkraut had been aged in large wooden barrels, the type of which I unfortunately wasn't able to determine.[154]

The reason for my visit to this beautiful part of Germany wasn't the oldest sausage stand in the world, although it surely was a highlight, but an appointment I had with the master brewer of Schneider Weisse on the site of the oldest Bavarian wheat beer brewery. The possibility for this most anticipated appointment had arisen due to a combination of some lucky coincidences. It had all started with a visit to the yearly Viennese craft beer festival, at which an ever-increasing number of breweries showcase their fascinating inventions. While looking and tasting my way through some fabulous creations, like a delicious amber ale aged in old rum barrels, a surprisingly balanced whisky beer made from peated malt and aged in former sherry and whisky casks, or simply one of Vienna's historically most successful exports, the Vienna Lager, I came across a curious creation at the most unexpected of all places: a Bavarian wheat beer that had been aged in former wine barrels at the booth of Schneider Weisse. Having attended high school in the Austrian Province of Salzburg, right next to Bavaria, I was familiar with this famous wheat beer from across the border. Yet with its long and distinguished history, and due to the popularity of its original wheat beer, I had expected Schneider Weisse to always play it safe by staying on the conservative side. That they had not only decided to experiment at all, but had also done it in such an outlandish way by putting wheat beer into former wine barrels, a technique I had never heard of before, was very unexpected indeed.

Generally, beer today consists of only four components: malt (grain that has been brought to germinate through the addition of water, initiating the formation of enzymes that will later convert its starch into sugars), water, hops (for flavoring and as a natural preservative), and yeast, which converts the malt sugars into alcohol through fermentation. Based on those simple ingredients, an incredible variety of beer styles have developed around the world. There are beers made from rice, buckwheat, millet, quinoa, rye, barley, maize, and wheat, which can be all malted differently. Depending on how long heat is applied during the malting process, there are different malts, ranging from very pale to very dark, almost or actually burned. The type of malt greatly influences a beer's flavor and color. Adding to the confusion is an astounding selection of different-tasting and varyingly bitter hops as well as different yeast and water with varying amounts of natural minerals. Also, additional flavorings like coffee,[155] chocolate,[156] grapefruit,[157] strawberry and rhubarb,[158] and yes, even bacon,[159] are often used.[160]

The brewing process is in its essence also very simple. However, it allows for an endless number of variations, each resulting in a different beer. It starts by the addition of copious amounts of warm water to the previously crushed malt, thereby activating the enzymes that convert the grains' starch into sugars. The result is basically a sweet grain tea. Filtered off from all solids, this solution is then brought to a boil, and the hops are added. It is quickly cooled and transferred into another vessel, and the yeast is added. Now, left to its devices, fermentation will start, converting the sugars to alcohol and CO_2 bubbles. After some days, the beer is ready to be drunk.

Unsurprisingly, it seems that humankind has been always very fond of fermented, beer-like beverages. The first solid historical evidence of such a beverage goes back to the seventh millennium BC in the province of Henan, China. Chemical analysis of the minuscule residue present in a pottery shard revealed a fermented beverage that was made from rice, honey, and fruits. The first beers made from grain probably go back to the area of Mesopotamia and Egypt, not far from where its main solid ingredient was initially cultivated in the region of north Levant, what is today the crescent-moon-shaped borderland between Turkey, Syria, Iraq, and Iran. The first written documents that mention beer are dated at around the third millennium BC, while the first description of its brewing process has been found in documents from the old Babylonian period dating to 1800 BC.

Grain cultivation had spread to Central and Northern Europe by the Neolithic period, in the fourth millennium BC. However, clear written evidence of the brewing of beer is first seen among the Celtic tribes who formed around 700 BC. By then it was, however, already a well-established and important beverage.

Funnily, the Romans and the ancient Greeks before them looked down at grain-based beverages, which they saw as a drink of the barbarians. Cultivated civilizations, like themselves, would drink wine—until the Roman Empire reached as far as Britain and the cultivation of grapes became difficult, they also drank beer. With the advent of the Middle Ages, beer spread over all of Europe and would later become an essential drink in every part of the world.[161] Curiously, the implication that beer is a somewhat less civilized beverage than wine seems to still exist today, although I think ever decreasingly.

Back at the craft beer fair in Vienna, I had just discovered the curious wine-barrel-aged wheat beer at the Schneider Weisse stand, which would have most likely resulted in a popular outcry in ancient Greek or Roman times. This experiment didn't appear on the stand's official beer menu; in fact, I overheard an employee of the brewery telling some fans about the curious creation as I was passing by their booth. I stopped in my tracks and joined what had by now turned into a tasting session and asked if I could possibly also sample the concoction. Most fortunately I could, and even before I actually tried it, an interesting conversation with the brewery's Austrian representative had begun. It would soon transpire that the brew master of Schneider Weisse was very adventurous indeed and had already been experimenting for years with barrel aging of their wheat beer. His newest creation I was tasting was called "Aventinus Cuvée Barrique" and was based on a mix between their dark wheat beer bock and their even stronger Eisbock. It had a quite unusual flavor combination of raisins, dark chocolate, banana, and prunes with a certain sourness and no carbonation. To be honest, it was not my favorite. Still, I was very intrigued and mentioned my interest into all things wood and its different flavors. After listening for a while, the brewery's Austrian representative told me that I should really talk with their master brewer, Hans-Peter Drexler, and gave me his contact details.

On my way back home from the fair I sent an e-mail to Mr. Drexler and he replied by inviting me to come by the brewery in Kelheim, Bavaria, to talk about barrel aging in the world of beer. Of course, I accepted the invitation, and so found myself driving one very early December morning toward Regensburg, sightseeing, and sitting down for a delicious lunch before my appointment at the brewery, some thirty minutes to the southwest. Besides specialty beers, I was most curious to find out if there was a place for wooden barrels in beer making today.

The Schneider Weisse brewery, which had been moved to the small Bavarian town of Kelheim after the original in Munich had been destroyed by Allied bombs in the Second World War, is a highly visible building complex with large production halls, offices, and laboratories. Yet when approaching from the old center of the town, the brewery looks as much the same as when it first opened its doors here in 1607. Not knowing which was the right entrance, I entered through the delivery gate, but nevertheless found the office very quickly. A friendly secretary called Drexler, and soon we were seated in his office talking about his experimental brews.

As it turns out, he'd started experimenting with different barrels some ten years before. Drexler told me his first inspirations for using barrels came from American breweries he'd visited, who had begun using the oak barrels from bourbon distilleries for initial beer-aging experiments. Liking some of the results, he returned to Schneider Weisse and ordered some barrels previously used for aging Jack Daniels, scotch, and calvados, as well as some fresh oak barrels. After filling them with his beer and sampling the results, however, he was not overly impressed. The Jack Daniels barrels completely masked the taste of his beer, the Calvados barrels added an overly sweet, fruity note, and the fresh oak barrels just added copious amounts of green tannins to his beer. Slightly disheartened by this first results, he set the idea aside for several years until one day he got into a conversation with a close friend, the brew master Jérôme de Rebetez from Brasserie des Franches Montagnes in Switzerland, who not only grew up in a wine-making family but was also an enologist himself. Somehow, they came up with the idea to age beer in wine barrels instead. Furthermore, they stayed the course and brought it to market. I would later find out that bringing an idea promptly to life was one of Drexler's specialties.

Using barrels that had previously aged Chardonnay and a variety of red wines, they, after several months of aging, created a cuvée that approached Drexler's idea of what a barrel should do. The aging supported his beer's taste, adding interesting notes to it but not overpowering it. Once he had found the right sales channels, mostly through specialty beer shops, he began to further work on the cuvée's taste. At the time of my visit, he had recently acquired some additional new German oak barrels that should add a certain tannic depth to the product. So, the previous experiments had a sense after all.

But what about using wooden barrels in beer making in general? Of course, historically the barrel has been immensely important in the industry. But most barrels used in continental Europe had been pitched, meaning that their insides were lined with a layer of tree pitch, preventing the beer from having direct contact with the wood and avoiding the loss of carbonation through the wood's pores. The large Czech brewery Pilsner Urquell uses pitch in its large oak barrels to this day.[162] Curiously, Drexler tells me that this practice was not common in the United

Kingdom, where even today some ales are aged in un-pitched wooden barrels.[163]

Seeing that I was really interested in the barrels, Drexler asked me if I wanted to see them. So, only a few minutes later we found ourselves in a cool, spotlighted room with stone walls lined with barrels. It looked more like a winery then a brewery, yet the smell was clearly that of beer, although with a slightly fruity note. Next, we walked on to the brewery's cooled treasury, which had samples from every beer recently made. He picked out one mono-variety that had been only aged in chardonnay barrels. From there we went to the tasting room just around the corner. After opening and pouring the beer into glasses, we waited a bit until it had reached the right tasting temperature, which was at around 54 to 59 degrees Fahrenheit. Surprisingly, it had a large amount of foam (called "head" in the beer world), which one wouldn't expect due to the usual loss of carbonation during barrel aging. There must have been some secondary fermentation going on in the bottle. The color was an opaque brown with a reddish tint, while the scent was somewhat sour with a hint of dried fruits and grapes. Like the one I had already tried at the craft beer fair, this beer had notes of raisins, dark red fruits, and bananas. But it was slightly less sour and had clear, fruity notes of chardonnay. This was quite a delight.

We continued to talk about the brewery, the possible uses of wooden barrels, and the making of wheat beer in general until it was time for me to leave—though not before agreeing to stay in contact and exchange ideas on barrel-aging beer.

On my return trip from Bavaria, I kept wondering which type of wood would fit best with Schneider Weisse's dark wheat beer. Back at home I immediately consulted my by now quite vast wood library and began experimenting with different wood extracts and the Aventinus beer Drexler had provided me with. Several experiments later I had narrowed it down to either larch or fir, as their quite resinous, yet still spicy notes really reverberated perfectly with the raisin, dark chocolate, and banana taste of the Aventinus. Later research revealed that the Celts, who also lived in

Bavaria, often used fir for their barrels, which of course were used to store beer.[164] So, without knowing, I had stumbled upon what their beer might have tasted like.

Quite sure that I'd created something worth sharing, I called Drexler. We agreed to meet after the holidays so I could let him taste my findings.

So, on an extremely bright, beautiful winter day, copious amounts of snow blanketing the landscape, I drove once again toward Kelheim. I drove onto the German Autobahn, past the world-famous bubble-shaped Bayern Munich Allianz Arena, first heading toward Ingolstadt and then my final destination. Flying by the car's windows were countless hops fields, identifiable by their power line–like trellises upon which the hops would grow come spring. Indeed, I was driving through the world's largest connected hops plantation region, famous for its Hallertauer varieties, also used by Schneider Weisse.[165] While imagining what this area must look like in the summer months, festooned with green hops, I suddenly came across an almost unbelievable display of nature's beauty. Due to freezing temperatures during the night, vast amounts of hoarfrost had formed on all the trees lining the Autobahn, making them look as though they had been dipped in ice. As the rising sun's rays hit those white ice sculptures, they began to sparkle and shine, contrasting sharply against the freshly salted, black asphalt of the road. This magnificent spectacle made it really hard to keep focusing on the road ahead. Fortunately, traffic was very limited.

Arriving safely at Schneider Weisse, I this time used the correct entrance and found Drexler's office right away. Together we walked the short distance to the tasting room, taking with us several Aventinus bottles for tasting. I had brought with me extracts from both larch and fir, which I mixed now with the Aventinus beer samples. After letting the mixture sit awhile so the unfamiliar aromas could mingle, they were ready for trying. We both tried the samples, and I tried really hard to interpret Drexler's facial expressions. Would he like it?

Not giving away too much, he tried both samples, sipping slowly, until he finally gave his verdict. He really liked the slightly resinous, spicy notes the larch added to his dark wheat beer. Even the fir grew on him, though he liked it more in combination with their classic wheat beer. Yet the most exciting part for me was that he was absolutely willing to try entrusting some of his valuable beer to a larch barrel. I couldn't believe it—I had, essentially, just landed my gig consulting on the flavor of wood!

Minutes after I had left the brewery, still buzzing with the excitement of Drexler's approval, I phoned Paul Schneckenleitner, the incredible talented barrel maker I'd previously met, and asked him if he could actually make some larch barrels. I had discussed the idea with him in the abstract before, wanting to be sure I wasn't suggesting something completely impossible. But now it needed to be certain. He had to call me back, but when he did he told me that his father could actually remember making one years ago, and although it was a bit tricky due to the softer wood, they would manage. Perfect.

Not even a month later, the barrels, one sixty-gallon Barrique and one Zigarillo, named for its elongated shape reminiscent of a cigar, holding around twenty-nine gallons, were delivered to Schneider Weisse and filled with Aventinus dark wheat beer. The Zigarillo was an additional experiment, as due to its larger surface area it would impart even stronger flavors on the beer within. However, to avoid overly strong flavors, I had asked Schneckenleitner to toast them very carefully and once done even steam them on the inside to extract any strong tannins and resins.

Now, the long waiting period began. Finally, nearly ten months later just around Christmas, Drexler told me that they not only were about to bottle the result and that he would send me some bottles to try, but also that an American beer specialty distributor liked the idea so much that he had bought all of them. Beginning in December 2015, the beer was available in the United States market under the name "TAP X Aventinus Barrique – Matured in a single Grand Cru Larch Barrel." The reactions it received were most interesting—the first real-world reviews for what could be a fantastic variety of wooden flavors. The average score across the largest beer-rating sites ratebeer.com,[166] beeradvocate.com,[167] and untapped.com[168] was about 3.5 out of 5; not too bad, but there was still room for improvement. The reviews hinted at the incredible variety of notes people tasted: tart berries, wet and moldy wood, earthy licorice, plum, juniper berries, prunes, cedar, what you taste when licking a newly built wooden boat, tannins reminiscent of a rich red wine, mushrooms, birch bark, resiny, malty, piney, papery, and sprucey. Some really liked it while others absolutely hated it, but for most it seemed to be a somewhat acquired taste.

For Drexler the resinous notes were the dominating ones, reminding him of the typical Greek white wine Retsina, which has a recognizable sappy taste produced by its freshly pitched barrels. For me they were also definitely at the forefront, but accompanied by strong notes of red fruits and cedar (resinous and slightly spicy with cloves and sandalwood). The "new wooden boat" note was a bit hard to find, but then again, I had never licked one before. Although the beer was quite flat, as many reviewers had pointed out, I was nevertheless very pleased with the results, which showed strong similarities to my first kitchen experiments; maybe too strong, as the larch definitely needs to take a step back in possible further iterations—something that can be easily done by a shorter aging period or by the use of more depleted barrels.

Overall, this most public experiment was tremendously exciting for me, as it clearly showed that people are interested in giving the different flavors of wood a try. Who knows? Maybe it was the beginning of wonderfully woody flavors to come.

CHAPTER 14
Black Gold of Modena

Childhood memories are a strange thing. Many events you simply forget. Some you know vaguely must have happened, but you are not able to pinpoint them exactly. And then there are certain things you remember clearly. You recall every little detail, from the weather outside to the color of the surrounding walls, the smell and sounds of the place, and maybe even the taste of the meal you ate. I certainly have several of these memories, and a large proportion of them, maybe unsurprisingly, have to do with food. One such moment was sitting on the train to Vienna on a late fall day; I must have been around eight, while my mom was telling me about an exciting article on Aceto Balsamico di Modena in a weekend newspaper supplement. It went into the details of how the vinegar was made, how long it actually took to be finished (back then simply an incomprehensible amount of time for me), and how to cook with it. The article ended with a list of some of the best types of balsamic vinegar and the shops in Vienna where they could be bought. To this day I don't know why this article impressed me so much, but I really wanted to go to one of the Viennese delicacy shops mentioned and see the vinegars up close and personal. I imagined it like a visit to a museum, but for foodstuffs.

Since one shop was almost on our way, my mum wasn't too hard to convince. Soon, there I was, standing in front of a seemingly sky-high shelf filled with shiny black bottles. After having seen them in person my suddenly flaring curiosity was somehow satisfied, even without trying or buying a single one. We could continue with the normally scheduled program, a visit to an actual museum. Needless to say, Aceto Balsamico di Modena was something special for me from that day on, although strangely I never engaged with it properly, besides always making sure to have a relatively good one in the house. Of course, I can't say if this instant alone was the reason why I started studying food many years later. However, it must have been a contributing factor. Why would I remember it so clearly otherwise?

Imagine, then, how excited I was when, in the first few weeks of studying at the University of Gastronomic Sciences, I had the opportunity to try the best Aceto Balsamico I have ever tasted. This I can also remember as if it were yesterday, although it was four years ago. Our Piemontese classmates organized a dinner, where they prepared the most typical Piemontese dish for us: *bagna cauda*, a hot dip made from anchovies, garlic, oil, and butter in which mostly raw vegetables are dipped. Everyone from our class of twenty-four contributed to this feast with a food or dish of their choosing: salads, wine, beer, bread, cheese, vegetables for dipping, and much, much more—a true feast. Cate, a classmate from Modena, brought a very small bottle of a brownish liquid and told us that this was from her grandparents' personal *batteria* (back then I had no idea what this was) of Balsamic vinegar, which was for the family's consumption only. Everyone was immediately intrigued. However, it was a while before she let everyone have a taste in the form of a small, black drop on the back of our hands. When it was my turn to try it, I was very quiet for a moment as I processed the immense complexity of its taste, then remained so because I was simply missing the correct words to describe this divine liquid. I truly had never tasted a balsamic vinegar this good before, from Modena or otherwise.

This first fix made me long to see how Aceto Balsamico was actually made, as I had only read about it quite superficially at this point. Although Cate and I talked about visiting Modena and her family's private balsamic vinegar operation, we somehow never found the time during our year at the University of Gastronomic Sciences. So when I began to look seriously

into the flavor of wood, I straightaway recalled her family's hobby operation in Modena and knew I had to try to visit, because I vaguely knew
that the actual flavor of the finished product was by some degree influenced by the type of wood in which it was aged. Yet by how much and
in which way I had no clue.

Since both Cate and I were busily working and traveling after grad-
uation, it would take us a full two years until we finally managed to meet
in Modena. Even this nearly didn't happen; when I had barely arrived in
the outskirts of Modena I had to overcome an unexpected hurdle. The
automatic tollbooth at the Modena highway exit on the autostrada from
Milano simply refused to take my money, no matter which combination
of coins I fed it. Every time I inserted one, the machine would reject it
immediately. After a while it very reluctantly started to accept my money,
but only in ten-cent increments. With a growing line of numerous cars
impatiently waiting behind me, it took around fifteen aggravating minutes until the machine finally accepted the last of my coins before I was
able to rush to the address Cate had sent me.

Once underway again, I didn't fully know what to expect when I
met with Cate; the only thing she had told me was that she was going to
show me a friend's professional *Acetaia,* or vinegar manufactory. What
she didn't tell me was that it was one of the best, if not *the* best, Acetaia in Modena. Their balsamic vinegar won Best Traditional Balsamic
Vinegar of Modena D.O.P. in 2011, had many fans around the world,
and had been used, among other illustrious places, in the White House
by the Obamas.[169]

Having researched Modenese Balsamic Vinegar before making the
trip I realized for the first time that there was a crucial difference between
the reasonably priced "Balsamic Vinegar of Modena IGP," readily available in supermarkets worldwide, and the rare, expensive "Traditional
Balsamic Vinegar of Modena D.O.P." While the first is produced in large
quantities using a host of different industrial processes, the latter is only
manufactured in small quantities and has to adhere to a very different
and lengthy process regime.[170] How distinctly different I would only fully
comprehend after visiting Cate's friends' manufactory.

The manufactory is called Acetaia di Giorgio and is housed in a beautiful villa a few miles from the city center of Modena. Back in 1870, when the ancestors of today's owner, Giorgio Barbieri, took over the villa, it was still in the countryside and surrounded by fruit trees. Today the city of Modena has grown much larger, and the former countryside villa is now surrounded by rather unimpressive looking factories, roads, and railways. One would not expect to find this gastronomic gem in such an industrial-looking area. But there it is, hiding away behind a high brick wall, overgrown by a beautiful violet wisteria tree. Only a small mosaic sign on the wall next to the entrance hints at the treasure hidden within.

Cate was already waiting for me in front of the house together with her friend Carlotta, the owner's very friendly and knowledgeable daughter. Upon entering the house, I immediately noticed the beautifully preserved mosaic floor, the painted walls and ceilings, as well as the slightly acidic but also sweet and altogether pleasant smell of vinegar. Carlotta led us up the stairs into the attic of the house, where traditional Modenese balsamic vinegar is aged. Contrary to many aged food products, like beer, wine, cheese, or sausages that need a rather stable temperature and humidity, balsamic vinegar thrives under the strongly fluctuating climatic conditions of an attic. Only when it has very hot summers and cold, but not freezing, winters will the vinegar mature to become this delicious brownish liquid. But does it also need the influence of wood?

It all starts in the family's vineyards, where both the white Trebiano grape variety and the red Lambrusco variety (from which the famous Lambrusco sparkling wine is made) are harvested in September. The grapes are carefully pressed, taking care not to extract any bitter flavors from the stems, and the resulting juice, called must, is transferred to large open vats. For nine to ten hours the must is cooked slightly below the boiling point and reduces thereby by more than 50 percent. This cooked grape juice is called "saba" and is a common flavoring and sweetening ingredient in many local dishes, such as *Pane di Natale*, a delicious Christmas bread made with heaps of dried fruits and nuts. In fact, saba was already a kitchen favorite during Roman times. Once reduced to the desired percentage, the now very dark-colored grape syrup is then transferred into the so-called "Mother Barrel" made out of wood, which can be seen as the last outpost before it gets transferred to the *batteria*. It has a volume of around fifty-three gallons and contains all the naturally occurring essential yeasts as well as bacteria needed to transform the grape juice sugars into alcohol and further into vinegar. This process is, according to Carlotta, almost frightening to observe, as there seems to be a living, constantly bubbling and foaming, monster inside the barrel. It is also essential that this monster be always fed. If it runs dry, all the valuable microorganisms inside, essential for the vinegarization process, will die. The fermentation process takes around two to three years. Even in this beginning phase, Traditional Balsamic Vinegar of Modena demands serious patience.

After the fermentation is over, the vinegar finally rests in the first and biggest barrel of the *batteria*. The *batteria* is a row of around eight wooden barrels (there is no fixed number), each smaller than the last. Hearing about the process in more detail I could vividly imagine that the first balsamic vinegar developed by accident when one of the containers filled with saba was forgotten and the natural processes took their course. First whisky and now Aceto Balsamico—it seems like happy accidents gave us some of the best things in the food world!

Either way I was delighted to hear that barrel aging is not only the most important part of the balsamic vinegar–making process but also the most complex one. Most interesting to me was the art and science behind choosing the type of wood the barrels are made from and how it actually influences the product. Historically oak, cherry, ash wood, mulberry, juniper, false acacia (black locust), and chestnut were used, all of which grew in and around Modena. All, with the exception of mulberry, of which there are almost no remaining trees, and, increasingly, juniper, of which it is very difficult to find machinable pieces, are still used today. The different types of wood are used because of their varying densities and the unique flavor profiles they give to the vinegar. Traditionally there are two types of *batterie*, one comprised of different types of wood and one with only a single type, which includes the mother barrel. The type made of a single wood has the name "*riserva*," meaning "reserve," as this type is relatively rare. The more common vinegar is aged in the multi-wood *batteria*, whereby the order of wood types is chosen by the vinegar master. Everyone has their own sequence they swear by; however, there is a rule of thumb. At the beginning of the *batteria*, the barrels still have a comparably large volume (thirteen to twenty gallons), and the focus is on the further reduction of the liquid. This is best done with soft and porous wood, like cherry or mulberry, which facilitates greater evaporation. Toward the end of the *batteria,* it's common to want less reduction but more refinement, which can only be supplied by the much harder and less porous wood types like oak, chestnut, ash, and acacia.[171]

However, this rule of thumb has to be weighed against the different flavors delivered by the woods depending on their position in the sequence. At the Acetaia di Giorgio there are several multi-wood *batterie* which have oak at the beginning and cherry in the middle. If it were the other way around, a different taste would result. For example, if a sweeter wood, like cherry and chestnut, is put at the end, the final flavor will be sweeter. If mulberry and juniper are at the end, the flavor will be more intense, berry-like, and smoky. Using oak at the end yields a richer product with more vanilla aromas, Carlotta told us. If each barrel is made from a different wood type, then mathematically there are 40,320 possibilities for different flavors from the number of possible barrel sequences alone.

The most mesmerizing thing for me to hear, however, was that the older the barrel of a *batteria*, the stronger its taste. How is this possible? If the oldest barrels are a hundred-years-plus (which many of them are), how are they still emitting wood flavors? Conventional wisdom from the spirits industry suggests that wood flavors are washed out with every fill, ever reducing their intensity. The first hypothesis I imagined to explain this discrepancy is that the barrels of a *batteria* can never run dry, as this would kill the valuable microorganisms inside. This means that, in contrast to barrels used for aging spirits, they are never fully emptied, always leaving behind a highly concentrated "soup" full of wood extracts. However, with every draw-and-refill cycle this soup gets diluted practically by half, with its taste influence moving asymptotically toward zero. So something else must be occurring, possibly involving the very community of microorganisms that is individual to each barrel. I could imagine that, depending on which wood type the barrel is made of, a slightly different community of microorganisms forms, resulting in a different taste from the liquid it interacts with. So, hypothetically, the unique wood flavors in Traditional Aceto Balsamico di Modena are as much from the barrel itself as they are from the microorganism community living on and from it. Proving this would be an amazing experiment, yet it could take the better part of a century.

Carlotta told us that traditionally the *batterie* used to have up to nine barrels, which results in a more "universal" taste, as many wood types and flavors are mixed, with none becoming especially pronounced. Today the trend is for fewer barrels (a minimum of five) and fewer types of wood, which give the final product a stronger, more distinctive taste. Carlotta let us try seven different types of their precious product. The difference was in the woods used and in the age. The official consortium of traditional Modenese balsamic vinegar D.O.P producers distinguishes only between two age groups: over twelve and over twenty-five years. This is in stark contrast to "Balsamic Vinegar of Modena IGP" which only requires producers to age it for a minimum of sixty days (often in enormous wooden vats). If it is aged for three years it can be labeled as "invecchiato" (aged).[172]

All of the seven balsamic vinegars we got to try, which spanned in age from twelve-plus to an unbelievable hundred-plus years, tasted amazing, but two stood out by far. One was the hundred-plus-year-old, which had been aged only in oak and chestnut. It not only had an incredibly thick texture and very dark color but also an intense sweet flavor, which was strongly influenced by the oak's vanilla note, and a hint of marzipan, most likely from the chestnut, with very little acidity. I could immediately imagine it being paired with coconut cookies or, maybe more interestingly, with grilled snails.

The second one, and probably my absolute favorite, was the Juniper riserva twelve-plus. This amazing balsamic vinegar was only aged in barrels made from very rare juniper wood, and this over a timespan of more than twelve years. This vinegar seemed to have a very slightly green tint, like greenish-black obsidian, and a slightly more acidic smell. Its taste had some similarities to classic gin, also infused with—amongst other botanicals—juniper berries, but paired with a perfectly balanced sweetness and the roundness of a wood-aged product. This one I would absolutely love to try with some milk-based dessert, like vanilla ice cream, but I imagined it would also taste amazing with roasted lamb.

Additionally Carlotta proudly showed us her personal *batteria,* which, in accordance with a Modenese tradition, her father started when she was born. Carlotta's *batteria* contained a twenty-nine-year-old balsamic vinegar made with only sweet woods, including oak, chestnut, ash, and cherry. Secluded in a small room, all the barrels' openings (which are in general square in shape, in contrast to a wine barrel) were covered with beautiful crocheted linen covers made from Carlotta's great-great-grandparents' bed sheets. Although it was such a highly cherished *batteria*, we were most fortunately allowed to try a very small drop of the vinegar. It was indeed very sweet, yet it also had a surprisingly distinct sherry aroma, of course paired with a slight but pleasant acidity.

Overall, I was very much impressed by the importance of wood in forming this world-renowned product; it was probably only rivaled by that of the weather, which in Modena is generally excellent for balsamic vinegar production. The region's long, dry summers are perfect for promoting evaporation, and its rainy, yet not freezing, winters allow for continued and essential microbial activity in the barrels. But at Acetaia di Giorgio, the effects of climate change are already felt; ever-hotter summers are causing the vinegars to become increasingly viscous. Let's just hope that it won't have a more severe impact in the future—a world without Modenese black gold would be bleak indeed!

Extremely happy, but also extremely hungry, we thanked Carlotta profusely before we drove into the city center, parked our car, and followed Cate, who knew the perfect place for lunch. Walking through a myriad of small side alleys and even smaller squares only a local would know, we suddenly reached an inconspicuous set of stairs leading up into a building. At the top of those stairs there was a wooden door, and next to the door hung a simple sign announcing it to be a *trattoria* (which means "inn" in Italian) and listing the dishes of the day. There were very few specials—always a good sign. Upon entering we immediately saw that it was the most traditional *trattoria* imaginable, with marble floors, classic wooden chairs, and tables covered with simple white cloths. The room was full of locals engulfed in lively conversations, with laughter coming from all sides. I knew right away that this had to be an amazing place to share a meal.

Fortunately, Cate was acquainted with the owner, and so we got a table within minutes, in stark contrast to some unfortunate tourists who came right after us and were refused immediately. (At least in their local *trattoria* the locals want to be only amongst themselves.) The menu consisted of ravioli, stuffed zucchini with mashed potatoes, and a pumpkin crème brulèe, all relatively simple dishes but outstanding in taste. I will especially remember the ravioli, handmade of course, filled with fresh ricotta and stinging nettle, for the rest of my life. In German we have the saying "was für ein Gedicht!" (literally, "what a poem!") if a dish is especially good. A gastronomic poem it was indeed!

Over dinner, Cate asked again whether I really wanted to see her grandmother's *acetaia*. After the visit to the professional Acetaia di Giorgio, she said, it would probably be a disappointment for me since it was just in the old attic of her grandmother's apartment house. But vividly recalling my first taste of her family's treasured *balsamico*, I assured her that if she was still willing, I would very much love to see the place. So, after a quick detour to the beautiful Modena cathedral, we went to her grandmother's apartment building and took the elevator to the top floor. My excitement grew every minute as the old elevator ascended at a painfully slow speed.

When we arrived at the top floor and stood in front of an inconspicuous wooden door, Cate retrieved her set of oversized, medieval-style keys (an Italian standard), and after a few tries found the right key to open the door. Within, an absolutely normal and slightly dusty attic awaited us. It consisted of two fairly big rooms, the bigger one containing three *battiere* of the Modenese black gold. The barrels were neatly lined up against the wall, largest to smallest, and clearly numbered to assign them to one of the three *batterie*. Each barrel rested on a specially made stool that would raise its rectangular bunghole (the pluggable opening through which a barrel gets filled and emptied) to a consistent height across each barrel. As with Carlotta's special *batteria*, these bungholes were also covered with sheets of linen, though they were not crocheted. The back wall had several shelves filled with all the tools, containers, and bottles needed to run an *acetaia,* while the whole scene was lit by a simple bulb hanging from the ceiling at the end of a yellow extension cord. The setup was the Modenese equivalent of a Silicon Valley startup, with the difference that this "startup" was more than a hundred years old, run from an attic rather than a garage, and had no interest whatsoever in going public, ever.

While fetching the keys Cate had also brought up some spoons, so we could try the *balsamico* straight from the barrel. This time I was able to actually taste the intense transformation the cooked grape must undergo. Beginning with the biggest barrel and slowly sampling my way through the ever-smaller barrels, I could vividly experience the influence time, bacteria, and wood had on the product within. It was very interesting how the acidity decreases and transforms while the sweetness grows ever stronger. The clear grape flavor was also quite noticeable at the beginning but was almost nonexistent toward the end. It was replaced by many other flavors, most of which stemmed from the different kinds of wood used. The old-fashioned *batteria* used many types of wood, including cherry, linden, ash, oak, mulberry, walnut, and chestnut. Cate wasn't sure about the exact order, and as the exteriors of all the barrels had blackened over time, it wasn't possible to tell purely by eye. However, during the tasting I was at least able to detect the flavors of oak (with its signature vanilla taste), chestnut (marzipan), and cherry (sweet). For the others, I unfortunately couldn't be sure. However, I caught unexpected flavors like a tiny hint of cabbage, licorice, propolis, and black pepper.

I have always been fascinated by the smoothing effect wood has on many food products. I can best describe it with a process from the world of carpentry. Once a piece of furniture is roughly ready, the tedious but absolutely necessary process of sanding and finishing the surface begins. One normally starts with a quite rough sandpaper. Over several steps, which (unfortunately) can last days, a series of finer sandpapers is used. This process smooths the surface, removes any tool marks, and rounds off all the previously very sharp corners. Additionally, it adds a slightly glossy look and makes the wood very pleasurable to touch, without having to fear splinters.

In my opinion, this is exactly what happens to the balsamic vinegar in the wooden barrels. The sharp corners of acidity, grape flavor, and sweetness become increasingly rounded, while "tool marks" like unwanted caramelized sugars stemming from the reduction process are absorbed or transformed. In the end, a very refined product with a smooth surface remains, which presents the underlying design, craftsmanship, and quality of the material in a most flattering light.

Cate's grandmother's *balsamico* presented itself in the most flattering light possible when I finally reached the smallest barrel in the oldest *batteria*. It easily outmaneuvered nearly all the balsamic vinegars I had tried before (except for the juniper riserva from Acetaia di Giorgio, an absolute masterpiece) and, at least in my opinion, sits firmly in a category of its own. The mix of sweetness, vanilla, licorice, and marzipan, with a hint of black pepper resulted in a complex flavor unmatched by any other balsamic vinegar I'd tasted, and its slightly higher acidity gave it a certain unrivaled freshness. I was immediately transported back to that moment in Bra at the potluck with my classmates where I had tried it for the first time.

CHAPTER 15
Sugar Moon Rising

Shaped like a Christmas tree toppled over sideways, the native range of the flamboyant sugar maple stretches from Canada's Cape Breton Island in the east to Missouri and Kansas in the west. Tennessee's former moonshining hot spot, the Smokey Mountain region, marks its most southern point, while the Canadian provinces of New Brunswick and southern Quebec mark its most northern distribution.[173] For now, one might add, a rapidly changing climate is pushing the sugar maple continuously farther north, transforming it into a shape that has yet to be defined.[174]

Sugar maples usually grow in the company of other broad-leaved species like red maple, yellow birches, ash, and beech,[175] but occasionally they are found near evergreen species, like red spruce and hemlock. In all cases, the forests they create are delightfully airy and light-filled, particularly when one encounters them after walking for hours through (or rather climbing through and over) a dark, aromatic thicket of balsam firs and spruce trees, which are the first ones to return en masse after a clear cut, as one comes across in eastern Canada so often these days.

If you're lucky enough to find yourself encountering a maple forest in autumn, on a cool, sunny day, the sugar maple has another dazzling surprise for you. What a staggering sight it is when the ever-cooler autumn nights finally convince the tree to retract all its vital energy into its roots in wait of winter, leaving behind brightly colored deposits that make the leaves glitter and gleam in each and every red and yellow color on the spectrum. Beside a smooth body of water this scene becomes almost unbearably beautiful, as everything is mirrored, thereby more than doubling its effect. Throw some mist silently floating above the water and a loon's eerie cry (a living fossil of a bird, featured on the Canadian one-dollar coin, "the Looney") into the mix, and you have an almost indescribably otherworldly experience.

No wonder, then, that the Canadians chose the leaf of this beautiful tree as their flag symbol in 1965 and, before that, proudly wore it at Olympic games.[176] That it would be inadvertently replaced by a Norwegian maple leaf (an invasive species in eastern Canada) on the country's new polymer currency introduced in 2012 is just a small hiccup in the grand, albeit short, story of this iconic flag.[177]

But the sugar maple is extraordinary not just because of the all-around beauty of the tree itself but due to an immensely valuable and flavorsome food product it provides. Discovered and refined by the Native Americans long before any written history, and produced in a very similar way to this day, the sugar maple's treat has sustained the people of Northern America for possibly millennia. I am, of course, talking about delicious maple syrup.

As to exactly how it was discovered there are many stories and legends, but all have a similar motif: a sugar maple tree was somehow wounded at the time of its sap rise in early spring (a chief's tomahawk that missed its intended target often being the perpetrator), and it started to drip profoundly from this gash. Someone decided to collect this liquid and use it for cooking, which in turn reduced it and intensified its pleasant, sweet taste. Soon people would purposefully cut the sugar maple with a V-shaped incision, at the bottom of which they placed a peg to channel the sap flow into a watertight vessel below.[178] The natives collected the sap in containers created from birch bark and then reduced the syrup over an open flame—which is, incredibly, possible to do without burning the bark[179]—or in wooden troughs in which heated stones were placed. Often, they reduced the sap not only to a syrupy consistency, but further to a solid sugar cake, gum, candies, or even granular sugar. Many tribes, like the Chippewa, who lived mostly to the north of the Great Lakes, used to mix the reduction with everything from wild rice (the cultivation of which they are famous for) to corn, fruits, and even meat. It was utilized in hot and cold drinks, for the preparation of medicines, and as a seasoning. Beautifully molded and decorated miniature sugar cakes were even used as gifts or money.[180]

Many rites and rituals revolve around the sugar maple and its sap to this day, some of which derive from the use of a lunar calendar describing the seasonal phenomena or human activities occurring within a particular month (e.g., maple syrup production) by many Native American tribes.[181] In midwinter, some Native American communities celebrate a ceremony to "wake up the earth" in which they pray for the new products of spring, which include maple syrup. Once the "sugar moon" rises between March and April and the maple's sap starts flowing, for them a new year or cycle begins.[182] The sap flow is very soon accompanied by the thawing of snow and ice, gushing rivers, the first young buds on trees, and a chorus of birds heralding the arrival of spring. Now that is a proper start to a new year, in contrast to the dreary, bitterly cold midwinter version we adherents to the Gregorian calendar celebrate today each January 1. No firework, however bombastic, can hide this fact.

Most fortunately, though, it wasn't January but rather an intensely sunny, late summer day when I drove together with my father along the famous Trans-Canada Highway somewhere between the small but very charming university town of Antigonish and the city of New Glasgow in the province of Nova Scotia. Our destination was a most curious farm in the heartland of the province whose owner, Scott Whitelaw, I had met some days before at a regional Slow Food event. He is an actual, real-life sugar farmer who made a prosperous business out of producing maple syrup at his appropriately named "Sugar Moon Farm." I was immediately interested, as I have always been a huge maple syrup fan and, of course, maple syrup is the very essence of a tree's flavor.

He most kindly offered me a tour of his operation, so on that sunny

Saturday afternoon my father and I were cheerfully heading his way. As strongly and repeatedly recommended by my navigation system, we took exit 18A and found ourselves after just a few miles in the middle of a dirt road flanked by nothing but seemingly endless forest. This is quite common in Nova Scotia, as the population density is rather low, so it wouldn't be financially possible to cover and maintain all the roads with costly asphalt. However, I have never driven nicer dirt roads than the ones in Canada. Even in our rental (a fine car, yet, with its five-inch ground clearance and rear-wheel drive, one definitely not built with dirt roads in mind) we had no problems whatsoever driving the twelve-odd miles toward Sugar Moon Farm.

After passing large blueberry fields that offered superb vistas into the surrounding undulating countryside, we found ourselves in front of a large log house that seemed to be Whitelaw's base of operation. Surprisingly, many people were in and around the building. They turned out to be a group of tourists who first took a tour of the farm and then had some delicious pancakes at the farm's dedicated pancake house.

Whitelaw arrived just a few minutes later, coming from a nearby farmers market where he sells his products on Saturday mornings, and we started the tour of the operations at the maple syrup's point of origin, his sugar maple forest, also generally called a "Sugarbush." As we went uphill through designated pastureland, which had been beautifully bounded by stone walls by the first European settlers in 1821, who were of Scottish origin, we were walking along what seemed to be a power line with an unusually large diameter. Soon I would realize, however, that it actually wasn't a power line but instead the pipe that in spring transported all the freshly tapped maple water directly from the forest to the sugar shack where it was turned into syrup through the process of evaporation.

We passed through a somewhat protective thicket of young balsam fir trees and found ourselves amidst a most beautiful mature hardwood forest. Dominated by the sugar maple, it contained a mixture of yellow birch, ash, and some red maples that were, judging by the trunk diameter, more than 150 years old. Spots of sunlight drifted across the forest floor, covered with a green carpet of next-generation sugar maple trees broken up by a small creek. Looking around further, I spotted opaque blue plastic tubes running all through the forest from maple tree to maple tree. I wasn't surprised at all when Whitelaw told us that in all likelihood this beautiful spot had been used by the eastern Canadian Indian tribe of the Mi`kmaq as a wintering and hunting ground, which surely must have included the making of maple syrup in spring.

After walking a bit of further and crossing the tiny creek, we suddenly found ourselves in front of a small log cabin built right below a towering yellow birch. Here Whitelaw began to tell us his story. Originally from Rhode Island, he moved to Nova Scotia right after high school. He enrolled in forestry school and worked as a forestry technician for many years, mostly in the area surrounding what is now his sugar farm. One day, he came across a house with a "For Sale" sign in front of it. As he was looking for a house to rent, Whitelaw contacted the owner and inquired about the property and, to his surprise, learned that the property had a large maple tree stand on it and had been used for the production of maple syrup. Bob Williams, the former owner, had come to Nova Scotia particularly looking for a nice stand of maple trees to produce maple syrup. Once he had found the property he immediately started to tap the trees on it and built the first small log cabin we were standing in front of now. For many years he produced maple syrup off the grid, much like the first settlers did when they initially came to North America and learned the craft from the Native Americans. With the help of two beautiful Clydesdale horses he was actually living the picture depicted on a great many of the maple syrup bottles sold worldwide, a snowy landscape featuring a man collecting small wooden buckets hanging on maple trees with his horse and a sled.

Typically, the man in the picture also wears a red-and-black-checkered jacket and some sort of a fur hat, while in the far distance one can see a blockhouse with a very inviting smoking chimney. Now, I do not know if Mr. Williams wore this hat and jacket combination; however, the house before me looked exactly like in the pictures. Whitelaw told me that Williams used up to eight hundred wooden or metal buckets (the European take on the birch bark vessel) to collect the sweet sap dripping from small holes drilled into the trunk of the maple trees. He would then collect the sap in a huge metal pot, where it was brought to a boil over a roaring wood fire. The water would start to evaporate and, together with the smoke from the fire, must have sent huge quantities of smoke billowing from the small blockhouse in the middle of the woods. One can only imagine how mouthwatering this cloud of smoke must have smelled as it drifted toward the sky, dispersed by the tree branches above. If I were a bird, I would specifically migrate to maple syrup–producing regions in spring and land above a different sugar shack every day. The question is, would I be able to smell the difference between them?

After a first in-person meeting, Williams got along very well with Whitelaw and his wife Quita Gray. So he offered to let them rent the house for two years while he taught them everything he knew about maple syrup. After this time, they then would take over the property and continue the land's proud maple syrup production. They both jumped at the opportunity, and this is how Sugar Moon Farm began. Fortunately for them, Williams had in the meantime already upgraded to a gravity-fed tube system, which means that the sap was no longer dripping into individual buckets but rather into a network of tubes that ended directly in the sugar shack, saving them from having to individually collect the contents of eight hundred or more buckets.

As Whitelaw spoke, we walked deeper into the woods and stopped at one sugar maple tree that was tapped and connected to the intricate tube system spanning all the forest. He explained that they only tapped trees with at least a diameter of ten to twelve inches, which, due to the slow growth of sugar maple in Nova Scotia, would be eighty years old. On average one tree would thereby yield ten to thirteen fluid ounces of syrup (for reference, a typical store-bought glass bottle holds 8.5 fluid ounces), half of what trees in Vermont or Quebec typically produce. There are several theories as to why the trees produce so much less in Nova Scotia, but the rather thin, rocky, and acidic soil seems to play a major role. Either way, as a consolation, Whitelaw's sugar wood seemed to be one of the most productive in the region.

As we walked on, he began to introduce us to the work of a maple sugar farmer, which typically starts in February, when the snow is still waist-deep. This is the time when the sap run, or the wakening of the trees, if you will, normally begins. Curiously, scientists are still not completely sure as to how the maple and related species are able to pump copious amounts of water from the soil into its branches at a time when most of the landscape is still frozen. Normally, a tree circulates water by utilizing the negative pressure (suction) that is generated by the evaporation of water from its leaves. However, in the freezing conditions of late winter, the maple has no leaves it could transpire from. Experiments have shown that after several days of temperatures oscillating above and below thirty-two degrees Fahrenheit (warmer days but still-freezing nights), the maple starts to increase the pressure in its trunk, which ultimately results in the flowing of sap. In some cases, the positive pressure can reach up to 30 PSI, equaling that of a car tire. The precise causes behind this phenomenon, called "exudation," are still actively debated, but scientists have several hypotheses to explain the occurrence that involve a combination of osmosis and the freezing and thawing of sap in the tree's trunk and branches. Together, these processes seem to transport water absorbed by the roots into the endmost of tiny branches, taking with it sugars and amino acids that the tree had stored in its vast network of roots in fall. Curiously, the sap dripping out of a tap hole seems not to come directly from the roots but rather downwards from the crown of the tree, where it had frozen solid in the days before and been released by the warm rays of the sun.[183]

Catching the exact moment when this exudation first happens is part of the art of sugar farming. Tapping the tree too early means exposing the delicate interior of a tree to bacteria and fungi too early and thereby risking not only diminished sap yields[184] but even the life of the tree itself. Tapping too late, on the other hand, results in missing several days' worth of sap, which ultimately means having less maple syrup to sell.

I was most interested to learn that one of the most important tasks of the sugar farmer is to know when to stop tapping a tree. The flavor of sap changes dramatically toward the end of the season, which at Sugar Moon Farm can last anywhere from ten days to seven weeks. The change of taste is due to the increased presence of a variety of amino acids in the sap as the trees initiate the growth of buds. Only through constantly monitoring the taste of the sap can one determine when the season's end has come. So, in essence, a sugar farmer has to actually walk through the woods and taste the trees.

Whitelaw described late sap as tasting a bit like a Tootsie Roll, with it buttery, caramel, molasses-like taste mixed with a certain grassy greenness swerving into various degrees of bitterness. In books on maple syrup production it is also described as a "buddy" off-flavor, meaning that one can taste the trees growing buds in the sap.[185]

Catching those perfect moments to start and stop tapping has, however, become increasingly difficult in recent years. The season seems to start ever earlier and sometimes ends abruptly with unusually warm days, resulting in an early budding of trees. Whitelaw now considers starting his season in late January, whereas Williams never began before March 1. The climate is clearly changing, and this might have a very real influence on the future of maple syrup in Nova Scotia.

At the outset, each individual tree is tapped, a process which requires drilling a new hole each year; this can be particularly difficult with old trees that have been tapped for a long time, as the area around the previous years' holes has been compromised and won't ever bear sap again. Once tapped, each tree is connected to the tube system. Then it is time to fire up the evaporator in the sugar shack. At Sugar Moon Farm, "firing up" can be understood quite literally, as Whitelaw uses a wood-fired evaporator whose running is an art form in itself. In contrast to evaporators that run on fossil fuels, a wood-fired one needs careful stocking, which ensures a consistent distribution of the heat across the whole floor of the unit and prevents possible burning of the sweet sap, never mind the backbreaking work that goes into preparing the firewood in the summer and fall before.

Most interestingly, Whitelaw also told us that the evaporator is essential to the syrup's taste and its color. Without it the sugar won't caramelize, resulting in a very mild flavor.

We had by now returned to the sugar shack, and after I spent a while marveling at the towering walls of firewood before its entrance, Whitelaw showed me the shiny heart of his operation: A mirror-polished stainless-steel evaporator fed by an outside tank connected to the tube system coming from the forest. It looked like an enormous rectangular kitchen sink with a hood, whose floor was very slightly tilted toward one corner and filled with a labyrinth of dividing walls. These walls let the sap flow very slowly over the heated floor, thereby evaporating most of the water and finally resulting in maple syrup, which by law has to contain at least 66 percent sugar. (This means that on average, ten gallons of maple sap yield only 0.3 gallons of syrup.) What a spectacle it must be to see and smell the huge plumes of sweet water vapor as well as feel the immense heat radiating from this shiny beast in action. One day I'll have to return during sugar season!

The final step is filtering and bottling the syrup, followed by the immensely laborious task of cleaning the evaporator and the tube system in the forest. Each tap must be removed so the trees can close the small tap holes, which a healthy tree manages in only one season.

Having gone through all the fascinating steps that go into making delicious maple syrup, it was now time to finally try the result. I was most curious to see what different wood tastes there were to discover. Would there be a difference in taste between producers, terroir? And if maple syrup had terroir, would there be a difference between individual trees? I couldn't wait to find out.

Generally, I knew that there were different grades of maple syrup and that their differences had something to do with at which point of the season the syrup was made. However, I had never completely understood the difference. Luckily, Whitelaw had devised a very ingenious way of describing it. In a south-facing, sunny window, he set up a small shelf that held fourteen glasses filled with maple syrup. Each had its very own specific color, ranging from a very transparent golden yellow to an opaque mahogany. Now he explained its taste gradations, which are for the sake of easier production consolidated into four seasons. We started the tasting with an early-season, golden yellow syrup. This first syrup had a very creamy and fresh consistency followed by a complex sweetness with hints of a floral dark chocolate made from the superb Ecuadorian *Arriba* variety, milky coffee, vanilla, and a note of caramel. This wonderful bouquet of flavors paired with an almost startling freshness, the likes of which you just don't expect in maple syrup. No wonder it was Whitelaw's favorite for pancakes.

Next was an early-mid-season, darker golden syrup, which shared several flavor notes with the first syrup but had a more intense sweetness and an altogether heartier character.

The real difference came with the third syrup, a late-mid-season, amber-colored specimen whose sweetness and robustness really overpowered many of the previously noticeable flavors. I also noticed, for the first time, certain flavor-parallels to molasses. This impression was really reinforced upon trying the end-season, mahogany-colored syrup. This one had a pleasant, molasses-like sweetness but still had a range of detectable flavors, from buttery and caramel to a hint of raisins and even a very slight saltiness. Although certainly distinctive, this last version was a favorite of mine and would be perfect for cooking.

So, if there was such a strong flavor difference during a sap run, was there also one between producers? Does maple syrup have terroir?

Whitelaw was absolutely sure of it. In fact, he told us that an employee of his could detect a difference in flavor between his syrup and that of the producer on just the other side of the hill, less than a mile away. Of course, much of it has to do with how a producer runs the evaporator, as everything from how fast you heat the sap to which exact sugar concentration you reach ultimately influences the flavor of the syrup. Nonetheless, the location and the soil of one's sugar bush have an undeniable influence.

Though I couldn't explore the differences on the spot, I went on a maple syrup shopping spree some days later. What huge differences I would discover among syrups of the same or similar categories! Not only were the textures very different, from creamy and light to sticky and very viscous (which one could attribute to the handling of the evaporator), but so were the flavors. Tastes ranged from dark coffee and roasted notes to very light, delicate milk chocolate aromas. One syrup even had a fruity sensation reminding me of very ripe red fruits like cherries or plum. Fortunately, I was even able to find a bottle of refrigerated Nova Scotian maple water, which had been only slightly reduced to enhance its sweetness. This was the closest I would come to tasting sap directly from the tree during sugar season. Its flavor was indeed very different from the syrup, as it had not only a very delicate sweetness paired with a greenness but also reminded me slightly—but not negatively—of the taste of cardboard.

At Sugar Moon Farm, in the meantime, I had said goodbye to Whitelaw, thanking him profoundly for all his generosity, and had some delightful buttermilk pancakes with copious amounts of maple syrup in the farm's pancake house. One thing that Whitelaw mentioned, however, stayed in my mind. When we were in the sugar bush, he had told me that, theoretically, all maple varieties in the world could be used to make maple syrup; they just don't have as high of a sugar concentration as the sugar maple, which averages 2 percent. On his farm, in fact, he had tapped several red maples, which he said had a distinctive taste that was hard for him to define. Furthermore, he had heard of people making syrup in the Canadian Prairie Provinces or British Colombia using Manitoba maples or, respectively, big leaf maples. In South Korea, maple trees are tapped in spring, and the fresh sap is drunk as a tonic.[186]

So, according to Whitelaw there was a difference in taste not only between the syrup producers but also among different maple species. He had, however, never tried to identify a taste difference between individual trees of the same species. As the time of the yearly sap run was unfortunately already over, I couldn't try it for myself in Canada, but back in Austria I had an idea. I had read many times that in northern and eastern European countries people used the sap of birch trees in a way very similar to North American maple sap.[187] Fortunately, there are many birch trees around my house. I decided to tap two different birch trees in early spring, not only to taste their sap but also to compare their flavors.

Early spring was, opportunely, just around the corner. So as soon as I could be sure that the birch's sap run had commenced, which is based on the same complex processes as in the maple,[188] I selected two birch trees in close vicinity for tapping. As I didn't want to damage the trees profoundly by drilling too deep or in the wrong spot of the trunk, I just cut off the end of a branch as thick as a thumb on each tree and tied glass bottles around them. Their weight bent the branch so the bottles hung almost upright in the air. I returned the next day while walking the dog to find both bottles already overflowing with clear sap and ready for immediate tasting. Once I had managed to deter the dog, which was curiously sniffing at this strange contraption dangling at nose level, I could untie the first bottle from the branch and try it on the spot. Much like the maple sap, it had only a very delicate taste; it began with a slight sweetness that only moments later revealed a very feeble greenish, grassy taste, which reminded me of willow bark. Once I had untied the second bottle, which hung a little higher, out of the dog's reach, I was finally able to compare their tastes. Would there be a difference?

Upon first sampling the sap from the second tree, I couldn't find any. When tasting them in immediate sequence, I did detect a difference in the intensity of flavors. However, this could probably be explained by a higher immediate availability of water to the second tree diluting its sap's flavor. So, overall, I couldn't detect any strong difference in flavor between the two birch trees of the same type, a result that would be in all likelihood similar when done with maple trees. Nevertheless, I was happy with the outcome of my experiment, as I had not only discovered a marvelous refreshing spring tonic but also tried yet another tree flavor.

As some dark clouds brought a sudden flurry of snow, I was already thinking about how I could incorporate this wonderful tonic in my spring cooking. Recipe ideas for birch water risotto with microgreens, wild trout filet with a reduction of fresh birch water and a light mist of birch leaf perfume or even a delicate birch water ice cream came to mind as I walked home through a whirlwind of snowflakes.

I could see it becoming as important as maple syrup, which I had already used for everything from salads and cocktails to planked salmon and desserts. A wide variety of uses that was only going to broaden now that, with Whitelaw's wonderful help, I had discovered a multitude of additional maple syrup and tree flavors.

CHAPTER 16

The Count and His Wine

Although for a long time my interest in wine was superficial at best, I have known about the South Tyrolean wine estate Manincor for many years. Back in my high school years, one of my best friends, Clemens, would sometimes mention the wine estate, which consisted of vineyards and a winery, of his great-uncle, situated in South Tyrol near the beautiful city of Kaltern. Even though I knew absolutely nothing about wine—besides there being a white and a red version—I really loved the taste of the wine from Manincor. It would, however, take several years before I unexpectedly came across the name of the estate once again while doing research for an article on wooden barrels. Now very interested in wine, and especially its use of wooden barrels, I was very intrigued to read that Manincor actually makes some of its barrels from oak sourced right on their property. Not only that, but they also age some of their white wines in wooden barrels, a practice which I had never heard of at the time. I had many plans to visit Manincor from that point on, but, for various reasons, I never actually made the trip, though I drove through South Tyrol several times.

Finally, while working at the Milan World Expo 2015 for the Austrian Pavilion in October, I was invited by a friend and colleague on a weekend trip to her parents' home in Tramin, South Tyrol. I realized that this was the perfect opportunity to visit the estate. Through Clemens, I managed to get ahold of Count Michael Goess-Enzenberg, the owner of

Manincor, who warmly invited me to come by for a visit and a talk about the estate as well as their interesting approach to aging wine in wooden barrels.

So a few days later, I was driving along the winding road leading up to the estate. More than once, I found myself wishing I were driving a convertible, though I typically consider them terribly uncomfortable. Yet there was something this countryside, with its winding, grapevine-lined roads, apple orchards, sparkling lakes, quaint little towns, and towering snow-covered mountains, that made the prospect seem bearable.

This landscape must have looked very different during the times of the Rhaetian people, who are believed to have lived in the area beginning in the late Iron Age. However, archeological findings of wild grape seeds as well as historical written sources seem to confirm that even back then wine production was already underway, long before the region was invaded in the first century BC by the Romans,[189] who were known champions of grapevine dissemination. They in turn had gotten hold of the domesticated grape through the Phoenicians, who are believed to have brought it and the knowledge of wine production from ancient Greece to Italy before the ninth century BC. And before that, the ancient Egyptians doubtless enjoyed the grapes' fermented juices, as did the Mesopotamians. In fact, the first cultivation of the grape appears to have happened even earlier, between 7000 and 4000 BC somewhere in the area between the Black Sea and Iran.[190]

Captivatingly, the production process of this alcoholic beverage, enormously cherished and idolized as a cultural symbol for millennia, has in its most basic form never changed. It always involved the collection of the grapevine (wild or cultivated), the extraction of its sweet juice through a form of pressing, and its fermentation through natural yeast.[191] Of course, if you visit a winery today, you are initially overwhelmed by all the extensive equipment used, the exact differences between the types of wine, the distinctive fermentation processes, the aging in diverse containers, and the various bottling and corking methods, yet the basics stay the same. Growing, harvesting, pressing, and fermenting—that's it.

Although I have never been much of a wine drinker, I've always been intrigued by its production process and by the cultured aura that surrounds it. Wine has its own language, procedures, and traditions. Particularly fascinating to me is the vocabulary used to describe wine's taste. After all, I think it's fair to say that wine is by far the single food item most described in terms of taste. If one searches "wine taste" on Google Trends (a public web facility that allows one to find how often a particular search term was used relative to the total search volume across various regions of the world[192]) and compares it to "beer taste," "cheese taste," "chocolate taste," and "whisky taste" wine always comes out on top by a huge margin.[193]

As it is initially quite difficult and maybe even intimidating for most to describe wine flavors, an entire device in the form of a wheel with color-coded aroma groups was created to help people express what their tongue and nose are sensing. One of the first so-called "aroma wheels" that displays all the different aromas that one can detect in wine was thereby developed by Dr. Ann Noble. It was the first curriculum material I received at the University of Gastronomic Sciences, featuring basic tastes like honey, lemon, and almond, as well as more particular ones like burnt match, cedar, or even dust.[194] Apparently Noble was inspired to make her aroma wheel in order to democratize and make accessible the vocabulary used to describe wine, which had heretofore been described using many adjectives that reflect social class, like "rich" and "fine." The idea was that anyone can have access to fruits, stones, and vegetables, so describing tastes using more common objects is in a sense much more accessible.[195]

Of course, over-the-top taste descriptions of wine like "*Profound, deeply complex, truffle-sprinkled sponge cake, burnt orange, liquorice. Sexy and chic with bravado. Tannins are velvety soft, but the body is still pretty tight*" have sparked sometimes-deserving ridicule from comedians and regular people alike, yet in essence describing wine is a worldwide language experiment.[196] How can we describe the signals we perceive with our tongue and nose in the most precise way? It is nothing less than a new descriptive taste language in the making.

I arrived at the Manincor estate, which lies directly on the famous South Tyrolean Wine Road. Its slightly elevated position overlooks Kaltern Lake on the one side and looks up to the Leuchtenburg castle ruin on the other. In fact, the ruin is part of the Manincor estate and sits in the center of the forest that provides oak for the barrels. The manor house is surrounded by vineyards as well as orchards and consists of several buildings constructed between the seventeenth and eighteenth centuries in the fabulous South Tyrolean *Überetscher* style. Count Goess-Enzenberg would tell me later that when he took over the estate in 1991 from his uncle there was no winery on site, a problem that was solved some years later with the addition of a vast underground winery and a small above-ground shop.[197] It was built mostly underground so as to not interfere visually with the beautiful manor house and the picturesque landscape beyond. The result is architecturally extremely interesting; only once you are in the center of the original building complex do you see the large access road leading down toward the subterranean vinery. The whole thing seemed to be straight out of a James Bond movie, with a secret base hiding in plain sight in one of earth's most beautiful settings. I was half-expecting to see an Aston Martin shoot out of the large metal door of the vinery, pursued by a dark SUV, villains leaning out of its side windows with guns blazing. Fortunately, though, only a small vineyard tractor came my way, and at a very leisurely pace, as I walked across the access road to the office.

As soon as I met Count Goess-Enzenberg, we began a lively conversation on wine, barrels, and wood. Amusingly, we realized soon into our conversation that we had attended the same high school and had both trained as cabinetmakers. I immediately got the sense that wood was occupying an important part of his life, too, though I would only realize later how true that was.

Goess-Enzenberg told me how, having completed the mammoth task of building the winery, he began to transition the estate to a biodynamic operation in 2005, a radical idea at the time. His grapes never seemed to obtain the highest quality he desired, which he needed in order to produce his wine, so he realized that, much as his family kept healthy through wholesome food, fresh air, household remedies, and individualized attention, his grapes required the same natural care. He consulted an expert, and, to the initial shock of many of his employees together, completely changed the estate's methods for growing grapes. They stopped using any industrially produced chemicals and began to build up the topsoil by sowing a variety of beneficial plants between the vines, letting hedges regrow, planting trees, using compost for fertilization, tending the grapes by hand, and generally bringing back life and biodiversity into the vineyards.

And it has come back in full force. When I later walked through the rows of vines, there was bustling animal activity everywhere. Bumblebees were buzzing back and forth, birds were singing, and chickens scratched the dirt. In winter, herds of sheep even roam the vineyard, Goess-Enzenberg told me. All this individualized care finally produced the kind of grape quality the count had always imagined, and with it he was able to craft the wines he had dreamed of, which have won many prestigious awards since. Even the strongest skeptic among his employees, someone who has worked on the estate for more than sixty years, is now fully convinced of the value of a biodynamic approach.[198] And to Count Goess-Enzenberg, it was important that everyone be convinced, as he is certain that the taste and the quality of a wine depend on every hand that has a part in its making, from the initial planting of the vines to the tending of the vineyard and its soil, the conditions in the wine cellar, and the artwork of the barrel maker. He attributes at least a third, if not half, of the final taste of a wine to human influence.

So, what about the concept of terroir, then? After all, it was the wine industry (specifically, the French wine producers) that coined this notion in the first place.[199] According to Count Goess-Enzenberg, the type of soil, the specific microclimate, and the exact orientation of the vines relative to the sun all play their crucial part, yet for him terroir also encompasses human activity.

As you might expect, I was eager to ask how important wood was in this context. It is an important part of his wine, he told me, and his concept of terroir certainly influenced his idea of using wood from the estate's forest to make barrels. Yet, somewhat surprisingly, Goess-Enzenberg has a very measured and careful approach to wood in wine. He gave the common example of winemakers' ability to determine in which type of oak barrel a wine has been, tasting the difference between a French Limousin oak and one from Allier. If this were to happen to his wine, he stated, it would mean that he had done everything wrong. According to his philosophy, one should taste the superb taste of his grapes and not the wood of the barrel. Everything else has just a supporting role in helping make the grapes' flavors more perceptible.

This wasn't what I had anticipated. Having researched Manincor's use of wood in the making of its wines, even whites, I'd thought that he would be very fond of the flavor of wood. The more the better, if you will. This was most interesting.

In Goess-Enzenberg's opinion, the point of making a wooden barrel is to match it to the wine. A vessel should let the wine breathe, making it thereby more stable and less in need of excessive preservative agents. Wood does that by facilitating microoxidization that practically saturates the wine with oxygen, so later it will oxidize very little, if at all. (Later oxidation results in a flat taste after the wine is open for a while.) A wooden barrel also rounds off certain unwanted-flavor high notes and helps in harmonizing the wine. Carefully barrel-aged wine is much more alive, yet it shouldn't have a wooden taste. But was it even possible to use wood in making wine without tasting it in the finished product?

All my conversations with experts of various alcoholic beverages about the correct use of wood could be put into two basic categories: (1) Yes, we want wood and its flavor (in varying degrees) or (2) No, we don't want wood and its flavor. So far, I had come across only one approach similar to that of Count Goess-Enzenberg, and that was regarding sherry production, which only uses very old barrels going into the hundreds of years of age. This way the wooden flavor of the barrels has been so strongly leached out that the only perceptible effects on the final product are the ones stemming from microoxidation. Yet the barrels used at Manincor are surely not that old. So how do they manage this feat?

The count explained as we left the conference room in the office and walked to the courtyard of the old manor house. To one side of the house there were stacks of boards, which I straightaway recognized as the raw staves used in the making of barrels. By their dark greyish-black color, it was evident that they had been sitting there for years. Indeed, Count Goess-Enzenberg told me that it had been a little more than three years since the trees had been felled in his forest and the trunks carefully extracted with winches from the often steep and treacherous ground common in his mountainside forest. Vividly recounting the runoff of yellowish tannins and the strong vanilla-like smell of the staves as they sat in the rain that first year, he is now certain that all of those harsh flavors have been washed out. Having even been split and sawed in the area, they were now awaiting their delivery to his trusted barrel maker in Austria. Not only harvesting the oak trees on his own estate but also letting them age right next to the winery is all part of his concept of terroir. If the cooperage had a mobile workshop, I am sure that he would also ask him to make the barrels on the premises, too.

After testing several barrel makers, the count made his selection for the estate, and this barrel maker now processes all of the estate's own wood. However, the estate's wood only amounts to 20 percent of the total barrels it uses; felling more oak trees unfortunately wouldn't be sustainable. The remaining 80 percent of barrels needed are sourced from a *tonnellerie* (cooperage) in Bordeaux, France. What they both have in common, though, is that the staves have been matured outside for a minimum of three years and the barrels are toasted only lightly and carefully on the inside. This results in very toned-down wooden aromas and no unwanted smoky flavors in the wine.

In contrast to the aesthetic of the wood barrels was the contemporary architecture of the newly built underground winery. Formed in its entirety from light grayish, almost beige concrete that contrasted with doors, stairs, large wall panels, fixtures, and fittings made of rusty sheet metal, it spread across three stories and housed everything from the wine presses to the large fermentation vats (also made from oak), the vast barrel storage rooms, the bottling plant, the bottle storage, and even a spacious garage for all the machines and tools. The space was striking, yet also literally cool and toned down. No frills, straight lines, nothing overly decorative—functionality was clearly the denominator.

As I was visiting right in the middle of the busiest time of year—the harvest and the subsequent making of the wine—the winery was full of commotion. The wooden fermenting vats were bubbling from the frantic activity of the natural yeast and releasing a fantastic smell, with notes of fresh grape juice, sourdough, alcohol, and a certain nuttiness floating through the room. The grand hall was filled with new barrels waiting their turn to be filled, and in the garage people were prepping machinery, tools, and boxes for the final harvest. We navigated through all this activity, with a short stopover in the immense barrel storage room, filled with evenly spaced oak barrels bathed in cool spots of light, until we reached some long metal stairs at the end of the building. We ascended toward an ever-brighter light source, which I realized only halfway up was not artificial but daylight. Passing through a large door, we found ourselves in the tasting room, having emerged out of the underground winery much like a periscope on a submarine. It offered wonderful sweeping views over the estate's vineyards in the forefront, the Kaltern Lake in the medium distance, and in the background the mountainous forests framing the castle ruins. Looking out from the room's high windows, I found myself looking straight into the eyes of a colorful rooster standing on a patio table just outside of the room.

Count Goess-Enzenberg invited me to sit on a chair made from barrel staves. I have seen others before, but they all have been horribly clunky; this one, however, was surprisingly elegant. Goess-Ezenberg told me that finding uses for barrels that have reached the end of their lives in the winery is a pet project of his. His desire not to see the excellent-quality wood in a barrel go to waste was a clear sign that he still had a passion for cabinetmaking; one can only hope that more wineries will begin to think of similar solutions. He also offered to let me taste some of his wines. I was really curious by now how it was possible for a wine to age in wood but not taste like it. Since I came by car and would later need to drive home, I could only take minute sips, but what they revealed was remarkable.

The tasting began with a wine called "Moscato Giallo," a white made from the Muscat grape that was, unconventionally, left in contact with the grapes' skins for twelve hours after pressing to extract a variety of flavor compounds. (Most white wines have as little skin contact as possible.) Part of the juice was then fermented in oak barrels, which is also atypical, while the other part was fermented conventionally in stainless steel tanks. The wine's color was intensely yellow, a result of its longer contact with the grape skin, but the smell was very fresh and reminded me slightly of a pomelo, a large citrus fruit. Upon tasting, the freshness came immediately to the foreground, joined by a slight acidity, a certain citruslike fruitiness, and a slight hint of bitterness. Remarkably, there was no typical oaky vanilla aroma. However, the taste was curiously long-lasting, and the wine was missing any intense flavor spikes, which are undesirable yet fairly common in white wine. Was this the doing of the wood?

Next, we tried another white wine called "Réserve della Contessa." This was a name I knew well, as my friend Clemens would occasionally bring a bottle of it over when he visited. Made from a mix of Pinot Blanc, Chardonnay, and Sauvignon Blanc grapes, it was again left in contact with the grape skins after pressing, yet for only six hours. Fermentation happened this time entirely in oak barrels.

This wine also had a beautifully intense yellow color and a wonderful fresh scent reminiscent of apricot and cantaloupe, yet I could also detect a hint of vanilla. The taste was extremely smooth, surprisingly full bodied, and strong for a white wine, with a very toned-down acidity and a slight, pleasurably bitter aftertaste. The taste was faintly similar to that of the first wine, with notes of honey and apricot that were only ever so slightly joined by a hint of oaky vanilla. Particularly impressive was how long its taste lasted. This remarkable wine did have hints of oak, but they were so delicately interwoven with the other tastes that one could easily miss them.

The final wine was a red called "Cassiano" made from seven different red grape varieties all individually pressed and fermented in wooden vats together with their skins (as traditionally done with red wine) and then aged in sixty-gallon barrique barrels, of which half were new—and therefore yielding a stronger wood aroma—and half used. The plum red color was joined by the smell of dark red fruits and, yes, a noticeable oaky vanilla scent. The taste also went in the plum direction, joined by a freshness and lightness, uncommon for red wine, that only later revealed tannins and the accompanying astringency. In this wine, the oaky vanilla flavor began to appear, although again this was toned down and accompanied with a pleasurable sweetness.

While there were obvious notes of oak, particularly in the second white and the final red wine, I was impressed by how well they were integrated and balanced with the other aromas. The oak aroma wasn't isolated, but was speaking, laughing, and strongly gesticulating with everyone else.

I now understood Count Goess-Enzenberg's approach to the use of wood in winemaking, which did not yield any immediately noticeable wood flavors in the finished product. Much like a perfectly fitting perfume the wood was only accentuating and supporting the wine instead of competing for attention. When combined masterfully with a very refined and toned-down wooden flavor, this most ancient of fermented drinks truly shines.

Just like that, in Manincor's wines I had found the contemporary flavor of wood.

CHAPTER 17
Truffle Hunters of Piedmont

After working for eight months at the Milan Expo, my girlfriend and I both desperately needed some respite from the crowds, so we withdrew for several tranquil days to a remote national park in Liguria. Refreshed, we decided on the day of our departure not to catch the boat that would bring us back to civilization but rather to take the scenic, yet slightly more challenging, hour-long hike back to our car.

Departing the hotel around ten in the morning, we shouldered our thankfully light luggage and began our climb up hundreds of stairs along the rocky coastline. Although the air was very humid from an impending thunderstorm, we enjoyed walking along the steep, stony coast of Liguria and looking out to the sea, where ocean and sky seamlessly interweaved. Only the distant silhouette of a ship distinguished the two.

Back in the town of San Rocco some 1.5 miles down the coast, we found our car still parked under the Mediterranean pines that characterize Liguria's rugged coastline like no other; they are even indispensable in the region's cuisine. The world-famous pesto Genovese, made with copious amounts of basil, Parmesan, olive oil, salt, sometimes garlic and the all-important pine nuts couldn't exist without this tree. Another staple of Liguria, infamous amongst tourists, are its extremely narrow roads. Driving in Italy in general was an adventure, but navigating through the narrow, dimly lit tunnels drilled through the protruding rock formations that hindered the path of the highway (itself carved out of the sometimes vertical coastline), always produced a certain feeling of unpleasant adrenaline—particularly when a truck decided to pass me as I, incomprehensibly to him, adhered to the 80 mph speed limit.

After driving through these tunnels, one really starts to look forward to the exit for Turin—our next destination—and its much wider roads. But before arriving at the plain surrounding Turin, one has to first venture over or through the mountain range alongside the Ligurian coast. With its mountains and valleys parallel to the coastline, Liguria offers one of the most diverse climatic and ecological zones of Italy. Despite its poor soils, the coastline can produce everything from oranges to sloe berries (a fruit best known as a component of the sloe gin fizz but also called blackthorn, whose fruits need frost to become palatable) in the span of a few miles.

Three hours after leaving Liguria, we arrived in Turin and parked the car in the center of the city. From there we set out to explore what had once been the capital of Italy and visited some of the city's many grand buildings and streets, all monuments to a bygone era. Our sightseeing was followed by an excellent dinner in one of the city's many new, inventive restaurants that comprised the thriving vegetarian food scene now shaping Turin's restaurant scene.[200] Some university friends happened to be in town as well, so after dinner we met for a drink at our favorite wine bar.

It was midnight when we finally returned to the car, the last one remaining in the parking lot. As we approached, I realized that someone had broken the driver's side window in a pitiful attempt to steal the few things of value that were in the glove box. We would soon realize that the only thing he'd taken was our membership card for roadside assistance, yet he'd left behind a hell of a mess. With glass shards sprayed over the car's interior, driving would be impossible, or at least very risky. Thankfully, an amazing friend who lived in Turin was still awake and had an extra garage space for our vehicle at her apartment building, which meant it would be safe from the elements and further burglary, at least for the night.

The following morning began early, as I wanted to be one of the first at a local windshield repair shop, and the drive there—the wind whipping through the broken window on what proved to be an incredibly beautiful, yet somewhat chilly, fall morning—woke us up immediately, no coffee needed. Following long discussions at the repair shop and many phone calls, we managed to find a replacement side window for the car. However, it would take several hours to install it, eating into our schedule and derailing our main reason for returning to Piedmont, visiting La Morra. After waiting half a day for the repair, there was no way we'd make it to La Morra in time.

La Morra is a small but spectacularly scenic town perched atop one of the highest hills in the Langhe area of southern Piedmont, which is home to some of the best red wines Italy has to offer. The region's native grape variety, Nebbiolo, is the base for outstanding wines, including the eponymous Nebbiolo, the Barbaresco, and, most importantly, the world-famous Barolo. My wine professor at the University of Gastronomic Sciences would probably call Barolo a "meditation wine," as it is very full-bodied, heavy, and tannic, and therefore demands time from the person drinking it.

However, I hadn't planned to visit the Langhe area for its wines but for another world-famous product of the region: the white truffles of Alba. More particularly, I had been able to set up an appointment with a seasoned truffle hunter, Marco Varaldo, who lived in La Morra, only a few miles from Alba. As truffles are a fungus that grows in symbiosis with several tree species, I was dying to know if the different trees had any influence on the taste of the truffles. Maybe they would hold the secret to the flavor of wood within them?

Yet this meeting was now in jeopardy thanks to the moronic car burglar. I was furious!

Going for a sweet Italian breakfast of a jam-filled cornetto and an espresso helped to calm me a bit. A surprising yet most welcome coincidence, however, made me believe in miracles. Phil, a good friend from university and a fellow food enthusiast, texted me while we were venting our disappointment over breakfast and told me that he was in town for holiday. I immediately called him back and not completely selflessly asked him if he had any specific plans for the day. Luckily, he hadn't and was more than interested in going truffle hunting. He even had a car. So, only thirty minutes later, we were flying along the highway to make the appointment in La Morra.

It was a glorious November day, with bright autumn colors on display in every direction. Both the flat landscape of the Po valley around Turin as well as the Piemontese hills we entered thereafter were clad in monochromatic dresses. While rows of almost obscenely brilliant golden-yellow poplar trees dominated the scenery in the valley, reddish-hazelnut bushes and grapevines defined the Piemontese hills. On this day the colors appeared particularly vivid against the distant snow-covered mountain ranges that surround Turin. These mountains are normally only faintly visible due to strong haze, but on a clear day like this, however, they rise spectacularly out of the plain like a huge snow-covered wall without any visible foothills in between.

We arrived in La Morra just in time for our appointment and found the parking lot slightly outside the village, which Varaldo had suggested as a rendezvous point before heading deeper into the forest to hunt for truffles. When we arrived, he was already there waiting in front of his original iconic Fiat Panda 4x4, which held his two excited truffle dogs. We had barely gotten out of the car and donned our trekking shoes before he got into his car again, telling us to meet him somewhat below the town in the vineyards and small patches of forest. Walking there was a delight, as the footpath led through rows of grapes—their leaves now up close revealing an ongoing change from green to reddish-brown—on the left and tall, evenly spaced hazelnut bushes with their brownish red foliage on the right. The mixed broadleaf trees' pre-winter loss of leaves allowed for relatively unobstructed views into the slightly misty Langhe valley below and only hazy glimpses of the increasingly mountainous hills beyond. A silent breeze above our heads agitated the dry leaves, giving way to the illusion that our long shadows, projected by an already low sun into the hazelnut plantation, were somehow plucking some of the stems like the strings of a rustling harp. Accompanied by this symphony on all sides, we silently enjoyed the last strong rays of the sun before winter would filter them anew.

Absorbed by thoughts of tasty truffles hidden beneath our feet, we soon reached the entrance to a small patch of forest where Varaldo once again awaited our arrival. Before we began our trek through the forest, he gave us a brief orientation on the secretive subterranean world of the truffle, a tuber-forming fungus renowned and revered the world over whose human consumption goes back millennia.

Descriptions of truffles can be found in Sumerian inscriptions dating between 1728 and 1531 BC, and also in works by classical Greek authors ranging from Plato and Aristotle to Plutarch and Theophrastus. Varaldo tells us that many ancient Greeks magnificently assumed that truffles were a result of thunder and lightning, a belief that is still alive and well amongst the nomadic Bedouins of the Sahara today. And many today believe the vibrant descriptions in the Bible and the Quran of manna, the foodstuff God allegedly provided for the Israelites during their travels in the desert, refer to truffles.

All those early truffle references most likely refer to the desert truffle, which is part of the same taxonomic order as the European truffle but grows in the arid and semi-arid regions of the Middle East. It also grows much closer to the surface than the European variety, which is buried by as much as twelve inches of earth, which means the fruiting body of the desert truffle often breaks through the surface, making it visible to the naked eye—no truffle dog needed.[201] Direct references to the European truffle begin in the seventeenth century, when the truffle hunt was a popular pastime among the Italian and French aristocracy. This gastronomic enthusiasm continues to this day, as our expedition into the Piemontese hills superbly demonstrates.

The biology behind this mushroom tuber is no less interesting. Much like mushrooms that you find either naturally growing in the landscape or in prepackaged form on supermarket shelves, the truffle itself is only the fruiting body, or simply the fruit, of the mushroom. The actual mushroom is a rather inconspicuous whitish net called "mycelium" sometimes spanning many square miles.[202] The mycelium consists of many fine filaments called hypha, which have a thickness of 2–10 μm[203] (millionths of a meter). By comparison, a human hair measures somewhere between 30–80 μm in width.[204] The truffle lives, like many mushrooms, in an ectosymbiotic relationship with specific trees. Its hyphae enclose the tree's roots on a cellular level like a very tight-fitting sock. This effectively lets it tap into the tree's nutrient cycle, allowing the tuberous mushroom to receive essential nutrients, like sugar or amino acids, which the tree produces through photosynthesis.

However, the truffle is not a nutrient leech that always takes but never gives. Quite to the contrary; mycorrhiza (the symbiosis between tree and mushrooms) is highly important for trees and forests in many ways. By forming a protective layer around the tree's roots, they enable the tree to fend off pathogens and protect it from drying out. Furthermore, the mycorrhiza act like a root extension that delivers faraway nutrients and water to the tree.[205] The mushrooms also have several physical and chemical properties that allow them to break up tough organic materials like wood and even rock, unlocking nutrients for the tree.[206] Finally, mycorrhiza form vast networks in forest soils, connecting most trees and plants through their roots and allowing the exchange of nutrients, water, minerals, and possibly even information. Due to its similarities to our Internet, the ingenious term "Wood Wide Web" has been coined to describe this network.[207]

Utilizing nutrients from the tree, the truffle mycorrhiza is able to form its highly valued fruit, which can range from the famous Alba white truffle and the French black Périgord truffle to the European summer truffle. Most interestingly, different types of truffles need specific trees to grow. According to Varaldo, the Alba white truffle, for example, only grows on the roots of oak, poplar, elm, willow, and linden trees. So, would there be a difference in taste?

Overall there are an estimated 180 different types of tuber-forming mushrooms in the world. Only a few are used in gastronomy. Those that are, however, are worth their weight in gold, as an Alba white truffle weighing 1.3kg that was sold in 2010 for USD $417,200 ($321 per gram!) impressively demonstrated.[208] As we were just ten miles from Alba, in the middle of the Alba white truffle hunting ground, there was a slim chance we would find one today. You never know.

After our introduction into the science and history of truffles, we were keen to start the hunt. Varaldo's two dogs definitely couldn't wait to get going, as was evident by their excited barking. We began to walk into the forest while the two white dogs, the older one called Rocky and the younger one Lila, straightaway began to search the forest floor with their highly sensitive noses. Varaldo in the meantime let us in on some secrets of the truffle hunter's trade. He told us that, because truffles live symbiotically with only very specific types of trees, you have to first look for the right trees, which fortunately were all here. The next telltale sign is the presence of other mushrooms on the forest floor, particularly the one he called "priest's hat," a mushroom commonly called "elfin saddle" in English due to its tiny, saddle-like shape.[209] And finally, much like hunting or fishing, it's of the utmost importance to hunt without haste. Slow and steady wins the race—or potentially thousands of dollars, in the case of truffles.

Almost on cue, Lila began to dig at the root of a medium-sized oak tree, her short tail wagging like crazy. Mr. Varaldo threw a treat by her side, diverting her attention, and began digging carefully with a small foldable truffle spade no larger than a smartphone. Within seconds he indeed unearthed a small black truffle the size of a walnut. Although none of us had done anything to find it, we were still excited. We passed around the little, shriveled black thing carefully, trying to smell its faint scent. Varaldo would later tell us that a freshly dug truffle is like a good bottle of wine: it first has to be opened and allowed to breathe for a while before it develops its full aroma.

Interestingly, there is a negative correlation between the quality of truffles and wine produced in the Piedmont region and beyond. Years that produce a lot of truffles normally coincide with really bad years for wine. The reason behind this is actually not too far off from the beautiful ancient Greek belief that truffles are a result of lightning. Born in late spring or early summer, the tiny truffle needs copious amounts of water throughout the summer to reach its full potential in the fall. Grapes, on the other hand, thrive on sunshine. So while the truffle hunter looks forward to rainy, thunderous summers, a wine grower dreams of the opposite.

Varaldo began to talk about his two dogs, which obviously meant the world to him. Both were crossbreeds, Rocky an eclectic mix of Labrador, Spinone Italiano, and Brittany and Lila almost pure Spinone Italiano; both had pedigrees for hunting. However, to be an excellent truffle dog, he passionately told me, the hunting dog DNA is not enough; a dog also needs to have truffles in its heart and spirit. Indeed, these dogs seemed to have that in spades. Not even ten minutes after our first find, both were digging again, tails wiggling. Fortunately, a treat diverted their attention once again, and moments later we were passing around a sizable Alba white truffle, this time carefully wrapped into a red-checkered handkerchief. From a smashed car window in the early morning to a white truffle in the early evening—what a day!

Looking a little more appealing than the black truffle with its smooth skin, this one also exuded a slightly stronger earthy, musky smell with a slight hint of garlic. The aromas were strange but at the same time very gastronomically intriguing.

Both dogs now earned a second treat, as each white truffle counts for a double reward. The older dog, Rocky, had figured this out a long time ago and had therefore become an exclusive white truffle–hunting dog. Lila, in contrast, still had youthful enthusiasm on her side and eagerly searched for any truffle.

As we continued our so far very successful hunt, I asked Varaldo if there was a difference in taste depending on which type of tree a truffle grew. To my amazement, he not only affirmed this theory of mine but also listed very specific distinctions and how they paired with different dishes. He told me that truffles growing on the roots of poplar, linden, and willow trees are much lighter, while the ones growing on oak and elm are darker. The same is also true for their taste. The lighter-colored ones are more delicate, pairing well with eggs or fondue, while the darker ones have a more intense, longer-lasting flavor that pairs very well with meat dishes. For pasta dishes, he said, both are fine.

However, he told me with a twinkle in his eye, the best ones are those that have been nibbled on by worms or any other forest creature, as these animals are clearly not stupid and always select the tastiest. In fact, if you happen to stumble on an earthworm that has eaten a truffle, he strongly recommends barbecuing it, as it is extremely tasty. Needless to say, I just took his word for it. Although I did wonder . . . would the worm then also taste different depending on which tree the truffle had grown on?

Our mesmerizing hunt continued, and we even found another small Alba white before the sun became very low and visibility became an issue. On our walk back to the car, I pondered how I could possibly try the different flavors of trees as captured in a truffle without spending hundreds, if not thousands, of dollars. Low-cost truffle oils were out of the question; Varaldo had strongly advised against them because many contain artificially enhanced flavors. Besides, even if I were to find one that didn't, it still wouldn't be made from different single-tree varieties but rather all mixed together. A difficult problem.

Unfortunately, we couldn't stay and try one of the truffles we had found, as we had to race back to the repair shop in Turin before it closed so I could collect my repaired—and hopefully now watertight—car. Driving into the sunset down the winding roads of Piedmont, with the colorful, ever-misty Langhe valley below us, I vividly remembered the birthday dinner I had in the first few weeks of my time at university here in Italy some years before. As the university is just a twenty-minute drive from Alba, some friends suggested having a truffle dinner in the town. No sooner said than done, we found ourselves in a restaurant a friend of a friend had highly recommended and ordered the truffle menu. The *black* truffle menu, I might add—we were students, after all.

The dish that I most vividly remember was the pasta, which consisted of freshly made, exceptionally yellow tagliatelle, which must have been prepared with an incredible amount of egg yolks, served with butter and black truffles grated on top. The smell of fresh pasta, melted butter, and the earthy, slightly sulfuric aroma of black truffle was extraordinary itself, but the taste was otherworldly. The sweet starchiness of the pasta paired with the fatty creaminess of the butter, on top of which the intense, earthy taste of the black truffle was floating, was indescribable. And not just in the proverbial sense—I was literally unable to describe the taste of the black truffle. So even if I were to somehow find the same type of truffle from different trees, I couldn't properly articulate the difference. Not an ideal situation for someone writing about food and its flavor, is it?

But as luck would have it, a friend came to the rescue. Sarah, the wonderful friend from university who introduced me to Tim from Postcard Teas had just opened a concept restaurant in Tokyo. Called OUT, it served nothing but fresh, homemade pasta topped with copious amounts of truffle, to be enjoyed with a glass of red wine and Led Zeppelin playing in the background.

Since she was surrounded by truffles day in and day out, I asked her if she could share some of her vast truffle-tasting knowledge. She did, and could actually describe the truffles' tastes. She described it as a mix of deep smoky notes, a hint of wood chips, earth, mushrooms, damp soil, sulfur, and even sweet notes like chocolate and burnt caramel. If a truffle is slightly off, it fascinatingly produces a real chemical sensation akin to kerosene, according to Sarah. Curiously though it was quite difficult even for her to describe the aroma and taste of a truffle. That's why she prefers to explain it as a feeling of complete exhilaration.

Exhilarating it was indeed to have found yet another bouquet of tree flavor hiding inside one of the most expensive and sought-after food items in the world.[210] A subterranean flavor wonder only made possible through symbiosis. There would be no truffles without trees.

CHAPTER 18
A Very Swiss Rock Star

It all began with a link to an online Austrian cheese shop sent by a friend and University of Gastronomic Sciences classmate. He knew about my obsession with the flavor of wood and had come across a cheese that had been wrapped and aged in a piece of spruce cambium (the soft, inner part of tree bark). I was intrigued, but for some reason didn't follow up on it right on the spot, so the message became buried in my mailbox. Yet only a week later, and completely unrelatedly, my parents sent me a link to a BBC documentary called *A Cook Abroad*, in which London-based chef Monica Galetti visits a French cheese producer making a very similar cheese. I duly saved the link in my calendar, this time even setting a reminder to view it in the course of the upcoming week. Of course, the reminder got muted, and that should have been the unfortunate end of it. However, yet another week later while I was catching up with a friend who was helping a Swiss cheese company set up shop in Vienna, she told me about their tree-bark-wrapped cheese. I couldn't escape it!

In German we have the saying *"mit dem Zaunpfahl winken,"* which directly translated means "to wave with the fence post"—German is a strange language—and really means "to give a broad hint." In this instance destiny was giving me a very broad hint; from all possible directions, Austrian, French, and Swiss fence posts (probably made from spruce) were waving. So, on my way back to Milan, where I was living at the time, I began researching the topic of the cambium-wrapped cheese on my phone. Somehow, I soon stumbled across the name "Sanglè" which seemed to be the French name for this type of cheese. A quick search in a dictionary revealed it to mean "belt" or "band," most probably in reference to the band of spruce cambium that wraps the cheese. Unfortunately, my French is limited to the point of being practically non-existent, so I very soon hit a dead-end in my research on Sanglè. However, once back in Milan and reunited with my computer I started unearthing the fabulous links sent from friends and family. Of course, all the information I could possibly need was already there. One lead seemed to be particularly promising, as it involved a Swiss cheese maker famous the world over. His name is Willi Schmid, and he is the rock star of cheese producers in Switzerland. After starting his own shop in 2006 he quickly became known as Switzerland's most innovative cheese producer, and by 2010 he had won an award for the best Jersey cheese, a blue cheese, in the world—a feat he repeated only two years later.[211]

He also produces two variations of the Sanglè cheese. One is called "Bergficht" ("Mountain Spruce") and is made from unpasteurized cow's milk, and the other one is called "hölzerne Geis" ("wooden goat") and is made from unpasteurized goat milk. On top of all of that, he spoke German, and his cheese dairy was east of Zürich, in the Canton St. Gallen, just a few hours' drive from Milan.

I managed to find the number to his shop and called him straight-away. He answered the phone himself and was very welcoming when I asked him if I could come by for a visit. Once I told him that I wasn't sure if I would come by car or public transport he immediately recommended the latter and even told me the best way to get to his place by bus. However, against his recommendation, I decided to drive there by car once I had found two days off from work at the Expo, since I wanted to be independent from public transport schedules. I soon came to regret this decision after I had to purchase an annual motorway permit sticker at the Swiss-Italian border for forty francs (about forty US dollars), the only permit they offered, even though I'd only be in the country for two days. (Switzerland must make a lot of money from tourists visiting the country for just a few days . . . well played, Switzerland!)

Entering Switzerland from Italy, I immediately noticed the profound difference in driving. Not only was the road in perfect condition (thanks to the generous contributions of people like me buying annual stickers, no doubt), but traffic itself seemed different. It took me a while to pinpoint the exact difference, but when I finally realized what it was I had to laugh out loud: Everyone drove very carefully and actually adhered to the speed limit—something rather unthinkable in Italy—because of the draconian speeding fines one can receive in Switzerland. Driving 1–3 mph over the speed limit equals a fine of forty francs, whereas driving 7–9 mph over the limit would result in a fine of 160 francs.[212] Those are not just hypothetical fines on paper, either; they are rigorously enforced; the little canton of St. Gallen received 17.4 million francs from speeding fines in the year 2014 alone.[213]

To further reinforce what a mistake it was to drive myself, a construction site in front of the Gotthard tunnel brought traffic to a full stop for two long hours. That'll teach me a lesson to drive a car in a country with one of the best public transit systems in the world!

All of this meant that I was running dangerously late for my meeting with Willi Schmid at his cheese dairy, Stätlichäsi Lichtensteig. Now driving with an increased sense of urgency, but still carefully staying within each and every speed limit, I couldn't help but marvel at the ever-changing, beautiful scenery flying by my window. Within a few miles I would often pass through at least one valley surrounded by steep mountains, lower-lying pastures with small herds of brown- and white-spotted cows lining the winding road left and right, charming little farming villages built around a church, and, surprisingly, several rather industrial-looking warehouses and factories. In a sense these tableaux perfectly portrayed Switzerland, the country where, stemming from a farming background, a myriad of highly specialized but often world-leading industries developed. Nonetheless, the original farming landscape persists. One story that never ceases to amaze me is the way the now world-dominating Swiss watchmaking industry developed. Some of the first watchmakers in Switzerland were actually farmers looking for a side income during the slow winter months.[214] Can you imagine working all through the growing season in the fields and then going to your house in winter and, instead of resting a bit, sitting on a table under the dim light of a candle and starting to make the minuscule metal parts necessary for a watch? With captivating stories like this, it is absolutely no wonder that products made in Switzerland are sought-after the world over.

Cheese is one of those famous Swiss products with a long and distinguished history dating back to at least the Celts.[215] For this reason, I was particularly surprised to hear from Schmid that the brand of Swiss cheese had suffered immensely both in quality and reputation amongst cheese aficionados in the twentieth century. I had reached his place of artisanal cheese creation by now, and we were already engulfed in a very interesting conversation on the history of cheese made in Switzerland. Until the 1930s the Swiss cheese landscape was still relatively diverse, and many still made blue cheese (his reference cheese), he tells me. The demise of Swiss cheese diversity had, however, already started some years before, in 1914, with the start of the First World War. At this time Switzerland established the Swiss Cheese Union, effectively a government-sanctioned cartel between milk producers, cheese makers, and exporters, which would prevent the industry from collapsing during the war years. This measure was completely understandable; after all, the milk industry was an essential food provider for the country.

Milk and cheese prices were fixed, and so were production quotas, which posed a real problem for maintaining cheese diversity. Initially, production was restricted to only three types of cheese: Gruyère, Emmentaler, and Sbrinz, all hard cheeses. And in the turbulent years between the wars, the union effectively stayed in place, continuously trying to stabilize the industry. Standards loosened slightly but still favored the big three hard cheeses. Then came the Second World War, raging all around Switzerland and forcing the little country into self-sufficiency yet again.

Once the war was over, Schmid told me, farmers were so used to giving all their milk to the Cheese Union that they demanded that this practice continue. The state agreed, but only if the farmers were willing to produce the types and amounts of cheese decided by the Union. It soon became clear that only durable cheeses (e.g., Gruyère, Emmentaler, and Sbrinz) with longer shelf lives were wanted. There was no place for soft cheeses of any kind, or cheese diversity, for that matter. The union's exporters needed cheeses that wouldn't spoil quickly and could be sold in large quantities. This problem was soon taken advantage of by buyers, who simply had to wait for huge discounts when the union's warehouses were full.

Fascinatingly, the Cheese Union was also responsible for creating the mythos of fondue, which had once only been a regional dish in Switzerland. Through decades of strong advertisement, with a real breakthrough moment at the 1964 New York World's Fair, those campaigns made everyone believe that the Swiss practically lived off of fondue—well, that and chocolate, of course.

Only when the Cheese Union was finally abolished in the late 1990s, due to its incompatibility with global trade agreements, did the Swiss cheese landscape begin to gain back some of its former diversity.

In 2006 Schmid started his own cheese dairy, and some might say that this was actually the day that Swiss artisan cheese production came back to life.[216] The cambium-wrapped cheeses, my reason for coming to visit him, were part of his lineup from the beginning. He told me that cheeses wrapped in tree bark go right back to the roots of cheese making itself.

In order to understand the use of the tree bark in the making of cheese, it is important to first talk about the very basics of cheese making. Every type of cheese starts with some kind of animal milk, whether it be from cows, sheep, or goats. This milk (the fresher the better) is then slowly heated in a container until it reaches the desired temperature, around 89 to 91 degrees Fahrenheit. At this point the so-called "rennet" is added, a substance that clots the proteins in the milk, called curd, and separates it from the liquids, called whey. Once the curd has fully formed, it is cut into pieces, heated once again, drained, and finally pressed into a porous mold.[217] The mold has two functions: to form the cheese and to get rid of the excess whey. Those molds are now made from plastic with holes in it, but Schmid tells me that historically they used to be made from tree bark, specifically from spruce tree bark. In spring, the cheese maker would go into the woods, select a spruce tree with the desired diameter, make two horizontal cuts around the tree separated by the height of the mold, and finally connect those two with a vertical cut. Then he would carefully peel away the bark (easily done because of all the sap circulating through the bark in spring) until he had an open cylinder of tree bark. This cylinder was then sewn shut with a quartered piece of flexible tree root, and the cheese mold was ready. Spruce trees were used not only for their thick yet still very elastic bark, ideal for the purpose of a mold, but also for their tendency to form very thin branches close to the ground which die off quickly due to lack of light. Those tiny branches form natural holes in the tree bark, perfect for draining off the whey. These holes can't be drilled artificially, because the structurally weak bark will rip as soon as it is put under any kind of pressure.

One curious example of such a tree-bark-molded cheese was the Swiss "Zigra" cheese, which was made on alpine pastures. The cheese maker would extract the curd from the day's fresh milk and fill it into a large tree-bark mold. Once it was full, which could take several days or even weeks' worth of milk, resulting in distinctly colored strata, he pressed and carried the cheese on his back, still in the mold, down into the valley for processing. He must have had an interesting whiff to passersby.

In those times, the tree bark seemed to be mainly used for its functional properties rather than its flavor-giving capabilities. Schmid explained that the same was true for the beginnings of the Sanglè. The Sanglè is a soft, red, moldy cheese that is very runny, almost liquid. To keep it from running off the aging board (the board on which cheese is placed during its stay in the aging room, which is also made from spruce), a ring of spruce cambium was placed around it. Cambium was used because it was easier to bend into a small circle, didn't make a mess, and didn't leave you with pieces of dry bark in your mouth. Over time, however, people seemed to appreciate the flavor the cambium introduced into the cheese, and so it became the trademark of the Sanglè.

Schmid enjoys the spruce flavor in the Sanglè. However, in his two interpretations of the cheese ("Bergfichte" and "hölzerne Geis"), he has a somewhat different approach. Traditionally, cambium is collected right after the tree is felled, quite often by the woodcutter himself, for whom it is a source of side income. He does that by first scraping off the top bark with a broad, chisel-like tool and then slicing off the cambium with a sharp, angular U-shaped tool. This results in a long belt of cambium already cut to the correct width. Later, in his workshop, he cuts the cambium belt to the appropriate length and lets it air-dry. Finally the dried strips are bundled and sold to the cheese maker.

Schmid likewise asks his suppliers, who are farmers and woodcutters from the surrounding area, to go through the same gathering process. However, he wants them not to dry the cambium but rather to freeze it. This way all the essential oils remain in the cambium and later release their fresh, sappy flavors into the cheese, in contrast to the dried cambium strips that release flavors that remind him of rotten bark. Next he prepares his cheese, using either cow's milk or goat's milk, presses it in plastic molds, and prepares it for the wrapping. Before he can wrap his precious cheeses, though, he has to sterilize the cambium strips by cooking them briefly in a pressure-cooker. Once the cheeses are wrapped, they are put on a spruce aging board and placed in the aging room with a constant temperature of around fifty degrees Fahrenheit. There they age for around three to five weeks before they are sold all around the world.

Historically the Sanglè could be only made in winter, Schmid tells me. This is not because of the colder temperature, as I suspected, but rather because of the flies, which simply couldn't be kept at bay in those days. Now, of course, he is fortunate to be able to make it all year long, a fact evident in one of his cold storage rooms, which is filled to the brim with frozen spruce cambium.

Amazingly, even though he makes several thousand pieces of cambium-wrapped cheese every year, its flavor is still one of his favorites. He speaks passionately about the fresh, sappy flavors transferred from the spruce into the cheese. Anecdotally, he told me that even when walking about the Swiss forests he likes to chew on fresh spruce needles.

After spending more than four hours at his brand-new cheese dairy, where everything is still made by hand (except washing the aging board, which is now done by his most prized possession, an industrial washer), it was time for me to leave, but not before buying some of his amazing cheese.

After I had stored the cheese in what I hoped was the coolest part of my car, I headed into the city of Zurich, where I was meeting with a good friend of mine from university. We spent an enjoyable evening in the city, which included a great dinner at Restaurant Volkshaus. I left for Milan the next morning, though not before strolling through this charming village of a city alongside the river Limmat, admiring the shiny church spires against a backdrop of white cumulus clouds, grand houses, and ancient chestnut alleys that have formed formidable green archways above sidewalks. I also, of course, had to buy some chocolate from Läderach chocolatier, my favorite.

With a car full of Swiss chocolate and cheese, I began the drive back to Milan, this time carefully planning my trip so that I would avoid the Gotthard tunnel at all cost. I decided on what I hoped would be a scenic route over the San Bernardino Pass, although it looked particularly rainy. (If that name sounds familiar, it's because this is the area where the St. Bernard rescue dog, complete with clichéd Swiss-branded wooden spirits barrel around his neck, a complete fabrication,[218] is from.) Indeed, when I was barely a few miles out of the city it started pouring. But as soon as I reached the twisting mountain roads leading up to the pass, equally spectacular to look at and drive on, the sun began to shoot bright rifts of light through the still-harshly-dark cloud cover. These illuminated the intensely white fog patches that the wind blew in front of the gloomy, towering mountains.

Once I returned to Italy, I began to weigh the best way to taste my two cambium-wrapped cheeses. In the end, I decided to follow Schmid's suggestion of eating one as it was and melting the other in the oven, accompanied by a very dark and flavorful rye bread.

Starting from the center, the wonderful creaminess of the "Mountain Spruce" cheese was paired with an ever-increasing sappiness the closer I came to the cambium-banded outside. The strong flavors reminded me of fresh lemons and turpentine while still retaining a certain nuttiness. Its pleasure was only topped by the warm gooiness of the hearty and more musky "wooden goat" cheese that I baked in the oven and scooped onto different types of bread (the rye one was indeed the best). The slightly musky flavor note that my cheese-tasting professor at the University of Gastronomic Sciences would call "the flavor of a horse blanket" mingled extremely well with the fresh tastes of a spruce forest warmed up by the intense rays of the mountain sun—or the oven, in my case. This was Swiss cheese meeting the flavor of wood at its best, made by a true rock star of cheese.

CHAPTER 19

Edible Wood

In my hunt for the flavor of wood I had discovered a spectacular abundance of wooden flavors in most unexpected places and food items, yet I hadn't found the holy grail of tree flavors: actual edible wood. Wherever I looked and whatever I tried, it seemed to only exist in my imagination. Sure, I had tried leaves, bark, tree sap, and cambium as well as extracts from many different types of wood, but wood in its pure, technical meaning wasn't one of them.

After having come so close to it—tasting and experimenting with ash to make Pokot ash yoghurt—I was determined to find a way to finally taste pure, unadulterated wood. How I could possibly accomplish this seemingly impossible feat was the subject of many a daydream and numerous sleepless hours.

I set out to try the many various methods I'd brainstormed, starting with the simplest one, cooking. No matter how long I cooked the ever-thinner pieces of pinewood, which I had chosen for its relatively low density, the result was always a slightly soggy piece of inedible wood. Frying, which had proved to be such a success with tree cambium earlier in my research, and even numerous carefully timed blasts with a blowtorch, which I hoped would sear the wood but not burn it, couldn't render it even slightly edible.

Alright, I thought to myself, it's time for more drastic methods.

With the help of a newly sharpened handsaw, I reduced several inches of both a beech wood and a pine plank to two small heaps of fine sawdust. Having already had the questionable pleasure of eating practically raw teak wood sawdust only mixed with water, this time I opted for a slightly more refined approach. While researching the book I had come across many references to "famine bread" that was partly made from sawdust, tree bark, or even straw during times of food scarcity over the centuries.[219] Several of those sources had mentioned the use of beech wood sawdust, hence my first wood selection; the pinewood one was my own innovation.

I chose a regular whole-grain bread recipe from the basic recipe book that came with my bread machine and substituted the fine, sifted beech sawdust for a third of the recommended amount of whole-wheat flour. Curiously, after a few hours in the machine the dough leavened just as well as a normal, wood-free version. After baking for several hours, it emerged as a slightly smaller and denser loaf than usual. The bread smelled delicious, with no recognizable additional scent that would hint at the presents of beech sawdust. I immediately tried a piece, first plain and then with butter. Initially, to my surprise, it tasted exactly like whole-grain bread. However, after a while I began to notice a slightly crunchier, gritty texture, paired with a somewhat stronger dryness. Slowly but surely, the faintly astringent beech wood flavor—rolled oats with a milky note—began to surface. It was not altogether unpleasant.

Next was the pine sawdust bread, whose intense, resinous smell began floating through the kitchen within the first hour of baking. Once done and removed from the hot machine, it exuded an intense fragrance that reminded me of roaming through a thicket of young balsam firs in Canada. When I tentatively tried a bit, I was very pleasantly surprised. Its sappy, marginally bitter note balanced perfectly with the sweet, starchy taste of the whole-wheat flour. Best of all, there was no grittiness whatsoever. Adding butter enhanced this positive sensation; never in my wildest dreams had I thought that famine bread might taste so good.

As you might imagine, I was tremendously happy with this result. I had finally found a way to eat actual wood, and it wasn't an altogether horrible experience. Quite to the contrary. Yet to do so, I had to first reduce it to dust and then hide it in copious amounts of all the other ingredients that make up proper bread. It clearly wasn't a main ingredient. Was there really no way to make it one?

Having recently acquired a pressure cooker, adding to my already extensive collection of small kitchen appliances—and not just any brand either, but one made by the German company Fissler, the supposed "Mercedes of pressure cookers"—and being impressed by its early results, I saw a new possibility for cooking wood. Again, I chose a comparatively soft pinewood, sliced it into 1/32-inch-thick pieces, and put it, together with some water, in my new pressure cooking silver bullet. Two hours later, under a relatively constant high-pressure environment of 12 psi and temperatures exceeding 242 degrees Fahrenheit, I impatiently released the pressure, resulting in a spectacular cloud of water vapor that engulfed the whole kitchen with a loud hiss. But as soon as I began picking the slices of thin pinewood out of the still-boiling water with a pair of kitchen tongs, I could feel that they were as tough as ever. A quick test with the teeth regrettably reaffirmed my initial feeling: soggy, but still inedible.

Disappointed but even more determined, I started to consider my other options. Inspired by several YouTube experiments with liquid nitrogen, or LN2 (normally gaseous, atmospheric nitrogen that has been liquefied by cooling it down to -320 degrees Fahrenheit), I forged a somewhat elaborate plan. Provided I could somehow procure LN2, I would combine several attempts into one, starting with a type of wood I hadn't considered using before: willow. To improve my odds of success, I had revaluated every part of my earlier attempts and realized that the wood species I had previously used, pine and beech, might not be ideally suited for what I wanted to achieve.

Although pine had a relatively low density, it still wasn't the softest wood out there. Beech was very dense, which in all honesty made it a terrible choice for a wood eating experiment in the first place. Willow, in contrast, is a very soft type of wood that predominantly grows in rather wet spots alongside rivers and streams. Its low density makes willow a poor choice for furniture making but a perfect choice for my experiment.

With the type of wood decided, I would now need to find the LN2. This, it turns out, is not an easy feat if you do not want to spend hundreds or even thousands of US dollars on getting a large, super-insulated canister filled with hundreds of gallons of liquid nitrogen delivered to your house. As I didn't want to turn my whole house into a spooky haunted house or cryogenically freeze myself for all eternity, I had to look for options outside of the general market. After all, I only needed a maximum of seventy fluid ounces for a single experiment. Thankfully one of my amazing friends worked at a laboratory that regularly uses liquid nitrogen for the preservation of samples, and he agreed to let me have a small amount of this ultra-cool liquid. He also had a Styrofoam cube with top cover on hand that would prevent most of the liquid from evaporating during the transport to my kitchen.

My plan was to immerse the willow wood first in the LN2, rapidly cool it to -320 degrees Fahrenheit, and then swiftly transfer it to my already boiling pressure cooker to quickly heat it up to 242 degrees Fahrenheit. I was hoping that this massive cold shock, followed by a serious thermal shock, with a total temperature difference of 562 degrees Fahrenheit, would pry the rigid molecular structure of the willow wood fibers wide open, effectively breaking it down and making it edible.

No sooner said than done, I found myself walking carefully through Vienna's streets with my hands gripping a large white Styrofoam cube. The puffs of steam that emerged as small amounts of escaping nitrogen gas froze the surrounding air surely caught me some curious looks by passersby, but thankfully no one seemed alarmed by the sight. Having finally reached my kitchen, without accidentally freezing anything or anyone along the way, I immediately fired up the pressure cooker.

I had collected some willow wood the day before from a tree right next to a stream not far from my house. To further improve my odds, I had not only cut a thin branch, which I then later sliced into 1/32-inch-thick pieces, but also fresh new shoots, barely older than a few months, sprouting from the base of the tree. Their even lower density would significantly increase my chances—or at least that's what I hoped when I set all the wood out to soak in jam jars overnight.

As soon as the water in the pressure cooker showed signs of imminent boiling, I removed the cooler's cover, releasing a cloud of steam into the room, put on my safety gloves and glasses, and submersed one piece of fresh willow wood after another into the liquid nitrogen. The liquid inside bubbled and steamed furiously as the room temperature object hit its surface. The wood pieces soon reached -320 degrees Fahrenheit and were now easily breakable. One after another, I fished them out of the cube and threw them into the by now vigorously boiling pressure cooker, locking and sealing the lid after the last piece of wood went in. I kept them boiling for more than two hours before I switched off the stove and let it cool down slowly. My excitement upon opening the cooker was eclipsed only by my disappointment when the soggy willow wood was just that—soggy, inedible wood. The only curious thing was the intense red color of the water, courtesy of the willow bark, whose use as a natural clothing dye by the Native Americans I had already come across in my earlier research. Even repeating the wood torture once again, with the same piece of willow, didn't change the results. Likewise, simply freezing it and then letting it thaw to a safe temperature wouldn't solve its inedibility. What a disappointment.

Having basically run out of ideas about cooking methods, I remembered that I could always utilize the power of other organisms like bacteria or mushrooms. After all, even if I were to find a way to make it edible by making it first chewable, due to the wood's high cellulose and lignin content I wouldn't be able to digest it anyway. Some other mammals, like cows, had solved this problem by extending their digestive system and having symbiotic bacteria that could break down the tough fibers they encountered in their plant-based diet[220] colonize their stomachs. Termites use the same symbiotic relationship with bacteria to extract nutrients from actual wood.[221] Due to the glaring limitations of my gut, this method was clearly not an option for me. And recreating the anaerobic environment in which the wood-eating bacteria would thrive would have required a laboratory setup I simply didn't have. So, my only option was to work with organisms that could break down wood in a normal outside environment, for example fungi.

Fungi were actually an often-reoccurring topic while reading and researching all about the flavor of wood. No matter whether the goal was to break down fibrous agricultural or gastronomical waste to be used as nutritive animal fodder[222] or to recreate the unmatched tone of Stradivari violins,[223] fungi were the tools of choice to break open the strong cellular structure of wood. With their fine penetration hyphae, they are the only organisms that can completely spread through solid wood.[224] Stumbling across this possibility more by chance than by design, I was visiting friends who were working extensively in edible and medicinal mushroom cultivation when I came across a beech log that had been colonized by Shiitake mushrooms for several years. As a result of the Shiitake enzymes, the ligneous parts of the wood[225] had become very light and almost flaky. Out of curiosity I tried one of those flakes. Incredibly, it was quite easy to chew. Its taste was dominated by that of a raw shiitake mushroom; there were clear meaty, slightly fatty, umami notes followed by an incredible dryness, as if I were eating cardboard. So, although I had found chewable wood, it tasted overwhelmingly of mushrooms—not exactly what I was looking for.

At this point I was becoming increasingly frustrated. Whatever I tried didn't give me the longed-for result, although I had come across some gastronomic delights, like the pine dust bread, along the way.

I set off searching library catalogues, bookshops, and the internet once again using different search terms. This time, surprisingly, it didn't take long before I came across a blog that talked at length about an edible wood from Argentina.[226] I couldn't believe it! Supposedly there was even a small company by the name of Yacaratiá Delicatessen producing and selling it as a curious delicacy. I found their website within seconds, and a few minutes later I sent an inquiry in English, asking for an interview.

Several weeks later, I was still waiting for a reply. English seemed to be the problem. The website also listed a phone number. Unfortunately, my Spanish was way too basic for an actual conversation on the phone, but Carmen, most fortuitously, did speak Spanish. So a few more weeks later, when all my experiments had reached dead ends, I asked her if she could kindly make the call. One or two rings later, Vanina Pascutti, the company's owner, answered the phone and was very excited that some-one from Austria had somehow discovered their highly regional product. She agreed to an interview later that day and even gave us her mobile number so we could arrange everything via WhatsApp. As we exchanged messages, we found out that there would also be the possibility to do the interview in English.

So, not even a few hours after our first phone call, I was having a video call with a woman who turned out to be Vanina's mother, Marisa Pascutti, the English speaker in the family.

During our video call, I would learn that the whole idea of making wood edible was born by Marisa's late husband, Roberto, who was a chemical engineer as well as a forestry engineer and professor of forestry sciences at the University of Misiones in northern Argentina. While work-ing with the region's indigenous people, the Guaraníes, he discovered that they ate worms that fed on the wood of a medium-sized tree (fifty to fifty-two-feet tall) that seemed to only grow in one area of northern Argentina. Called *Yacaratia spinose,* it had a most curious wood that was completely different from any other tree he had seen before. Its stem was extremely soft, naturally saturated with water, and began to decompose within hours of being cut. Taking some of the wood to the university for further analysis, he realized that the tree had very low cellulose content, giving it an exceptionally low density quite similar to that of a soft sponge. The worm consumed by the Guaraníes gave him the idea of try-ing to make the wood directly edible, basically cutting out the wiggly middleman.

Many experimentations later, he'd found a process that worked. He would first use steaming hot water to extract the tree's resinous sub-stances that impart an unpleasant flavor from the wood and then have it undergo a hydrolysis with weak organic acids to further break up the al-ready weak structure of the wood. He then immersed and cooked the now edible, but supposedly pretty bland-tasting wood in a sugar syrup, sometimes with the addition of lemon juice or further natural flavorings. Having discovered this remarkable process, his daughter is now contin-uing her father's legacy by producing a wide variety of *Yacaratia*-based sweets that include everything from chocolate-covered wood bonbons to wood preserved in sugar syrup.

Listening to this mouthwatering description I became more and more eager to try it and therefore asked Marisa Pascutti if she could possibly mail me a sample. This however proved to be much more difficult than I could have ever imagined. After a month passed without finding solutions for both sending the actual sample as well as transferring the money, I asked my Argentinian university friend Angie for help. Incredibly, she offered not only to meet with Vanina Pascutti at a food fair in Buenos Aires and buy a sample but even that she would take it with her to Europe on an upcoming trip she had planned. I was speechless!

Some weeks later she expedited two glasses full of preserved edible wood from her holiday stay in Croatia to my home in Austria, which we both expected would take a maximum of five days to arrive. But when it still hadn't arrived a week later I consulted the online parcel tracking system of the Croatian post. Supposedly they had already handed it over to the Austrian post, which I immediately contacted. The representative told me that it most likely was in one of the several containers full of parcels still sitting in their yard waiting to be processed, due to an extreme shortage of personnel—too many had gone on holiday at the same time. I'd have to wait a few more weeks for the postal service to work through the backlog. But when I called them some weeks after they'd processed the backlogged shipments, my parcel was still nowhere to be found. Sigh.

Back to the Croatian post. Initiating a search for the dearly missed parcel entailed filing an official request form in Croatian, a task I somehow managed thanks to Google Translate. Once filed, several months and a gazillion e-mails later it became clear that somewhere in Zagreb the parcel had seemingly vanished into thin air. At that moment I even surprised myself with some of the four-letter words I knew in German, English, and Italian.

It would take me the better part of a month to cool down and reattempt to procure another sample. Contacting several well-known international courier services, I finally found one that would pick it up directly in Argentina and deliver it to my doorstep—at a hefty price, of course.

Knowing that it was difficult for the Pascuttis to work with international couriers I asked Angie with a great sense of ineptness if she could possibly pick up another sample and hand it to the courier. She didn't reply for a while, but when she did I was once again without words. Not only had she already organized another jar of edible wood but also had arranged for a friend, who was going to visit her from Germany, to bring it back to Europe and mail it to me once again.

Finally, a few more weeks later (now just shy of one year from my first request) I held a jar of *Confituras de Madera*, the holy grail of wooden flavors, in hand at last.

One bright early summer morning I enthusiastically prepared everything I needed for trying the preserved *Yacaratia* wood. It included a plate, various kitchen instruments, my notebook, a pen, and my full photographic equipment (DSLR, lighting, flash and all) so I could document this exciting moment. Ceremoniously I set everything down on my dining table and carefully opened the lid of the brown tinted glass decorated with a colorful label depicting the *Yacaratia* tree, its bright green fingered leaves before a backdrop of vivid orange and red.

The glass opened with a satisfactory *plop* and released a whiff of sweetness. The chestnut brown syrup was peculiarly light and translucent, clearly showing the oblong pieces of wood lying at the glass' bottom. Taking a skewer I pricked a piece, much like a spearfisher in murky waters, and was immediately surprised by the firm consistency. It acutely reminded me of the perfect snappiness of the gherkins from the Spreewald.

I let some of the excess syrup drip off before I placed the piece at the center of the prepared white plate and examined its appearance. It looked like a wet, rough sawn piece of wood, distinctive grain and all, whereby the thinner parts let some light shine through. Smelling it at first revealed the expected sweet scent from the liquid preservative, but very soon it was joined by the distinct aroma of conkers (horse chestnut tree seeds) just peeled from their prickly, green skin, and a hint of artichoke.

Finally it was time to try it and taste actual edible wood. Would I be disappointed after all of this?

Cutting it into smaller, square pieces I attentively took a piece and placed it in my mouth. It had a nice snap, which was followed by a fibrous texture. Sweetness was the first, dominant note but was soon followed by an onslaught of delicate flavors. It included a hint of caramel that reminded me of a mid-season maple syrup, ripe banana notes like in some exquisite Caribbean rums, honey-preserved walnut flavors, a faint note of sweet artichoke (if such a thing exists), roasted chestnut aromas, and notably no bitterness whatsoever.

Just like that, I had discovered what was probably the only edible wood in the world and its extravagant flavor, all thanks to the incredible ingenuity of Roberto Pascutti and his family as well as the tremendous help of my friend Angie. To say that I was immensely happy was an understatement. This was the absolute pinnacle and the ultimate prize in my hunt for the most elusive of flavors: the flavor of actual wood.

PART III

Delicious Wooden Future

CHAPTER 20
Wood & Friends

As my wooden flavor hunt came to a close, I wanted to share all the fascinating things I had discovered through research, experiments, interviews, and even coincidences. It was great fun exploring this previously hidden world of flavors, meeting an incredible number of interesting people, experiencing breathtaking landscapes, eating dishes bursting with woody aromas, and finally capturing and condensing it all in writing. From the varied tangs of tree bark, the crispy yet simultaneously doughy textures and flavor rainbows of wood-oven pizza, the endless aroma variations of steeped tea leaves, the tannicly manifold essences hiding in the depth of a spirit-aging barrel, the wafting fragrance complexities lurking in woodland derived perfumes, and the milk-preserving savors of wooden ashes, to maple syrup's intricate sweetness, the contemporary interpretations of wooden notes in wine, the thunderous truffle-flavor exhilaration, the cheesy savors of spruce cambium, and finally the extravagantly delicious flavors of actual edible wood. Wonderfully complex yet at times shockingly simple, the flavors never ceased to amaze me.

Yet nothing beats sharing those riches with friends and family, exchanging thoughts, cracking jokes, and generally having a splendid time. Food thereby is the most superb facilitator there is for human interaction.

So, when all had been written it was finally time to invite a group of great friends to a wooden aperitif. Considered as a celebratory event but also as a final semi-public experiment of sorts, I was hoping to hear people's opinions and thoughts on the wood flavors I shared. After all, more than three years had passed since I had dived eagerly into this unexplored world and therefore could hardly be called objective. Was it all a bit in my head? Have my taste buds become so accustomed to the—in reality—potentially horrible flavors of wood that I found everything to be tasty?

After brainstorming for days to solidify a menu of the most representative, though not too experimental dishes, Carmen and I finally chose simplicity over complexity. No need to leave people confused, estranged, or, worst of all, with a literal bad taste in their mouth.

I had already collected and dried meaty spruce and pine cambium from a pile of logs coincidently felled at just the right time in early spring alongside a favorite dog-walking route, and the wood was quickly pulverized into a very fine flour, thanks to the ever-helpful kitchen blender. Ideally suited for the baking of cookies we incorporated it in an original recipe for pine bark Oreos from the Nordic Food Lab, a nonprofit organization exploring the food diversity of the Nordic Region.[227] To the 2oz cambium flour we added 3oz whole-wheat flour, 2.6oz sugar, 4oz butter, one egg white, 2tsp of baking powder, and a pinch of salt. Mixed together by first creaming the butter, sugar, and egg white before adding the dry ingredients, the resulting quite fatty dough was left resting in the refrigerator for an hour, before we rolled it out between two sheets of parchment paper. Finally, we cut out an assortment of cookie shapes and left it baking for only five minutes in an oven preheated to 266 degrees Fahrenheit.

Next on the menu was a pesto made with freshly picked mature pine needles, walnuts, olive oil, parmesan, and salt. To have something to spread it on, we also made some rolls with a handful of fine beech wood sawdust added. The guests would also be served a semi-hard sheep's cheese smoked with beech wood, roasted chestnuts, and a cherry-wood smoked salt.

For beverages, we had Manincor's "Réserve della Contessa" white wine aged in oak barrels; a northern German beer called Duckstein, which is aged with beech wood shavings; a black and green Assam tea; a 1985 Benriach scotch; a Corsair "Triple Smoke" American whiskey; a rye-based whisky aged in-house with an assortment of exotic woods, and an early-season, as well as late-season maple syrup for mixing with freshly pressed lemon juice.

The food and drinks were all prepared and spread on a table, the guests arrived just in time on a hot and thundery day in August. It was a diverse group of friends, including people from the world of art, sociology, linguistics, printing, and culinary arts. After everyone had cooled down a bit—it was a really uncomfortable muggy and hot day—I briefly introduced them to the idea of the flavor of wood, giving several examples from these very pages. Although most of them, with one exception, had of course already heard of my crazy experiments and knew that I was writing a book about it, it was still a surprise of sorts. (Imagine if one of your friends were to tell you that he basically had tried really hard to eat trees in the last few years!)

Nevertheless, they paid careful attention, and I could see them becoming positively curious once I introduced them to wooden-flavored foods we had prepared. Without hesitation, all the guests but one bravely tried the first of several peculiar food items; the one who declined said it was, quite understandably, all too strange for her. The cookies seemed to be the least intimidating item, as they were everyone's first choice. After a short moment of taste-probing silence, the first comments began as our guests described the cookies' flavor as "Christmassy" or "autumn-ly." One friend painted a beautiful mental picture comparing their taste to the smells perceived when splitting logs in winter and carrying them into the house. Overall, I think it was fair to say people actually liked them, many even helping themselves to several more.

Soon after, the pesto, rolls, and cheese were sampled, joined by maple syrup lemonade for most while a friend and I shared a beech wood–shavings beer. The pesto was also positively reviewed, with comments on flavor varying from sappy, fresh, sprucy, and green descriptors to nutty, fatty surprisingly savory, and non-acidic. The unexpectedly light beer reminded us of grapefruit rind and malt but unfortunately was also flat and watery. Historically aged in actual beech barrels, it was today aged in stainless steel ones with only a few shavings added. No wonder then. The original one must have been amazing though.

All recognized a certain gritty texture and a hint of dryness in the beech wood rolls, but no differing flavors. The only interesting thing for me was that the ones that were leftover were still unconventionally moist and edible two days later. Was this the effect of the wood?

Inspired by the cookies, a friend suggested the use of wood extracts in baking them instead of the actual dried cambium, a great idea that steered the conversation into the directions of perfumes and cooking. Fortunately, I still had some distilled teak extract, which I passed around for everyone to smell. While I had discovered many similarities between the teak and natural rubber, my friends were reminded of horse tack, old wooden furnishings, or raw iron. The most hilarious description given was surely "grandma."

Due to the heat, we all passed on the still slightly warm tea and went eagerly straight for the whisky. I first passed around the 1985 Benriach, which was considered simply too harsh by most. None of them were Scotch drinkers, which explains the reaction; I had the same reaction the first time I tried it. Also, the American whiskey was also deemed very harsh, yet after a while it was compared to smoked bacon with its strong, smoky, woody (old bookstore sensation) notes. Finally, it was time to try the whisky that I'd started to mature almost two years before. Using the white rye whisky from the Haider distillery I had visited as a base, I had split it over several smaller bottles and infused it with charred oak, teak, mahogany, and alder. Mixing it a year later in certain proportions, the result was surely interesting, yet in no way exceptional. My friends however really liked it, describing it as smooth, slightly sweet, and with notes of plum or roses. Even a comparison to cognac was drawn.

Leaning slightly back, listening to my friends talking about the flavors that wood or parts of trees had imparted on food items, was quite a special experience for me. It was great to see that they were interested in the subject, but it also meant that in terms of flavors I wasn't totally imagining things. There were different wooden flavors and some of them were actually considered to be good. So, my taste buds haven't been destroyed by all the experiments!

Additionally, it was most interesting to see the positive reactions of people who don't work in culinary fields, and their willingness to explore and even describe for the first time what they now consciously perceived with their tongue and nose. Actually, they were surprisingly intuitive, describing tastes perfectly by drawing parallels to things they had previously experienced. Was this yet another unexpected, monumental benefit of the lack of a dedicated vocabulary for the description of flavor? Does this make it easily accessible for everyone? I surely hoped so. With enthusiasm like this, there is clearly a great future in flavor linguistics—maybe even one for wooden flavors.

CHAPTER 21
Wood Revolution

Although trees are some 390 million years old, they are still the most striking embodiment of nature's beauty, formed over billions of years by the indefinitely artistic hands of evolution.[228] Defying gravity like no other, ever-growing skywards, they easily outdo most human work in sculptural art. Only powered by the sun, they draw the earth's water, purify, and enrich it before passing it on, one floating droplet at a time. Inhaling what we exhale, trees are the ones that keep us alive in so many ways. From the fertile soils below our feet to the actual food on our table, so much of it originates from a tree's nurturing branches. Their communities create a save haven for two-thirds of the Earth's species, still protecting many from undue discovery.[229] Tirelessly providing numerous cures already, their undiscovered biodiversity will undoubtedly save us from many unknown maladies yet to come.[230] As they are busily storing ever more of our carelessly emitted carbon, forests are the very buffer to a rapidly changing climate. In effect, they are the balance to a system, unsettled by humankind.

We can count ourselves lucky that there are still three trillion trees[231] vigorously fighting in our corner, cleaning and cooling[232] our ever-swelling cities and even calming our youth.[233]

Fortunately, an increasing number of people are realizing that trees are extremely important, not only valuing them for their inherent beauty but also for all the services they provide. Big and small investors alike are finally considering them something worthy of investment,[234] and even in agriculture the word agroforestry (highly productive farming in a three-dimensional forest system) slowly makes the rounds. By growing agricultural plants in a layered system that mimics forests, every story could offer something edible, from the nut trees in the highest layer, the apple trees and the blackberry bushes in the middle layer, and the rhubarb plant, mushrooms and potatoes in the lowest layers, increasing productivity. Scientists have begun experimenting with converting wood cellulose into edible starch or sugars.[235] Even NASA is investigating the conversion of fibrous plant material like wood into edible substances or fuels for their future manned mission to Mars.[236] Cellulose extracted from trees is already extensively used as an additive in processed foods today.[237]

Besides food, wood is already an important base for our chemical industry and will in the future become increasingly important. From the clothes that we wear to the bioplastics of our cars and machinery, everything will be created, to some extent, by using wood.[238] An innovative idea for the use of bark in the insulation of houses instead of petroleum-based material clearly shows what a sustainable future based on trees might resemble.[239] There is even a company making cozy blankets filled with the puffy seeds of poplar trees claiming it to be the warmest textile fiber in the world.[240] Also, technologically mimicking the abilities of some trees would allow for innovation, like copying the processes behind the self-healing properties of a rubber tree to create car paint that buffs itself.[241]

What an enticing future indeed, also in the context of the many flavor riches trees have to offer.

However, in order for this to be not only an alluring idea but actually a sustainable wood revolution, it is of the utmost importance for us to include trees in all aspects of our life. They not only have to be an essential part of our cities, gardens, parks, and landscapes but also of agriculture and industry. They need to be planted in the greatest quantity and diversity as possible. No street, square, road, driveway, or parking lot should exist without them. Roofs, balconies, and patios are also great planting spots and so are the planters in our houses and apartments. Even more important is switching large parts of agriculture to a three-dimensional, tree-based system, something absolutely possible with an ever-developing technology that already now outgrows the need for conventional tractors.[242] Also, replacing industry's need for petroleum with sustainable wooden- and plant-based resources and filling industrial parks with trees will not only be pleasing to our environment but also to the eye.

Only by allowing trees to thrive everywhere around us in much larger numbers and never using them beyond a point that exceeds their natural regrowth rate will ensure a sustainable and delicious wooden future—a future that goes far beyond the time frames we are used to thinking in now, giving us the capacity to thrive for generations to come.

Much like the trees who have been here long before us and will be long after.

Notes

1. Reinhard Trendelenburg et al., Das Holz als Rohstoff, (Berlin: J. F. Lehmanns Verlag, 1939); Fritz Hans Schweingruber, "What is 'Wood'?—An Anatomical Redefinition," *Dendrochronologia* 31, no. 3, (April 2013): 187–191, https://doi.org/10.1016/j.dendro.2013.04.003.

2. L. Vorreiter, *Holztechnologisches Handbuch*, Volume 2, (Vienna and Munich: Verlag Georg Fromme 1949). Republished in *Materials and Corrosion* 10, no. 8, (August 1959), 535–536, https://doi.org/10.1002/maco.19590100813; Schweingruber, "What is 'Wood'?—An Anatomical Redefinition," 187–191.

3. Editors of Encyclopaedia Brittanica, "Wood," *Encyclopaedia Britannica*, October 4, 2014, Online, http://www.britannica.com/EBchecked/topic/647253/wood.

4. Peter Raven and George Johnson, *Biology: Sixth Edition*, (New York: McGraw Hill: 2002).

5. Stephen Langdon, *Sumerian Liturgies and Psalms*, (Philadelphia: The University Museum, 1919).

6. A. C. Bhaktivedanta Swami Prabhupada, *Bhagavad-Gita As It Is*, (Los Angeles: The Bhaktivedanta Book Trust International, 2001).

7. *Nihongi: Chronicles of Japan from the Earliest Times to A.D. 697*, tran. W. G. Aston, (New York: Routledge, 2010); Genesis 8:11 (New International Version); Christopher A. Hall, *Worshiping with the Church Fathers*, (Illinois: IVP Academic, 2009); Quran 7:19.

8. Douglas Forrell Hulmes, "Sacred Trees of Norway and Sweden: A Friluftsliv Quest." Paper presented at A 150 Year International Dialogue Conference Jubilee Celebration, North Troendelag University College, Levanger, Norway, September 2009.

9. Carl G. Jung, "On the history and interpretation of the tree symbol," in *Collected Works of C. G. Jung*, Volume 13. (Princeton: Princeton University Press: 1967), 272–274.

10. Ma Velarde et al., "Health Effects of Viewing Landscapes – Landscape Types in Environmental Psychology," *Urban Forestry & Urban Greening* 6, no. 4, (November 2007): 199–212.

11. Sally Augustin and David Fell, "Wood as a Restorative Material in Healthcare Environments," FPP Innovations, February 2015.

12. C. Kelz et al., "Interior Wood Use in Classrooms Reduces Pupils' Stress Levels." Paper presented at the Proceedings of the 9th Biennial Conference on Environmental Psychology, Eindhoven Technical University, 2011; Hiromi Ohta et al., "Effects of Redecoration of a Hospital Isolation Room with Natural Material on Stress Levels of Denizens in Cold Season," *International Journal of Biometeorology* 52, no. 5, (May 2008): 331–340; David Fell, "Wood and Health in the Built Envi-

ronment," University of British Columbia, 2010; Yuko Tsunetsugu et al., "Physiological Effects in Humans Induced by the Visual Stimulation of Room Interiors with Different Wood Quantities," *Journal of Wood Science* 53, no. 1, (February 2007): 11–16.

13. Qing Li, "Effect of forest bathing trips on human immune function," *Environmental Health and Preventative Medicine* 15, no. 1, (January 2010): 9–17.

14. Karl-Hermann Schmincke, "Forest Industries: crucial for overall socioeconomic development," Food and Agriculture Organization of the United Nations. Accessed October 7, 2014, http://www.fao.org/docrep/v6585e/v6585e08.htm.

15. Arun Agrawal et al., "Economic Contributions on Forests," March 20, 2013, 4. Background Paper 1 for the United Nations Forum of Forests, tenth session, April 8–19, 2013, Istanbul, Turkey.

16. "Chemical composition of alcoholic beverages, additive and contaminants," *IARC Monographs on the Evaluation of Carcinogenic Risks to Humans* 46, no. 1 (1989): 419.

17. Bruce W. Baker and Edward P. Hill, "Beaver (Castor canadensis)," in *Wild Mammals of North America: Biology, Management, and Conservation.* Second Edition. ed. G. A. Feldhamer et al., (Maryland: The John Hopkins University Press, 2003), 288–310.

18. Baker and Hill, "Beaver," 288–310.

19. Baker and Hill, "Beaver," 288–310.

20. José Alvarez-Suarez et al., "The Composition and Biological Activity of Honey: A Focus on Manuka Honey," *Foods*, no. 3, (September 2014): 420–432.

21. "Aboriginal plant use and Technology," Australian National Botanic Gardens Education Service, (2000): 1 –8; Daphne Nash, "Aboriginal plant use in southeastern Australia," Education Services, Australian National Botanic Garden, (February 2004): 1–25; Frederick Webb Hodge, *Handbook of American Indians north of Mexico*, Smithsonian Institution Bureau of American Ethnology, Bulletin 30, Washington (1912); Caroline Sullivan, "Marula," in *Riches of the Forest: For health, life and spirit in Africa, report for the Center for International Forestry Research, edited by Citalli López* and Patricia Shanley, (January 2004): 13–16, http://www.jstor.org/stable/resrep02031.10 ; Citlalli López and Patricia Shanley, *Riches of the Forest: Food, spices, crafts and resins of Asia*, (Indonesia: CIFOR, 2004).

22. Mahdi J., "Medicinal potential of willow: A chemical perspective of aspirin discovery," *Journal of Saudi Chemical Society* 14, no. 3, (July 2010): 317–322. https://doi.org/10.1016/j.jscs.2010.04.010.

23. Hodge, *Handbook of American Indians north of Mexico.*

24. Lars Östlund et al., "Bark-peeling, Food Stress and Tree Spirits—the Use of Pine Inner Bark for Food in Scandinavia and North America," *Journal of Ethnobiology* 29, no. 1, (Spring/Summer 2009): 94–112.

25. Stephen B. Sulavik, "Adirondack of Indians and Mountains 1535–1838," Purple Mountain Press Catskill Blog, http://www.catskill.net/purple/sulavik.htm.

26. Lars Östlund et al., "Bark-peeling," 94-112.

27. Hodge, *Handbook of American Indians north of Mexico.*

28. Lars Östlund et al., "Bark-peeling," 94-112.

29. Jayaram Chandrashekar et al., "The receptors and cells for mammalian taste," *Nature* 444, (November 2006): 288–294.

30. "History," Erasmus Bond, http://erasmus-bond.be/history/; Mike Paterson, "Erasmus Bond, Victorian Man of Mystery," London Historians' Blog, November 15, 2010, "https://londonhistorians.wordpress.com/2010/11/15/erasmus-bond-victorian-man-of-mystery/.

31. Kal Raustiala, "The Imperial Cocktail," *Slate*, August 28, 2013, http://www.slate.com/articles/health_and_science/foreigners/2013/08/gin_and_tonic_kept_the_british_empire_healthy_the_drink_s_quinine_powder.html; Saul Jarcho, *Quinine's Predecessor: Francesco Torti and the Early History of Cinchona*, (Maryland: The Johns Hopkins University Press, 1993).

32. Asifa Majid and Stephen C. Levinson, "The Senses in Language and Culture," *The Senses and Society* 6, no. 1 (2011): 5–18.

33. Ray Jackendoff, "How did Language Begin?," Linguistic Society of America, http://www.linguisticsociety.org/content/how-did-language-begin.

34. Steven Connor, "The Menagerie of the Senses," *The Senses and Society* 1, no. 1, (March 2006): 9–26; Viktoria von Hoffman, "The Rise of Taste and the Rhetorics of Celebration," in *Celebrations: Proceedings of the 2011 Oxford Symposium of Food & Cookery*, ed. Mark McWilliams, (London: Prospect Books, 2012), 356–363; Viktoria von Hoffmann, *Goûter Le Monde: Une Histoire Culturelle Du Goût À L'époque Moderne*, (Paris: Peter Lang, 2013).

35. Giorgio Vasari, *The Lives of the Most Excellent Painters, Sculptors, and Architects*, tran. Gaston du C. de Vere, (New York: Modern Library: 2006).

36. Hoffmann, *Goûter Le Monde.*

37. Elihu Dwight Church and George Watson Cole, *A Catalog of Books Relating to the Discovery and Early History of North and South America Forming a Part of the Library of E. D. Church*, (New York: Dodd, Mead and Company: 1907), Archived online: https://archive.org/stream/catalogueofbooks01churrich/catalogueofbooks01churrich_djvu.txt.

38. John E. Staller, *Maize Cobs and Cultures: History of Zea mays L.*, (Berlin: Springer 2010).

39. Jennifer Meagher, "Still-Life Painting in Southern Europe, 1600–1800," in *Heilbrunn Timeline of Art History*, (New York: The Metropolitan Museum of Art, 2008). Online, June 2008, https://www.metmuseum.org/toah/hd/sstl/hd_sstl.htm; Walter Liedtke, "Still-Life Painting in Northern Europe, 1600–1800," in *Heilbrunn Timeline of Art History*, (New York: The Metropolitan Museum of Art, 2008). Online, October 2003, https://www.metmuseum.org/toah/hd/nstl/hd_nstl.htm.

40. Francois Pierre De La Varenne, *La Varenne's Cookery: The French Cook, The French Pastry Chef, The French Confectioner*, tran. Terence Scully (London: Prospect Books, 2006).

41. Hoffmann, "The Rise of Taste," 356–363.

42. De La Varenne, *La Varenne's Cookery.*

43. Hoffmann, "The Rise of Taste," 356–363.

44. *François Massialot, The Court and Country Cook: Giving New and Plain Directions How to Order All Manner of Entertainments*, tran. J. K. (London: Black Swan 1702). Original from The British Library, digitized April 2, 2015, https://books.google.com/books/about/The_Court_and_Country_Cook_Giving_New_an.html?id=7bhbnQEACAAJ.

45. Nicholas J. Enfield, "A Taste in Two Tongues: A Southeast Asia Study of Semantic Convergence," *The Senses and Society* 6, no. 1, (February 2011): 30–37.

46. Majid and Levinson, "The Senses in Language and Culture," 5–18.

47. E. E. Evans-Pritchard, "Ideophones in Zande," *Sudan Notes and Records* 34, no. 1, (1962): 143–146.

48. Mark Dingemanse, "Ideophones and the Aesthetics of Everyday Language in a West-African Society," *The Senses and Society* 6, no. 1, (2011): 77-85.

49. Majid and Levinson, "The Senses in Language and Culture," 5–18.

50. Johann Wolfgang von Goethe, *Italienische Reise*, (Germany: 1816), 151–240.

51. Wikipedia contributors, "Naples," Wikipedia, The Free Encyclopedia, https://en.wikipedia.org/wiki/Naples.

52. Wikipedia contributors, "Pulcinella," Wikipedia, The Free Encyclopedia, https://en.wikipedia.org/wiki/Pulcinella.

53. Goethe, *Italienische Reise*, 151–240.

54. Formisano SAS, "Formisano 'legnaioli Da Tre Generazioni' Facebook Page," Facebook, https://www.facebook.com/Formisano-legnaioli-Da-Tre-Generazioni -698805890212426/.

55. European commission, "Forests have long-term cooling effect during heat-waves," Science for Environment Policy News Alert, no. 220, (December 2010): 1.

56. Michael Sanderson et al., "Relationships between forests and weather," report for the European Commission, (August 2012): 1–36.

57. "Maple Tempura," Hisakuni Kousendou, http://www.hisakuni.net/process .htm.

58. Maya Hey (@heymayahey), "Sushi wrapped in persmission leaves," Instagram photo, December 7, 2015, https://www.instagram.com/p/_AV8fQKxCx/?taken-by= heymayahey&hl=en.

59. "Kakinoha-zushi: Nara's Local Delicacy that is a Must-Try for Visitors!" Japan Info, February 20, 2016, http://jpninfo.com/42873.

60. W.A. Janendra M. De Costa et al., "Ecophysiology of Tea," *Brazilian Journal of Plant Physiology* 19, no. 4, (October 2007), http://dx.doi.org/10.1590/S1677 -04202007000400005.

61. Tim Adams, "Portrait of the perfect dealer," *The Guardian*, March 1, 2008, https://www.theguardian.com/artanddesign/2008/mar/02/artnews.anthonydoffay.

62. Martha J. Miller, "Firsts + Lasts: Timothy d'Offay," Ethno Traveler, August 2012, http://www.ethnotraveler.com/2012/08/firsts-lasts-timothy-doffay/.

63. "Home," Postcard Teas, www.postcardteas.com.

64. Jeff Koehler, *Darjeeling: The Colorful History and Precarious Fate of the World's Greatest Tea*, (New York: Bloomsbury, 2015).

65. Iris MacFarlane and Alan MacFarlane, *The Empire of Tea*, (New York: The Overlook Press, 2003).

66. Koehler, *Darjeeling*.

67. M. K. Meegahakumbura et al., "Indications for Three Independent Domestication Events for the Tea Plant (Camellia sinesis (L.) O. Kuntze) and New Insights into the Origin of Tea Germplasm in China and India Revealed by Nuclear Microsatellites," *PLoS One* 11, no. 5, (May 2016), https://doi.org/10.1371/journal.pon .0155369.

68. Amy Hopkins, "Johnnie Walker is named most powerful drinks brand," The Spirits Business, June 3, 2014, http://www.thespiritsbusiness.com/2014/06/johnnie-walker-named-most-powerful-drinks-brand/.

69. "The Johnnie Walker Story," Johnnie Walker, https://www.johnniewalker.com/en/the-world-of-johnnie-walker/the-world-of-johnnie-walker/.

70. Giles MacDonough, "Walking Tall," *Cigar Aficionado, The Good Life Magazine for Men*, Winter 1996, https://www.cigaraficionado.com/article/walking-tall-7582.

71. Inge Russell, Graham Stewart, and Charles Bamforth, *Whisky: Technology, Production and Marketing*, (Massachusetts: Academic Press, 2003).

72. "Whisky," *Addicted to Pleasure*, season 1, episode 4. Directed by Tim Niel. Presented by Brian Cox. BBC 1: 2012.

73. Russell et al., *Whisky*.

74. "Whisky," *Addicted to Pleasure*.

75. Russell et al., *Whisky*.

76. "Whisky," *Addicted to Pleasure*.

77. Drinks International, "The Millionaires Club: The Definitive Ranking of the World's Million-Case Spirits Brands," Agile Media Ltd., 2018.

78. Doris Reinthaler and Eva Sommer, "Obstler in Österreich," Culinary Heritage Austria, report for the Federal Ministry for Sustainability and Tourism, June 11, 2010, https://www.bmnt.gv.at/land/lebensmittel/trad-lebensmittel/getraenke/obstler.html.

79. "Basic Information: Whiskey-Erlebniswelt," Whiskey-Erlesbniswelt, https://www.whiskyerlebniswelt.at/MEDIA/basic%20information_english.pdf.

80. Editors of Encyclopaedia Brittanica, "Distillation" *Encyclopaedia Brittanica*, February 21, 2016, Online, https://www.britannica.com/science/distillation

81. https://www.wikiart.org/en/marc-chagall/all-works.

82. Irving Lewis Allen, *The City in Slang: New York Life and Popular Speech*, (New York: Oxford University Press, 1995).

83. Tom Sandham, "Forget about old single malt – give No Age Statement (NAS) whisky a try," *The Telegraph*, June 22, 2016, http://www.telegraph.co.uk/food-and-drink/whisky/forget-about-old-single-malts—-give-no-age-statement-nas-whisky/.

84. Murli Dharmadhikari, "Oak Wood Composition," *Vineyard & Vintage View* 10, no. 2, (1995): 1–4.

85. Eric Meier, "Hardwood Anatomy," The Wood Database, http://www.wood-database.com/wood-articles/hardwood-anatomy/.

86. Dharmadhikari, "Oak Wood Composition"

87. J. R. Mosedale, et al., "Variation in the composition and content of ellagitannins in the heartwood of European oaks (*Quercus robur* and *Q petraea*). A comparison of two French forests and variation with heartwood age," *Ann Sci For* 53, no. 1 (1966): 1005–1018.

88. E. Dambrine et al., "Present forest biodiversity patterns in France related to former Roman agriculture," *Ecology* 88, no. 6, (June 2007): 1430–1439, https://doi.org/10.1890/05-1314.

89. Björn C. G. Karlsson and Ran Friedman, "Dilution of whisky – the molecular perspective," *Scientific Reports* 7, no. 1. (August 2017).

90. "Company," Velier SpA, http://www.velier.it/azienda/; "Luca you are my friend, you are my brother, you are my son," Interview with Luca Gargano, DuRhum, http://durhum.com/EN/LucaGargano_en.html; "The Institute," The National Institute of Origin and Quality, http://www.inao.gouv.fr/eng/The-National-Institute-of-origin-and-quality-Institut-national-de-l-origine-et-de-la-qualite-INAO.

91. "What is a Scotch Whiskymaker?" Compass Box Scotch Whiskymaker, http://www.compassboxwhisky.com/whiskymakers/index.php#wm_link.

92. Paolo Bernardini, *The Etruscans Outside Etruria*, tran. Thomas Michael Hartmann, (Los Angeles: J. Paul Getty Museum: 2004).

93. Steven A. Epstein, *Genoa and the Genoese, 958–1528*, (North Carolina: The University of North Carolina Press: 1996).

94. Epstein, *Genoa and the Genoese*.

95. Editors of Encyclopaedia Brittanica, "Genoa, Italy," *Encyclopaedia Brittanica*, June 1, 2017, Online, https://www.britannica.com/place/Genoa-Italy.

96. *Il Maestro della tela jeans*, Galerie Canesso, catalog, (Parais: 2013); "'Master of Blue Jeans' Holds Key to Fashion Riddle," *Independent*, September 25, 2010, http://www.independent.co.uk/life-style/fashion/master-of-blue-jeans-holds-key-to -fashion-riddle-2089247.html.

97. "Production," Clairin, The Spirit of Haiti, http://www.thespiritofhaiti.com /en/production/.

98. "Homepage," Mapa Da Cachaca, http://www.mapadacachaca.com.br.

99. "Trending: Why Old-School Drinking Vinegars Are Making a Comeback Now," Plated, https://www.plated.com/morsel/trending-old-school-drinking-vinegars -making-comeback-now/.

100. Henry H. Work, *Wood, Whisky and Wine—A History of Barrels*, (London: Reaktion Books, 2014).

101. "The chemistry behind the character of bourbon, scotch and rye," American Chemical Society, September 9, 2013, accessed October 20, 2014, http://phys.org /news/2013-09-chemistry-character-bourbon-scotch-rye.html.

102. Commission on Genetic Resources for Food and Agriculture, "The State of the World's Forest Genetic Resources," report for the Food and Agriculture Organization of the United Nations, 2014.

103. "The chemistry behind the character of bourbon, scotch and rye," American Chemical Society.

104. Ellen McCrady, "The Nature of Lignin," *Alkaline Paper Advocate* 4, no. 4, (November 1991).

105. Anna Ilnicka and Jerzy P. Lukaszewicz, "Discussion remarks on the role of wood and chitin constituents during carbonization," *Front. Mater.* 2, no. 20, (March 2015), https://doi.org/10.3389/fmats.2015.00020.

106. "Wood and Finishes," Glenmorangie Distillery, Paper presented at International Barrel Symposium, St. Louis, Missouri, May 1997.

107. "Chemical composition of alcoholic beverages, additive and contaminants," 419.

108. "Wood and Finishes," Glenmorangie Distillery.

109. Nirupa Chaudhari and Stephen D. Roper, "The cell biology of taste," *Journal of Cell Biology* 190, no. 3, (August 2010): 285.

110. Joel Beckerman and Tyler Gray, *The Sonic Boom: How Sound Transforms the Way We Think, Feel, and Buy*, (New York: Houghton Mifflin Harcourt, 2014).

111. Kate Fox, "The Smell Report: An overview of facts and findings," Social Issues Research Centre, Online, http://www.sirc.org/publik/smell_human.html.

112. David V. Smith and Robert F. Margolskee, "Making Sense of Taste," *Scientific American*, September 1, 2006, https://www.scientificamerican.com/article /making-sense-of-taste-2006-09/.

113. Christoph Borgans, "Scent of the Wild," *Frankfurter Allgemeine Zeitung*, January 1, 2015, http://www.faz.net/aktuell/stil/leib-seele/der-parfuemeur-severac-sucht-in-asien-nach-neuen-geruechen-13309248.html. [Translated from the German.]

114. American Chemical Society, "New Perfume Fixatives," *Chemical Engineering News* 19, no. 20, (October 1941): 1134.

115. Glen Brechbill, *Perfume Bases & Fragrance Ingredients*, (New Jersey: Fragrance Books Inc, 2009).

116. Brechbill, *Perfume Bases & Fragrance Ingredients*.

117. Mark Barton Frank et al., "Frankincense oil derived from *Boswellia carteri* induces tumor cell specific cytotoxicity," *BMC Complementary and Alternative Medicine* 9, no. 6 (March 2009), https://doi.org/10.1186/1472-6882-9-6.

118. Jeremy Howell, "Frankincense: Could it be a cure for cancer?" BBC News, February 9, 2010, http://news.bbc.co.uk/2/hi/middle_east/8505251.stm.

119. Howell, "Frankincense."

120. Masakuzu Kashio and Dennis V. Johnson, "Monograph on benzoin (Balsamic resin from Styrax species)," Food and Agricultural Organizations of the United Nations, Regional Office for Asian and Pacific Publication 21, (2001).

121. "The Mysterious Oud Wood & Its Ancient Heritage + M. Micallef 'Three Oud' Perfume Draw," Ca Fleure Bon, March 3, 2011, http://www.cafleurebon.com/the-mysterious-oud-wood-its-ancient-heritage-m-micallef-three-oud-perfume-draw/.

122. Robert A. Blanchette et al., "Growing *Aquilaria* and Production of Agarwood in Hill Agro-ecosystems," in *Integrated Land Use Management in the Eastern Himalayas*, ed. K. Eckman and L. Ralte, (India: Akansha Publishing House Delhi: 2015), 66–82.

123. Gerard A. Persoon, "Agarwood: the life of a wounded tree," IIAS Newsletter 45, no. 1 (Autumn 2007): 24–25.

124. Dinah Jung, The Cultural Biography of Agarwood – Perfumary in Eastern Asia and the Asian Neighbourhood," *Journal of the Royal Asiatic Society* 23, no. 1, (January 2013): 103–125, https://doi.org/10.1017/S1356186313000047.

125. Wikipedia contributors, "Incense Route," Wikipedia, The Free Encyclopedia, https://en.wikipedia.org/wiki/Incense_Route.

126. Persoon, "Agarwood," 24–25.

127. Huynh Van My and Ha Nguyen, "Local farmer taps into fragrant wood industry," *Vietnam News*, August 9, 2015, http://vietnamnews.vn/sunday/features/274326/local-farmer-taps-into-fragrant-wood-industry.html.

128. Dinah Jung, "The Value of Agarwood – Reflections Upon Its Use and History in South Yemen." Research paper, extended version of talk given at the workshop "The Use of Herbs in Yemeni Healing Practices," Halle, Germany, September 25–26, 2009.

129. Persoon, "Agarwood," 24–25.

130. Denyse J. Snelder and Rodel D. Lasco, Smallholder Tree Growing for Rural *Development and Environmental Services: Lessons from Asia, Advances in Agroforestry*, (New York: Springer, 2008).

131. *Der Duftjäger*, Film by Bernd Girrbach and Rolf Lambert, SWR: 2009.

132. "Home," That Hungry Chef, last updated 2018, http://www.thathungrychef.com/.

133. "Teak," The Wood Database, http://www.wood-database.com/lumber-identification/hardwoods/teak/.

134. Marco Biscella, "'Happy Villages' at the top on the Via del Brennero, *Il*

Sole 24 Ore, August 17, 2015, https://www.ilsole24ore.com/art/commenti-e-idee /2015-08-17/borghi-felici-top-via-brennero-063641.shtml?uuid=ACYQ8ai. [Translated from the Italian.]

135. "Überetscher Architectural Style," Kaltern Caldaro, http://www.kaltern .com/de/ueberetscher-baustil.html.

136. Elmar M. Lorey, "The Pharmacy in the Vineyard: The secret of the vine tears and their history as a folk remedy," *Rheingau-Forum* 14, no. 1, (2005): 13–23. [Translated from the German.]

137. "Google Maps," 2018, Google, Inc., https://www.google.at/maps/@46 .5169544,11.3570935,3a,75y,20.1h,78.62t/data=!3m6!1e1!3m4!1sQzzpCfTn0hK 72nLmC332Rw!2e0!7i13312!8i6656!6m1!1e1.

138. Armin Torggler, "Mittelalterliche Verkehrswege," *Interessantes aus Runkelstein*, 003.

139. Armin Torggler, "Von Handel und hoher Diplomatie," *Interessantes aus Runkelstein*.

140. "Homepage," Runkelstein Castle," http://www.runkelstein.info/curiosities .asp.

141. "Larch," Woodland Investment Management Ltd., Last updated 2018, http://www.woodlands.co.uk/blog/tree-identification/larch/

142. "Civic Crowdfunding / Art," Citta di Bra, http://www.comune.bra.cn.it /index.php?option=com_content&view=article &id=62&Itemid=268. [Translated from the Italian.]

143. "Goat Cheese Recipe with Ash," New England Cheesemaking Supply Company, http://www.cheesemaking.com/GoatWithAsh.html

144. W. Östberg, "We eat trees: tree planting and land rehabilitation in West Pokot District, Kenya. A baseline study," Uppsala: Swedish University of Agricultural Sciences, International Rural Development Centre, Working Paper 82.

145. Francesco Amato and Stefano Scarafia, "Living Food Communities: Kenya," Slow Food, YouTube video, 23:19. Posted November 25, 2011, https://www .youtube.com/watch?v=bCKmQlF9-C8.

146. Amato and Scarafia, "Living Food Communities: Kenya," YouTube video.

147. Ruth Spitzenpfeil, "The Killer Cucumber," The New Zurich Times, August 28, 2014, https://www.nzz.ch/gesellschaft/lebensart/genuss/die-killer-gurke-1.18372447. [Translated from the German.]

148. Marin Neumann, "Sorben (Wenden): A Brandenburg Minority and its Thematization in the Classroom," report for the Center for Teacher Education at the University of Potsdam, (February 2008): 1–56; Christel Lehmann-Enders, *Nicht rumgurken, sondern reinbeissen!: Das echte Spreewälder Gurkenbuch*, (Germany: Heimat-Verlag Lübben, 1998); "Homepage," Spreewald Lehde, http://www.spreewald -lehde.de/.

149. "The Year 1500," City Lübbenau, http://www.luebbenau-spreewald .de/760.html.

150. Lehmann-Enders, *Nicht rumgurken, sondern reinbeissen!*

151. Jørn Gry et al., *Cucurbitacins in plant food*, (Copenhagen: Tema Nord, 2006).

152. Brian A. Nummer, "Getting Crisp Home Pickled Vegetables," *Food and Nutrition*, Utah State University Cooperative Extension, (August 2016): 1–2.

153. "Die Steinerne Brücke," Stadt Regensburg, City of Regensburg, https:/ /www.regensburg.de/rathaus/aemterueebersicht/planungs-u-baureferat/tiefbauamt

/aktuelle-massnahmen/2010-2018-instandsetzung-der-steinernen-bruecke; "World Heritage Regensburg," UNESCO World Heritage Regensburg, https://www.regensburg .de/welterbe/welterbe-regensburg/geschichte.

154. "Homepage," Wurstkuchl, http://www.wurstkuchl.de.

155. "Cappuccino Stout," Lagunitas, https://lagunitas.com/beers/cappuccino-stout.

156. "Chocolate Stout," Rogue, http://buy.rogue.com/chocolate-stout/.

157. "Grapefruit Sculpin," Ballast Point Brewing Co., https://www .ballast-point.com/beer/grapefruit-sculpin/.

158. "Strawberry Rhubarb Sour Ale," Great Divide Brewing Co., https://great-divide.com/beers/strawberry-rhubarb/.

159. "Goose Island Maple Bacon Stout," RateBeer, https://www.ratebeer.com /beer/goose-island-maple-bacon-stout/119778/.

160. "Beer Styles Study Guide," The Brewers Association, www.craftbeer .com/beer/beer-style-guide.

161. Hans Michael Esslinger, *Handbook of Brewing: Processes, Technology, Markets*, (Hoboken: John Wiley & Sons, 2009).

162. "Pitching Barrels," Pilsner Urquell, http://pilsnerurquell.com/it/article/ pitching-barrels.

163. William Littell Tizard, *The Theory and Practice of Brewing: Illustrated*, (London, 1857), digitized by archive.org, https://archive.org/details/b28053412; Robert Scherer, Casein: Its Preparation and Technical Utilisation, tran. Charles Salter, (London: Scott, Greenwood & Son: 1906).

164. Work, *Wood, Whisky and Wine*.

165. "Welcome," Hopfenland Hallertau, https://www.hopfenland-hallertau.de.

166. "Schneider Weisse Tap X Mein Aventinus Barrique – Larchtree Barrel," RateBeer, https://www.ratebeer.com/beer/schneider-weisse-tap-x-mein-aventinus-barrique—larchtree-barrel/437023/.

167. "Schneider Weisse Tap X Mein Aventinus Barrique – Grande Cru Larch Barrel," Beeradvocate, "https://www.beeradvocate.com/beer/profile/72/241443/.

168. "Aventinus Barrique Larchtree," Untappd, https://untappd.com/b/weisses-brauhaus-g-schneider-sohn-aventinus-barrique-larchtree/1348827.

169. "Traditional Balsamic Vinegar of Modena," Acetaia di Giorgio, http://www .acetaiadigiorgio.it/en/.

170. "How It Is Produced," Balsamic Vinegar of Modena, Consorzio Balsamico, http://www.consorziobalsamico.it/balsamic-vinegar-of-modena/how-it-is-produced /?lang=en; "Excellent Quality: Grapes, Wisdom and Practice of Modena," Consorzio Tutela, http://www.balsamicotradizionale.it/prodotto.asp. [Translated from the Italian.]; "Rating Systems," Balsamic Vinegar Guide, https:// balsamicvinegarguide .com/rating-systems/.

171. "Consorzio Produttori Antiche Acetaie," booklet from Traditional Balsamic Vinegar of Modena P.D.O., 41-45.

172. "How It Is Produced," Balsamic Vinegar of Modena.

173. Shannon R. McCarragher et al., "Geographic Variation of Germination, Growth, and Mortality in Sugar Maple (*Acer saccharum*): Common Garden and Reciprocal Dispersal Experiments," *Physical Geography* 32, no 1. (2011): 1–21, https://doi.org/10.2747/0272-3646.32.1.1.

174. Jonathan Reynolds, "Will maple syrup disappear?," *Canadian Geographic*,

October 1, 2010, https://www.canadiangeographic.ca/article/will-maple-syrup
-disappear.

175. Bruce Stewart et al., "Selected Nova Scotia old-growth forests: Age, Ecology, structure, scoring," *Forestry Chronicle* 79, no. 3, (June 2003): 632–644.

176. "History of the National Flag of Canada," Government of Canada, July 25, 2018, http://canada.pch.gc.ca/eng/1444133232512.

177. "Canada's new $20 bill at centre of maple leaf flap," CBC News, January 18, 2013, http://www.cbc.ca/news/canada/ottawa/canada-s-new-20-bill-at-centre-of
-maple-leaf-flap-1.1343767.

178. Randall B. Heiligmann et al., *North American Maple Syrup Producers Manual Second Edition*, (Ohio: The Ohio State University: 2006).

179. John D. Speth, "When Did Humans Learn to Boil?," *PaleoAnthropology* 13, no. 1. (2015): 54-67.

180. Robert H. Keller, "America's Native Sweet: Chippewa Treaties and the Right to Harvest Maple Sugar," *American Indian Quarterly* 13, no. 2, (Spring 1989): 117–135.

181. Alexandra Marshack, "A Lunar-Solar Year Calendar Stick from North America," *American Antiquity* 50, no. 1, (January 1985): 27–51.

182. Annette Chretien, "Aboriginal Maple Syrup Values Report," (Article, Wilfrid Laurier University, Canada, 2014).

183. Isabell Graf et al., "Multiscale model of a freeze–thaw process for tree sap exudation," *Journal of the Royal Society Interface* 12, no. 111, (October 2015); D. Cirelli et al., "Toward an improved model of maple sap exudation: the location and role of osmotic barriers in sugar maple, butternut and white birch," *Tree Physiol* 28, no. 12, (August 2008): 1145–1155; Timothy R. Wilmot, "Maples under pressure," *Farming, The Journal of Northeast Agriculture* 16, no. 1, (March 2009).

184. Timothy R. Wilmot, "The Timing of Tapping for Maple Sap Collection," *Maple Syrup Digest 1*, no. 1., (June 2008): 20–27.

185. Heiligmann et al., *North American Maple Syrup Producers Manual Second Edition*.

186. Choe Sang-Hun, "In South Korea, Drinks Are on the Maple Tree," *The New York Times*, March 5, 2009, https://www.nytimes.com/2009/03/06/world/asia/06maple.html.

187. Ingvar Svanberg, et al., "Uses of tree saps in northern and eastern parts of Europe," *Acta Societatis Botanicorum Poloniae* 81, no 4. (2012), https://doi.org/10.5586/asbp.2012.036.

188. D. Cirelli D. "Toward an improved model of maple sap exudation."

189. Wikipedia contributors, "Räter," Wikipedia, Die freie Enzyklopädie, https://de.wikipedia.org/wiki/Räter#Das_.E2.80.9ER.C3.A4tergebiet.E2.80 .9C; H. L. Werneck, "Ur- und frühgeschichtliche Roggenfunde in den Ostalpen und am Ostrande des Böhmerwaldes," *Der Züchter* 21, no. 4–5, (April 1951): 107–108, https://doi.org/10.1007/BF00709562. [Translated from the German; article: "Prehistoric and prehistoric rye finds in the Eastern Alps and on the eastern edge of the Bohemian Forest."]

190. Jean-Frederic Terral et al., "Evolution and history of grapevine (Vitis vinifera) under domestication: new morphometric perspectives to understand seed domestication syndrome and reveal origins of ancient European cultivars," Annals of Botany 105, no. 3, (March 2010): 443–455, https://doi.org/10.1093/aob/mcp298;

Patrick E. McGovern, *Ancient Wine: The Search for the Origins of Viniculture*, (New Jersey: Princeton University Press, 2007).

191. McGovern, *Ancient Wine*.

192. Wikipedia contributors, "Google Trends," Wikipedia, The Free Encyclopedia, https://en.wikipedia.org/wiki/Google_Trends.

193. Google Trends, "Compare: wine taste, beer taste, cheese taste, chocolate taste, whiskey taste," https://trends.google.com/trends/explore?date=all &q=wine %20taste,beer %20taste,cheese%20taste,chocolate%20taste,whiskey%20taste.

194. Ann C. Noble, "What is the Wine Aroma Wheel?," The Official Website of the Wine Aroma Wheel, http://www.winearomawheel.com.

195. Bianca Bosker, *Cork Dork: A Wine-Fueled Adventure Among the Obsessive Sommeliers, Big Bottle Hunters, and Rogue Scientists Who Taught Me to Live for Taste*, (New York: Penguin Books, 2017).

196. Adam Conover, "Adam Ruins Everything—Why Wine Snobs are Faking it," YouTube video, 4:23. Posted October 26, 2015. https://www.youtube.com/watch ?v=5PeKcWCC-tw.

197. "History," Manicor, http://www.manincor.com/en/history.html.

198. "Biodynamics," Manicor, http://www.manincor.com/en/biodynamics.html.

199. Emmanuelle Vaudour et al., "An overview of the recent approaches to terroir functional modelling, footprinting and zoning," *SOIL* 1, no. 1, (March 2015): 287–312.

200. Katie Forster, "Turn, Italy's first 'vegetarian city'," *The Guardian*, December 11, 2016, https://www.theguardian.com/lifeandstyle/2016/dec/11/turin-italys-first -vegetarian-city.

201. Michael Loizides et al., "Desert Truffles: the mysterious jewels of antiquity," *Field Mycology* 13, no.1, (January 2012): 17–21; Wikipedia contributors, "Manna," Wikipedia, The Free Encyclopedia, https://en.wikipedia.org/wiki/Manna.

202. Paul Stamets, *Mycelium Running: How Mushrooms Can Help Save the World*, (Berkeley, California: Ten Speed Press, 2005).

203. Aziz Türkoglu et al., "New records of truffle fungi (Basidiomycetes) from Turkey," *Turkish Journal of Botany* 37, no. 5, (January 2013): 970–976.

204. S.V. Kshirsagar et al., "Comparative Study of Human and Animal Hair in Relations with Diameter and Medullary Index," *Indian Journal of Forensic Medicine and Pathology* 2, no. 3, (July–September 2009): 105–108.

205. Catarina Henke et al., "Hartig' net formation of *Tricholoma vaccinum*-spruce ectomycorrhiza in hydroponic cultures," *Environmental Science and Pollution Research* 22, no. 24, (December 2015): 19394–19399; Thibaut Payen et al., "Truffle Phylogenomics: New Insights into Truffle Evolution and Truffle Life Cycle," in *Fungi*. (Massachusetts: Academic Press: 2014), 70; Francis Martin et al., "Périgord black truffle genome uncovers evolutionary origins and mechanisms of symbiosis," *Nature* 464, no. 1, (April 2010): 1033–1038.

206. Lukasz Pawlik et al., "Roots, Rock, and Regolith: Biomechanical and Biochemical Weathering by Trees and its Impact on Hillslopes—A Critical Literature Review," *Earth-Science Reviews* 159, no. 1, (June 2016): 142–159.

207. Manuela Giovannetti et al., "At the Root of the Wood Wide Web: Self Recognition and Non-Self Incompatibility in Mycorrhizal Networks," *Plant Signaling & Behavior* 1, no. 1 (January/February 2006): 1–5.

208. "The Most Valuable Substances in the World by Weight," *The Telegraph*,

May 29, 2018, http://www.telegraph.co.uk/business/2016/05/18/the-most-valuable
-substances-in-the-world-by-weight/white-truffle/.

209. Wikipedia contributors, "Elfin saddle," Wikipedia, The Free Encyclopedia, https://en.wikipedia.org/wiki/Elfin_saddle.

210. Abby Rogers, "The 12 Most Expensive Foods on the Planet," *Business Insider*, May 8, 2012, http://www.businessinsider.com/most-expensive-foods-2012-5?IR=T #european-white-truffles-sell-for-up-to-3600-per-pound-truffle-farmers-use-dogs-to -hunt-for-the-truffles-which-grow-wild-underground-at-the-base-of-an-oak-tree-8.

211. "Homepage," Willi Schmid, http://www.willischmid.ch/.

212. "Disciplinary Fine Regulation," The Federal Council, Portal of the Swiss Government, last updated: May 7, 2017, https://www.admin.ch/opc/de/classified -compilation/19960142/index.html. [Translated from the German.]

213. Franz Welte, "Exhausted," *St. Galler Nachrichten*, November 26, 2015, http://www.st-galler-nachrichten.ch/st-gallen/detail/article/ausgeschoepft-0068710/. [Translated from the German.]

214. Jacek Rokicki, *Entwicklungen und Perspektiven der Schweizer Uhrenindustri*, (Germany: GRIN Verlag, 2007).

215. Judy Ridgway, *The Cheese Companion: A Connoisseur's Guide*, (New York: Running Press: 2004).

216. Catherine Donnelly, *The Oxford Companion to Cheese*, (New York: Oxford University Press: 2016).

217. Barry A. Law and Adnan Y. Tamime, *Technology of Cheesemaking: Second Edition*, (New York: John Wiley & Sons, 2010).

218. Thomas Burmeister, "The schnapps barrel of the St. Bernard is a legend," *Welt*, June 7, 2014, https://www.welt.de/geschichte/article128808857/Das-Schnaps-fass-der-Bernhardiner-ist-eine-Legende.html. [Translated from the German.]

219. Johann Heinrich Ferdinand von Autenrieth, Gründliche Anleitung zur Brotzubereitung aus Holz, 2 Aufl. 1834, 8.

220. John B. Hall and Susan Silver, "Nutrition and Feeding of the Cow-Calf Herd: Digestive System of the Cow," Virginia Cooperative Extension, Publication 400-010.

221. Samuel Chaffron and Christian von Mering, "Termites in the wood-work," *Genome Biology* 8, no. 11, (November 2007): 229.

222. Gunter Pauli, *The Blue Economy: 10 Years, 100 Innovations, 100 Million Jobs*, (St. Paul: Paradigm Publications, 2010).

223. Marusczyk I., Da Capo, Stradivari.

224. Francis W. M. R. Schwarze, "Wood decay under the microscope," *Fungal Biology Reviews* 21, no. 4, (November 2007).

225. F. C. Miller, "Production of Mushrooms from Wood Waste Substrates," in *Forest Products Biotechnology*, eds. Alan Bruce and John Palfreyman, (London: Taylor & Francis, 1998), 197–208.

226. "Edible Wood – A Modern Delicacy with Rustic Flair," Molecular Recipes, May 14, 2014, http://www.molecularrecipes.com/molecular-gastronomy/edible-wood-modern-delicacy-rustic-flair/.

227. Anna Sigrithur and Avery MacGuire, "Tree bark," Nordic Food Lab, November 24, 2015, http://nordicfoodlab.org/blog/2015/11/24/tree-bark.

228. Peter Thomas, *Trees: Their Natural History*, (Massachusetts: Cambridge University Press, 2000).

229. Xingli Giam, "Global biodiversity loss from tropical deforestation," *Proceedings of the National Academy of Sciences of the United States of America* 114, no. 23, (June 6, 2017): 5775–5777, https://doi.org/10.1073/pnas.1706264114.

230. Karin Pollack, "Medicinal Plants: 'There is really a treasure to raise'," *Der Standard,* July 4, 2015, http://derstandard.at/2000018540731/Heilpflanzen-Da-ist-tatsaechlich-ein-Schatz-zu-heben. [Translated from the German.]

231. Thomas W. Crowther et al., "Mapping tree density at a global scale," *Nature* 525, no. 1, (September 2015): 201–205.

232. Patrick Barkham, "Introducing 'treeconomics': how street trees can save our cities," *The Guardian,* August 15, 2015, https://www.theguardian.com/cities/2015/aug/15/treeconomics-street-trees-cities-sheffield-itree?CMP=Share_iOSApp_Other.

233. Christine Tragler, "Off to the countryside, aggressive youth!," *Der Standard*, July 2, 2016, http://derstandard.at/2000040209678/Aggressive-Teenager-b-ins-Gruene?ref=article. [Translated from the German.]

234. Tim Gray, "Forests Are a Treasure. But Are They Good Investments?," *The New York Times,* January 13, 2017, https://mobile.nytimes.com/2017/01/13/business/mutfund/forests-are-a-treasure-but-are-they-good-investments.html?emc=edit_th_20170115&nl=todaysheadlines&nlid=66720088&_r=1&referer=http://m-facebook.com.

235. Chun You et al., "Enzymatic transformation of nonfood biomass to starch," *Proceedings of the National Academy of Sciences of the United States of America* 110, no. 18, (April 2013): 7182–7187, https://doi.org/10.1073/pnas.1302420110.

236. Ruth Dasso Marlaire, NASA. July 30, 2009. "NASA Studies Cellulose for Food and Biofuel Production," https://www.nasa.gov/centers/ames/news/releases/2009/M09-93AR.html

237. Allison Aubrey, "From McDonald's to Organic Valley, You're Probably Eating Wood Pulp," *Morning Edition,* NPR, July 10, 2014, http://www.npr.org/sections/thesalt/2014/07/10/329767647/from-mcdonalds-to-organic-valley-youre-probably-eating-wood-pulp.

238. "Resource Wood," National Research Programme NRP 66, http://www.nfp66.ch/en; Rudolf Hermann, "Finland's forest industry reinvents itself," May 25, 2016, *The New Zurich Times,* https://www.nzz.ch/wirtschaft /wirtschaftspolitik/innovationen-aus-dem-wald-finnlands-forstindustrie-erfindet-sich-neu-ld.84529. [Translated from the German.]

239. "The Bark Visionary," Schrodinger's Cat, August 13, 2015, https://www.schroedingerskatze.at/der-rinden-visionaer/. [Translated from the German.]

240. "Pappelflaum," Pappella, http://pappella.de/pappelflaum/pappelflaum.php.

241. Diemut Klärner, "The self-healing power of plant juices," *Frankfurter Allgemeine Zeitung,* December 29, 2014, http://www.faz.net/aktuell/wissen/natur/bionik-die-selbstheilungskraft-der-pflanzensaefte-13337480.html. [Translated from the German.]

242. Anthony King, "EU's future cyber-farms to utilise drones, robots and sensors," reprinted from *Horizon Magazine,* August 24, 2017, https://phys.org/news/2017-08-eu-future-cyber-farms-utilise-drones.html.

Acknowledgments

I want to profoundly thank what was formerly the publisher Duckworth Overlook for jumping on board with my exploration of the tree's unknown flavors and making it accessible to the world. Thanks to Abrams Press for believing in my book, taking on the project, and bringing my book to the world.

In particular I would like to thank Chelsea Cutchens for her incredible ability to turn a rough-sawn timber of a manuscript into a smooth surfaced piece of furniture, Matt Casbourne for turning a simple inquiry about a tote bag into a chance of a lifetime, and Gesche Ipsen for believing in the success of my exploration already at the halfway point. Finally, I want to sincerely thank the late Peter Mayer for the most fascinating and positively challenging discussion about the then-still very rough draft of this book. This moment not only had a profound influence on how I continued to write this book, but also on my life as an author in general.

Index

A

Aboriginal Australians, 20
acacia, 96–97, 123, 156
Acetaia, 153, 159–60
Acetaia di Giorgio, 154–59
Aceto Balsamico di Modena,
    151–61
acetylsalicylic acid (aspirin), 20
"Adirondack," 20
Aftel, Mandy, 107
agarwood, 105–7
alder, 20, 98, 99, 132, 137, 222
Algonquin, 21
Amburana, 84, 88
Amedoim, 84
amphora, 92
Amruth whisky, 88
Angel Face cocktail, 70
angel's share, 86
Antigonish, 165
 "Aqua vinea nobilis," 112
aqua vitae, 58–59, 112
"Aquavit," 59
"Aqua vitis," 112
Aquilaria, 105–6
Aristotle, 25, 191
aroma wheel, 179
Asama, 77

ash, Kenyan cromwo, 122–23
ash wood, vinegar, 155, 156, 158,
    160
aspirin, 20
atirú:taks, 21
"Aventinus Cuvée Barrique," 145,
    147–49

B

bacteria, 95, 119, 127, 128, 155,
    160, 211
Bad Schörgau, 113–15
bagna cauda, 152
Bagòss, 122
balsam, 19, 103, 163, 166, 208
Barbaresco, 189
Barbieri, Giorgio, 154
bark, 20
barley, 59, 77, 120, 143
Barolo, 189
barrels, 91–100; aging, 64,
    82–89; Angelo, 84–89;
    charring, 98; cocktails,
    70; Cognac, 69; Cooper-
    age Scheckenleitner,
    93–97; Gargano, 82–84;
    gherkins, 134–35; Goess-
    Enzenberg, 182–86;